THE LONG JOURNEY

A REFUGEE BOY'S STORYFROM LAOS TO MINNESOTA

TOUAYIM THOJ

Copyright © 2022 Touayim Thoj.

All rights reserved. No part of this book may be reproduced, stored, or transmitted by any means—whether auditory, graphic, mechanical, or electronic—without written permission of both publisher and author, except in the case of brief excerpts used in critical articles and reviews. Unauthorized reproduction of any part of this work is illegal and is punishable by law.

ISBN: 979-8-88640-139-4 (sc)
ISBN: 979-8-88640-140-0 (hc)
ISBN: 979-8-88640-141-7 (e)

Because of the dynamic nature of the Internet, any web addresses or links contained in this book may have changed since publication and may no longer be valid. The views expressed in this work are solely those of the author and do not necessarily reflect the views of the publisher, and the publisher hereby disclaims any responsibility for them.

One Galleria Blvd., Suite 1900, Metairie, LA 70001
1-888-421-2397

CONTENTS

Thank You v
Foreword vii

Chapter 1   One People With Two Systems 1
Chapter 2   The First Jungle Home 24
Chapter 3   Short Year in Pha Daeng 66
Chapter 4   After the Country Fell 107
Chapter 5   The Rebirth of Chao Fa 123
Chapter 6   The Road to Phou Bia 156
Chapter 7   Running in A Circle 181
Chapter 8   Living With The Foes 220
Chapter 9   The Years in KM52 248
Chapter 10   The Refugee Camp 292
Chapter 11   Departure from Asia 325

Biography 338
Book Summary 339

THANK YOU

I want to thank my father, Nhia Tong, who taught me many lessons to be a good person to fit into society. His good discipline was an evidence to me not to steal in our poor community and not to cheat on others for my own greed. He always reminded me to work hard in life, even if we were in the agrarian lifestyle. When we did not have enough food to eat, it was not because he did not work hard to grow enough crops. It was because the long decades of war tore apart our homes. Thanks to my mother, Yer Yang, who was from a large family. She always disciplined me to keep my hygiene good because she was from a family with generations wealth and good leadership. She did not want me to be looked down on by others because then she would lose the good reputation of her good family. I always keep in mind one good lesson she taught me of not to be lazy, so my children would not go hungry and look up to others.

I also want to thank my wife with whom I have enjoyed married life for more than 20 years. I always was busy with my day job, and on the weekends too busy typing and revising this book, but she was very patient, not saying anything. She just kept on feeding our children to keep our lives moving, so we can catch up in the next decade to come.

Finally, a special thanks to my friend, Marlin Heise, who gave me the encouragement from the beginning a decade ago to write this book. His enormous support made my book come to life, from the start to the completion, including many hours of discussion. Without his guidance to shed the light on me for these many years, it would not be possible for me to see the light at the end of the tunnel. Thank you.

FOREWORD

As you read these pages, you walk barefoot with a little boy in his peaceful village in the mountainous northeastern Laos in the 1960s. Walk on the paths to the fields and forests of daily life. Enjoy the sun and bird's songs and the family life of secluded villagers who soon must cope with the world conflict of the Secret War.

Now you are a little older and learn to quickly abandon food, home and school, and flee up and down mountain trails, still in bare feet, as you try to avoid American bombers and Communist Pathet Lao soldiers. Birds still sing in the sunshine, but shelters are temporary and the meager harvests needed to survive often came from seeds planted by earlier farmers who have disappeared. Your flip flops wear out and have no replacements when Pathet Lao victory in May 1975 continued your years of frequent moves and hunger in Laos. Finally, put on Thai white tennis shoes as you struggle through Lao schools before your sudden successful escape across the Mekong to Ban Vinai Refugee Camp in Thailand.

Ban Vinai is where I met this quiet teenager in November 1982, perhaps somewhat shy or nervous because of his limited English. After a month together in that refugee camp, he was a relaxed, happier young man. However, his life in the refugee camp and then transit camp consumed several years before we met again in Minnesota. On the way "home" in Saint Paul, we stopped at Golden Arches for his first hamburger to bring to his first meal here.

Writing The Long Journey has been a long journey for Touayim, and a very interesting and emotional one for me as I have read his various manuscripts. So, please take off your shoes and experience the turbulent years of a young boy who became a teenager, years ago and far away.

Marlin L. Heise

Name and Meaning

Name	Meaning
Ban	Village
Chao Fa	King of Sky
Chao Khoeang	Governor
Chao Meuang	Mayor
Hoy	Valley
Khoeang	Province or State
Lao Lum	Lowland Lao
Lao Sun	Ethnic groups in highest elevations, the Hmong
Lao Theung/Karng	Ethnic groups who live in the middle elevation
Meuang	City
Nai Ban	Village Chief
Nai Kong	District Chief
Nam	River or water
Pha	Rocky cliff
Phou	Mountain
Phutong	Councilman
Taseng	Chief of Administrator
Viang Chan	Vientiane

Timeline

Before 1965	Tham Thao, Nong Het, Laos
1965 - 1969	Sala Village, Xieng Khouang
1969 - 1970	Pha Daeng, Viang Chan
1971 - 1975	Pha Hoi, Viang Chan
1975 - 1976	Pha Dang, Viang Chan
1976 - 1978	Meuang Orm, Xieng Khouang
1978 - 1979	Pha Ngun, Viang Chan
1979 - 1982	KM52, Viang Chan
1982 - 1984	Ban Vinai Refugee Camp, Loei, Thailand
After 1984	Saint Paul, Minnesota, USA

ONE PEOPLE WITH TWO SYSTEMS

*"Pom luag zoo ces xav **yuav**. Pom luag ntse ces xav **rhuav**. Ntseeg lwm haiv neeg **haub**, thaum kawg Hmoob thiaj li ciaj **khaub**."*

Our way of life uses the lunar calendar as a guide for our everyday life in small villages. We used to call the Julian calendar the French months because we were first exposed to the French when they came to Laos. Our livelihood in Laos was different from today. We earned our living by farming. January to February is considered a free time when most people stay home. March is the month to start clearing the fields to plant the new crops for the year. April is the month to get the fields ready by burning the dry brush and trees before planting. Sometimes if rain falls early, some families would begin planting their corn in April. However, the vast majority would wait until the last quarter moon of April to the first quarter of May, and rice in June. Mostly, from June to August would be the time to clear out the weeds to make sure our crops were growing well and we would have good quality at harvesting time. Since rainfall is very heavy from July to October, people tried to get as much field work done as they could and have time to stay home during these months. The weather was never too hot or too cold, but during this time of the year, it was very windy during the rain showers. Toward the end of October, the rain would slow down. It would be the time to harvest corn and plow the cornfields for opium poppies. Mid-November to mid-December would be the time to harvest the rice, depending on when the rice ripened. The last half of December was the preparation period for our New Year celebration. At this time the rice and corn should be stored in a good dry place, either at home or in the fields. Then the last day in December of the Lunar year is the celebration of New Year, which we called "Eat 30" *(noj peb caug)*. This was to send away the old year and the bad things and welcome the new year.

Traditionally, some families had killed animals and invited guests for a feast a few days before the month ended. On January first, young people, especially men, would prepare food and go from house to house to serve the elders which we called *"pe tsiab"*. This means the young wished the elders good health for the new year and asked for blessings from them for prosperity. The second day was the day people invited more guests to join their lunches. The third day they started the entertainment and ball tossing for the young to have fun for the year.

Our society was a different aspect for us. As I grew up, I realized that we were living in a homogeneous village which we never integrated with others. Each ethnic group was established and living in separate villages. Hmong people never lived in the same village with lowland Lao or the Lao Theung (Khmu), middle elevation people. One possible reason the Hmong liked to settle mostly in the mountains was that they knew other ethnic groups lived mainly in the lower valleys. So, living in the higher levels meant less interference. Second, they have survived for centuries in China by hiding in the mountains. As war penetrated our territory and some of our people started to move down to settle in the valleys, we started to integrate some small portions of our population with the lowland people. Once the integration began, languages started to mix while speaking. Some of the mixture words I remember in the early days were for garbage, normal, necessary, important, go, store, lost, etc. When they talked about a thing that related to these words, they used Lao words mixed into the Hmong sentence. Segregation from other ethnic groups was not just for the Hmong, but it was also true for most others. The Mien and Lao Theung also liked to live in valleys tucked in between the high mountains where they could make fields, and fish were abundant in the small rivers. They never integrated with the lowland people either.

The Hmong family rules used to be established and run by the father. The wife and children were taught to follow these family rules, but then the dominant rule was the clan. The house was considered to be the main institution while the parents were meant to be the first and best teachers. Traditionally and culturally, the parents were obligated to raise their children without letting them fall apart. Divorce in our previous society in Laos was rare. We believed that divorce caused hardships and led children to suffer and then poverty arose. Also, both parents had a bad image after the divorce.

In the subculture of birth, it was unacceptable for a child to be born to an unwed mother. The belief in the family structure was that in the poor society, the unwed mother would not be able to raise and provide enough support for her child without a father. This would also be a lesson for others to learn, so it would minimize community problems. Besides that, people were very sensitive about unwed mothers. The woman would lose her identity and dignity. The bottom line is that if no marriage, then no children. Another thing was that human beings have evil hearts. I called them in that way because abusive behavior was happening in front of my eyes. The children who were being humiliated the most were the orphans, born to an unwed mother, the poor kids, the skinny, and the blond. If you were a child from in a poor family, other kids hated you. They feared that you would grab their food in their hands. If you were too skinny, people insulted you. If you were an orphan or born to an unwed mother, other people humiliated you. If you were ugly, other kids ran away from you. One of those ugly and skinny kids is the author of this book. If you are blond then other kids called you "the French boy," "the American boy," or even "Russian." Genetically, some Hmong families happened to have blond kids. It was not that the mother slept with a blond foreigner to conceive that blond child. Maybe we inherited this type of mixed genes centuries ago from somewhere in northern China, Mongolia, or even Siberia which no one knows now. Any blond girl and boy in our community would have difficult time to getting along with other kids. They were always being humiliated and rejected from the group. It would be much harder for them to find a mate because of their skin color. These days we have too many fake blond youths. Whether they dyed their hair orange, brown, or tan, it will turn black again later. However, they don't face much discrimination like those natural blond kids I had seen before. I have seen some children, who had no fathers or both parents, were thrown out of the house by their foster parents. Some were being pushed against the corners of the fence or the walls of the house by other stronger children, without any reason. The word "bastard" came from people's mouths very easily when they saw these kids. I was a neutral person and stood aside, watching them being attacked, but could not say a word to stop the bullies. Sometimes there were some children pushing me around, hurting me, because they perceived me as a weak person, but not for the reason of being without parents. I was lucky to have both parents living. I have also seen some orphans, who were adopted by their uncle and aunt, but were used for heavy labor and given inadequate nutrition. Some had to work from dawn to dusk. Some were sent to stay alone in the isolated farm to take care of the animals and clear the weeds in the field throughout the crop season. When there was a little mistake, what I heard about them was yelling or name calling, "The bastard with a big belly." They treated their own children like princes and princesses while the orphans were treated like slaves. Under these conquering godparents, they lived powerless lives. Spanking commonly happened from the day they were adopted to the day they were old enough to be on their own. Some would die before reaching their teenage years if disease struck because they were too weak. Even though this did not physically touch me, it still hurt me deeply inside. I, many times, regretted that I could not help those children. I just could not understand why anywhere in this world, the disadvantage children always are the victims.

Family ties are considered very important within our culture. There were a few things we must learn in life. The marriage between a son and a daughter must be approved and chosen very carefully. Sometime parents only allowed their children to marry the children of families they have known for years because they knew the history of the other side well. *Noj nceb yuav tsum taug cav, yuav txij yuav nkawm yuav tsum xaiv neej xaiv tsav.* (If you want to eat mushroom, you must follow the tree trunk. If you want to marry, you must choose the good in-laws.) Often the roles and responsibilities of each family must be known as to how each functions prior to allowing their youngsters get married to each other. If the son was from a large family then he should marry a girl who was from a large family as well because large families tend to have similar roles and responsibilities and share similar burdens. The industrious son wants to marry only an industrious girl. This way the young bride, who was moving to live with the groom's family, would not have to make so much adjustment in her new family. Another thing some families did not like was drug addicts and alcoholics. It was a story being told that if you marry a man or woman from such a family, the in-laws certainly would pull you down in some way because they were not making much progress in life. The parents often told their daughters and sons to choose their partners carefully. *Qoob tsis zoo tsuas plam tas ib cim. Txij nkawm tsis zoo ces plam tas yus ib sim.* (If you have bad crops, you lost for one year. If you have a bad marriage, you lost for your entire life.) The two things our father often reminded us about were opium addicts and gamblers. Whoever was involved with these two things, that person would end up having no food to feed his children and have no house to live in. My mother used to say if you do those two things, it is better for you to die than be alive. This would not cause a longterm hardship for the children.

Genetic disorder was another great issue. Because of the diseases such as leprosy, Down's syndrome, short stature, and many others, our people tended to search further into the family trees before they allowed their children to marry each other. In an unfortunate case that a child was born with Down's syndrome, handicapped, or have more fingers than the normal condition, they believed it was from a genetic disorder. Thus, some families liked to practice the traditional way that their son and daughter should only marry the familiar people, or as close as second cousins. By doing so they knew best about the history of both sides that each family was healthy. Sometime if a woman gave birth to an abnormal child such as blind or not able to walk, the couple would turn their beliefs to other thoughts that maybe they owed someone money in their past lives. The baby was the person who they owed the debts to. Now that person was re-incarnated to be the baby for them to raise and take care of in order for them to pay off those old debts. Contrarily, some people believed in a different way for a different reason as well. They prohibited their children to marry their close cousins. Our father, for instance, believes that if the young couple could not maintain a good marriage throughout their lives, their bitterness fight would ruin the relationship of the seniors. The splitting of the young couple would cause such a distaste, leading to destruction of their good relationship or their family values on both sides.

I was born in Laos in the small village of Tham Thao, up in the high mountains of the Nong Het (ໜອງແຮດ) region, close to the Lao-Vietnam border. My grandfather and my father were born in that region as well. My great grandfather and great-great grandfather migrated from China to Laos.

We have ten children in our family, five sons and five daughters. I am the ninth child. We were all born before or at the beginning of the Vietnam War, without a hospital and immunizations present. We all were born with no complications and grew up healthy. The ten of us never suffered from the deadly illnesses of chickenpox and polio. There were no dental clinics, but we had no tooth decay. Unlike those children who died at a very young age, we were the lucky ones. My mother still believed that in those years there were fewer chemicals used and less exposure to the foreigners because we lived in a peaceful isolated village on the mountaintop. And cleaner air means less illness. The foods were organically grown in the fields, while livestock was raised on the farm to feed us. The clean water was carried from a small natural stream in the valley. The raw banana leaves were used as wrappers for our food preparation. It was a healthy way of life in those days. We always had enough to eat until the Vietnam War penetrated our home village.

I was born into a culture which I consider a complex one. In our culture once a boy is born, the culture, the rituals, and burden automatically fall on his shoulders. He would carry the family name. He would stay with the clan forever. As a boy growing up in this complex culture, I had to assume my role and responsibilities within the family and throughout the clan system. That is, as a man, I must know what kind of ritual our clan performs on a daily basis if there is something that needs to be done. Everything must be done correctly. If anything went wrong or was abused, our conscience would tell us that some day bad things will happen to us as a punishment. If you made a mistake, you made a sin.

Without any formal school in our early life, everything we learned was passed to us orally from our parents and others. There were a few good things we learned from Father, such as never cheat, lie, or steal. It was immoral in life to cheat, lie, or steal from others. If others cheated on you, lied to you, or stole from you, you would be angry, or you would curse them to have lightning strike on them. If you did such bad things to someone, later some bad things might come to you as a punishment. The second lesson from Father was that we must never humiliate the weak, the orphans, the disabled, and the poor. On earth, human lives are never created to all being the same. Those who have less advantage never wished to be that way. Besides these good lessons, I also learned silly stories from Father as well. When you peel off the shell of a hardboiled egg, there was a sinking spot in the white. It was eaten by your own soul. When two different colors of corn were planted next to each other, they usually mixed into bicolor. I was told that they exchanged their homes. The purple flew to stay with the white and the white flew to stay with the purple. A good discipline I learned when I was little was that you never pointed your finger at the moon because it would cut a line behind your ear when you were asleep. I also learned another thing from my mother that you should never be lazy unless you were very ill. You had to work hard to have enough food to feed your children. This way your children would not go hungry or have to look up to others. These were the lessons I learned within the family circle. They have stayed in my head for the longest time. And now it is time to move on to my long journey before the year is over, the next decade approaches, and my hair turns grey.

There were many things that happened to us which I did not know about it. Sometimes I wondered why Mother often mentioned that she missed her two daughters who went to Vietnam. What I knew was only my own small world, from the village to the farms, and there was the earth under my feet up to the empty blue sky. One thing I wanted to know was why we had to move out of our home in Nong Het area. Where was it? Until one day Father told me that Nong Het was where the sun rose because we kept moving west. I also wondered if Father ever knew how long our grandparents and great-grandparents had lived in Nong Het region before the French colonized Indochina. These were the things I always wanted to know. So, while walking to the farm or sitting in the backyard, I started to ask him about what happened to our lives before. Sometimes after dinner we sat outside in the moonlight, with plenty of stars flashing in the sky, and there were a lot of blood sucking mosquitoes for us to slap, he told me the story of his long difficult life in a remoted village. He said he was an orphan at a very young age. It was emotionally and deeply hurt because the kids from the rich families always looked down on him. Often, they verbally insulted and assaulted him because he was from the family without a father. It was not the way he chose to be, but it was because his father passed away from illness when he was nine years old. Life was very difficult for him to rise up since there was no a father in the house. One good thing was that before grandpa passed away, he had built a nice house for them. It was built with wooden walls and wooden shingles. From the time he and his siblings were born to the time he got married, they lived in the same house. Then the war arrived, and they moved away to a different place.

Even though Father had never been to school, later in life he had served the people within his community, both the public service and cultural activities. He earned great respect throughout his generation from the community for his cultural services as a marriage medium *(mej koob)*, funeral duty manager *(kav xwm)*, and shaman performing rituals. He also faced difficult times when he was working as a coolie for the French. It was often heavy labor beyond what human energy could sustain. It was either carrying supplies from one point to the other or pounding dirt to build the roads in the region.

They had to bow to the Japanese occupation when they arrived in Indochina during WW II. Mother said they were there very briefly, like from morning sunrise and evening sundown. After the Japanese were gone, the political climate had changed to the Pathet Lao's favor. The Pathet Lao and Vietnamese were pushing from the east into Nong Het. Then Father was transitioning to his second wave of work as a delegate to the *taseng* in his early life under the communist rule in our home. It was too much to bear, but inevitable. The war constantly penetrated the region, and the people had to bear two different political systems of Pathet Lao and French rules almost every day. Father's public service, however, was in this chaotic period when each day he had to face distasteful political activities. It was like the pattern of fog that touched down on your village each morning and cleared up as the sun rose. If one little thing went wrong, it could mean death. Serving people in a region at war with the interference of the Pathet Lao and the French, he had to deal with many difficult problems, avoid troubles, and try to get away from them. He said the communist system was much more difficult to deal with because you never knew what your crime was if you were accused or arrested. For you to be safe, you would have to praise or cheer for their system that it was the best all the time. At last, in the 1960s, he had to make the critical decision of moving us away from the danger. He chose to side with capitalism while others chose to be with the communists. That was why he had to abandon our century-old home to avoid persecution by the communist. He told me many times that life was the single most important thing. If you were alive, you could do anything to earn whatever you wanted. You may not always get everything, but you will get something if you work for it. Thus, on our journey from place to place, Father always looked for ways to get away from trouble before they came to us.

It seemed that the Hmong had not learned much about the political activities surrounding them. Father said some people believed that the shadows of the French were still cast over them even after they were gone. However, our home village was more under the control of the Pathet Lao because Nong Het was too close to the Lao-Vietnam border. The pro-Pathet Lao villagers gained greater advantage. Thus, the people in a small village were divided into two by political and ideological influences, Communism and Capitalism. Due to this disruption, we were not able to live a normal life in our mountain homes.

There were a few events that occurred longer than a half century ago now and that the 20th century is gone, but the pain is still felt on both sides. As I revealed these events in the next several pages, the hatred might come back to haunt me, or someone might just want to slice off my skin because people don't like to be criticized. One side will feel the pain from the old wound and the other side will feel themselves as being blamed and degraded. Our troubles in the villages remain because we cannot get rid of our egos and envies, and don't want to lose face. The loser will always carry on the hatred in his chest throughout his life, not letting it go and wanting revenge.

Since I grew up I learned that within our community we pretend we love each other so much. When one person died, we must gather all the loved ones from everywhere in the country to see the deceased person. Even if it would take two to three days for a relative walking on foot to get to see the dead person, the family still had to delay the funeral and wait for those guests to arrive. It seemed as if we cared about one another so much. But, at the same time we also hated each other so much. If one couple divorced, then we hated the entire clan like it was everyone's fault. When children fight each other in the playground, the parents sued each other through the clan system. When a couple got married, the two sides came to fight and dispute each other on the table of discussion with illogical reasons. Sometimes the fight was due to some little conflicts in the past. If the mediation went well and both sides agreed to the principle, then the wedding proceeded. They were happy together thereafter. They then loved one another as though both families came from the same mother. If the couple divorced later, the two sides hated each other for decades or even a century. They avoided eye contact or talking to each other.

Sometime in 1950's, a man named Tsa Jer Yang (*Tsav Ntxawg Yaj*), who was allied with the French and Royal Lao right wing, came to Tham Thao, our village in Nong Het area. He was my grandma's cousin from Xieng Khouang. His purpose of coming was the hope of taking over the *taseng* (ຕາແຊງ) of the Tham Thao area because the current *taseng* had passed away. He believed it was the right time and right place for him to seize the title as fast as possible. When he arrived, he appointed my mother's oldest brother, Tong Pao Yang, to be the *phutong*, a delegate who worked between the *taseng* in the village and the mayor in the city. He also appointed my father to be the *nai ban* to run and organize the people in our village. Father refused to accept the position because he had too many young children and he would not be able to handle it. However, Tsa Jer Yang insisted that he cared so much about Father, who was his nephew, and he wanted Father to be away from heavy duty coolie work for the French. In those days if a person held an official position, he would be released from doing heavy work. Even without my father's acceptance, Tsa Jer Yang ordered his own buddies to butcher one of Father's pigs to cook for the celebration of his appointment. They killed the pig maybe because the debate was too long and they were hungry anyway. Father had no other choice but to accept the responsibility. Tsa Jer Yang, however, did not think clearly and failed to predict the chaotic future of our village. The villagers were in the verge of living with an internal enemy since half of the people sided with communist Vietnam and the Pathet Lao while the other half sided with the French allies in Xieng Khouang. If the communist Vietnamese and Pathet Lao controlled the area, then those French allegiances would be in trouble. Soon after the appointment, the ordinary peasants like my father and his colleagues, who served under the communist *taseng* in the small village, faced many serious problems for more than a decade.

It was true that things did not go as well as they had planned. Each day the Pathet Lao kept pushing further into Nong Het region; the villagers lost connections with their Xieng Khouang allies. Also, Father, along with his colleagues, advised Tsa Jer Yang not to return to the village again since the pro-Pathet Lao villagers had gained greater strength from Vietnam. The risk was that he might be killed one day if he kept coming. The *taseng* position would never be his. They knew for sure that one of the Tham Thao villagers, who had been to school in Vietnam in 1951 and returned home in 1954, would soon take over the *taseng* position in the area. At the time they knew the position had already unofficially been transferred to him, Neng Vang. In order for Tsa Jer Yang to get the position, he had to fight for it, and it also depended on whether the people there would support him. If the people who sided with Pathet Lao gained full power, there was no way for him to get the position. Whoever was trusted by the communist Pathet Lao would earn the title. A few years earlier, Xai Phia Yang, who sided with Xieng Khouang, had traveled through there. The people who supported the Pathet Lao shot and wounded him badly in his knee. After hearing all these troubles, Tsa Jer Yang never put his soles on Nong Het soil again. Then another man, Nhia Chong Thao (*Nyiaj Txoov Thoj*), who had not had enough trouble for himself yet, took over the campaign to gain support for the *taseng*. After a couple trips, he used his metaphor to signal the villagers that he knew one day his kidneys might fall off. This meant that he would be shot dead. Once he was back in Xieng Khouang, he stayed quietly like Tsa Jer and did not come back to Tham Thao again.

Suddenly, in 1956, the new *taseng* gained full power from his Pathet Lao (ປະເທດລາວ) allies and took the helm. Thus, came the unforeseen problem of the establishment of Tsa Jer's small council in Tham Thao area to lead the villages. Father and his colleague officials, who allied themselves with *taseng* Tsa Jer, were in jeopardy. The new *taseng* stretched his iron fist to occupy the villages in his district and got stronger support from the Pathet Lao who supplied him with more guns for his bodyguard system while Father's people had only Hmong-made flintlocks. The *taseng* was very powerful in the way of compelling his own people who sided with his Xieng Khouang foes. The villagers clenched their teeth, scared to death of being punished for any wrongdoing as their dictator's body temperature rose. Maybe it was how a leader had to use his full powers to rule his people to deter his enemies during conflict, or it was a period when the *taseng* was appointed to the position without supervision.

They had their own chemists and blacksmiths, who made guns, but they thought the Western guns were more powerful. They abandoned their own chemists and blacksmiths and obtained the Western guns to use to deter their enemies, who were their own cousins. It was meant to appease their anger. It was their determination and ambition to gain power. One thing they failed to realize was that one day the weapons they got from the Pathet Lao would cause severe destruction to their own people. And finally, if they wanted to know about their own technologies, the chemists and blacksmiths who they had before, would never be found anywhere.

Soon, there was one bitter conflict after another among the villagers. One day Father, along with his Thao and Yang relatives went to hunt for elk. At that time a man in the village had a rifle from the Pathet Lao. Before leaving to the woods, the group persuaded him to go with them, but he said he did not want to go. After they were gone, he followed them into the woods, too. When Father's group was chasing the elk bull in the woods, Uncle Tong Pao *(Tooj Pov)* and Fai Dang (*Faiv Ntaj)* shot together with their flintlocks. The elk was wounded, but it did not die right away. It ran further down to meet him, the man who followed them, but they had no idea that he was there. He shot four times and the elk dropped dead. Then the group came to exam the angles of the shots and determined that even if his bullets had not hit the elk, it would have died shortly after anyway. So, the group decided to give the antlers to Fai Dang. Everyone was happy and agreed to accept this decision at the scene. In those days the elk antlers were worth a lot of money if sold to the foreign Chinese and Vietnamese. Somehow, very soon the elk antlers became the main cause of a problem against Fai Dang, which made relatives hostile toward one another. A week later, the man demanded Fai Dang to pay him 500 kip for the antlers, so he could divide the cash among the entire group. In those days 500 kip was too much for a person to pay. The entire group, including Fai Dang, was disappointed with the man's new decision. The group could not do much to resolve the case but were able to reduce Fai Dang's payment to 400 kip instead of 500. The man took the cash and divided it into little portions among everyone in the group. It was just such a very lousy idea. They thought the problem was solved. But in truth the wound was not healed.

Shortly after the 400 kip were paid, more internal troubles surfaced. The *taseng* accused Fai Dang of being a spy and conspiring with Xieng Khouang. In the charge, he stated that he saw and heard Fai Dang reading a letter from Tsa Jer Yang in Xieng Khouang. However, the communication between Xieng Khouang and Nong Het had been cut off and cold for a while. It was an illegitimate claim. They knew the reason he accused Fai Dang was because he was the only person in the village who received some basic education and was therefore able to read and write. The accusation was to create a good cause to arrest Fai Dang. It was also the *taseng's* intention to cut down the strength of the Xieng Khouang allies. Nevertheless, Father and Chia Xeng *(Txhiaj Xeeb),* who was Fai Dang's uncle, did not ignore the accusation. They started a further investigation into the case. Then the *taseng* twisted the accusation that it was another Green Hmong man, from another village, who told him so. Father and Uncle Chia Xeng did not stop there either. They went straight to ask the Green Hmong man if he had ever been in Tham Thao village to meet the *taseng* and tell him that he saw and heard Fai Dang read the letter from Xieng Khouang. The moment they questioned him, the Green Hmong man said it was ridiculous for the *taseng* to say so because he had not been to Tham Thao village for years. That was the end of the conversation.

Once they returned to Tham Thao, they went straight back to tell the *taseng* that the allegation was not true. Then he changed the story again by saying that it was from blond Pao Yang *(Pov Yaj),* another man who lived in another village close to Meuang Saen. At this point they knew for sure the angry *taseng* just wanted to bite them to appease his anger. The next morning, they went to see Pao Yang to question him further. They must find the answer to prove to the *taseng,* or else he could cut anyone's neck at any time. The moment Father and his brother-in-law Chia Xeng arrived at his house, Pao Yang said he did not say what the *taseng* had told them. What he was saying to the *taseng* when they both met was that if anyone was a suspect of being a conspirator with Xieng Khouang, that person must be put on the hot stove to reveal the truth. Once the person was burned to the butt, he would not hide any secret. He never told the *taseng* that he had seen or heard Fai Dang read the letter from Tsa Jer in Xieng Khouang. It was a very big pain-in-the-neck situation. They returned home with nothing.

On the way to Pao Yang's village and returning home, it rained steadily. Father and Uncle Chia Xeng were soaked with the heavy rain. In the afternoon before they arrived home, the *taseng* had ordered a man to go shoot his carbine across a stream from one side to the other and then roll himself around in the bushes, pretending that someone was shooting at him. Then he came back to report to the *taseng* he had done the job and ran to another village to lie to other people that the *Sak Tu*, meaning people allied with the French in Xieng Khouang, shot him. Then the *taseng* reported to the villagers what happened that afternoon as if it were a real situation. At the time, my father's cousin, Tong Pao, was at home and heard of the incident. He went to investigate based on what the *taseng* had told them. At the scene he found three carbine shells on the ground where the man stood to shoot to the other side. On the targeted side he also discovered only one person did the rolling action in the bushes because there were only one person's footprints. Once Father arrived home, his cousin told Father what had happened in the afternoon. Father and Uncle Chia Xeng were nothing but angry about one thing after the other. Just then they had not rested enough yet, but there were many Kong Lorne from the Pathet Lao side arriving from many places because the man told them the *Sak Tu* had attacked him. These Kong Lorne were civilian soldiers who had never been to military training and never wore uniforms, but were issued guns to provide security in the village. Because Father's cousin proved to them from his investigation the evidence was not *Sak Tu*, the Kong Lorne leaders apologized for the trouble and wanted to return home. However, Father, his cousin, and Uncle Chia Xeng insisted that the Kong Lorne must not leave until the next morning and the villagers would go with them to search the valleys and mountains if there were any *Sak Tu*, meaning enemies, around as they were accused. They wanted to find the truth, so they could throw mud on him after all. At last the Kong Lorne had no choice but stay in the village overnight. The next morning, the villagers took them to search for two hours as they had planned, but they found nothing. Then they were able to clarify that the *taseng* just wanted to punish those who previously sided with Xieng Khouang. It was such a bad fake idea he created against his own villagers. This was the end of the incident and they returned home.

A few months later, the *taseng* planned to arrest Fai Dang and his Uncle Blia Neng. He sent a letter with dried hot chili peppers, charcoal, and chicken feathers to Father and Wa Khue, who were his delegates, to arrest Blia Neng and Fai Dang, and send them to him. The dried red-hot chili peppers, black charcoal, and chicken feathers symbolized a hot situation, darkness and death, and must be done quickly, respectively. Before Father and Wa Khue responded to their iron fist *taseng*, Fai Dang and Blia Neng already knew that trouble was coming to them and escaped in the dark of night to see Nor Tou Lao in Phou Koua, a village inside Vietnam territory. The purpose of going there was to get help from him because it was impossible for them to get to Xieng Khouang at the moment. Even though Nor Tou Lao was just an ordinary peasant and they both were allied with the Pathet Lao, Nor Tou Lao had power over the *taseng*.

Throughout the night after Uncle Blia Neng and Fai Dang escaped, Father could not sleep and realized that the problem must be dealt with and cleared up for them to be safe in the village. It was a dangerous situation which they must handle very careful without taking any chances. What they needed to do was to find a good solution to appease their boss' anger. They must comply with the *taseng's* letter the next day before their necks were put under his sword. If they did not have a good reason to prove why they could not arrest the suspects for him, then their bodies could replace the suspects' bodies, either with prison or dead. If any one was arrested, there was no trial. If anyone got shot death, then that was it. Besides those things, Father just could not understand why the *taseng* pressed such unnecessary crimes against the two young men because they knew each other and cared for one another like one family.

The next morning Father and Wa Khue went to the *taseng's* house to respond to his letter. When they got to his house, the back door was left open. They looked inside the house and saw him walking back and forth, facing the back wall, with arms folded, and assumed he was waiting for them impatiently. They entered the house, but he neither invited them to sit down, nor turned to face them, nor said a word. Father called him softly twice, "*Taseng, Taseng.*" Then he made a noise from his throat like a lion roaring before turning to face them. Not sure how Wa Khue felt, but Father felt like his feet did not touch the ground. Instead of feeling his body temperature rise, Father's body was cold and sweating. The *taseng* was dressed in a Vietnamese army green uniform. By seeing him in his uniform and angry face, they were scared to dead. Father thought, "We are dead this time." *"Wb tuag zaum no lau."* He asked, "What happened to them?", he meant Blia Neng and Fai Dang. Then Father responded to him, "Well, *Taseng*...your letter arrived late last night, so by the time we knew about the situation, the uncle and son were already gone to Phou Koua." In fact, Father just made excuses to get them away from him because they did not want to arrest Blia Neng and Fai Dang for him anyway. Actually, Father and Wa Khue knew the problem prior to their escape. They believed the accusation was false. Wa Khue continued saying, "We will continue to investigate into the case and we will make sure they come back to face you for punishment." In truth, they just tried to appease his anger for the moment. They knew for sure that Nor Tou Lao would alter the accusation once he talked to Blia Neng and Fai Dang. He said, "Next time I don't want things to be loose again." He let them return home.

    Blia Neng and Fai Dang went to stay with Nor Tou for ten days as visitors without telling him what was wrong at home. On the tenth day Nor Tou realized there must be something going on at home, but maybe the two men did not want to reveal the problem. He asked them why they were there because they never before had visited him for so many days. They told him they were accused of crimes without any evidence by the *taseng* at home. They had tried everything to put out the fire, but it seemed the more they did, the bigger the flames got each day. Nor Tou asked them if they wanted to return home again. They said they wanted to come back home, but what if the *taseng* never set them free when they got home. He told them there must be no more problems if he was still alive. After they left Phou Koua, Nor Tou demanded the *taseng* to come to Phou Koua for a meeting, but he refused to comply with Nor Tou's request. He knew if he ever went to face Nor Tou, he would get enormous heat at the meeting.

As time moved toward the beginning of 1960s, there were more skirmishes in every direction. The Pathet Lao and Kong Pachai also went to war with Yang Shong Lue, the Hmong Mother of Writing, in Fee Kha village. The Pathet Lao wanted to wipe Yang Shong Lue out of the picture. They called him Chao Fa--King of the Sky. He invented his script in the wrong place and in the wrong time. It was also trouble in the village for Father. As the Vietnam War got boiling, combined with his own trouble with the *taseng*, Father knew he could not endure the problems any longer. The best way for him in life was to get away from the area. Then he decided to go to the house of an official in Nong Het to request a travel pass to go to Xieng Khouang. Father's purpose was to go to Xieng Khouang and not return home to face his foes again. The moment Father got into the house, the official pulled out an old rifle from the corner of the room and then told Father that they took it from the Chao Fa. They had just returned from defeating the Chao Fa people. Since Father did not want to engage in further conversation with him about the Chao Fa because he felt sad about the fighting, he cut short the conversation by asking the official to provide him with the travel pass. He told Father he would process it in the next few hours. However, Father waited at his house for more than half a day and he never returned from his workplace to give Father the pass. Then Father went straight back to his office to ask him again. He said he told Father that morning he was going to do it, but he changed his mind. The route from there to Xieng Khouang was dangerous to pass through. Therefore, he would rather not give Father the pass to go. In case something happened on the way, he might get into trouble. For Father, that was the end, and it had been such a waste of time. Father just returned home without the pass. It was hard to believe that in the communist area, civilians had to have travel passes to go from one city to the next, even though they traveled only within their own country.

Because Father was doing marriage medium work *(mej koob)*, he missed a few meetings conducted by the *taseng*. Then he told Uncle Tong Pao and Wa Khue at the meeting that there was an internal enemy in the village. They were startled to hear these comments from the *taseng but* said nothing. They just nodded their heads to appease his anger. It was their gestures of being obedient and loyal to him. The *taseng* did not say anyone's name, but my father could be the one. Another reason was that Father was the *nai ban* appointed by *taseng* Tsa Jer from Xieng Khouang. The *taseng* distrusted his own villagers who had previously affiliated with the French. Lastly, he was angry that father had skipped the meetings and used the marriage medium work as an excuse. All these troubles had built up in his head without venting. When Uncle Tong Pao and Wa Khue returned home, they told Father that what had popped out of their leader's mouth at the meeting was a bad signal that gave them a hint of Father's future. Then Father was panicked with sleeplessness. He knew he must flee for sure before the real trouble came to him, but he did not know how because the *taseng* ordered his soldiers to block every single route, not letting people sneak out. Our grandmother and three aunts had moved a year earlier to live in Phonsavanh, Xieng Khouang. Joua Yia Moua, who married one of our aunt's daughters, heard the bad news and was very concerned about Father's safety in Tham Thao village. He sent a secret message to Father to find a way out.

There was also something new they must learn of at the time. Father remembered in the 1930s and 1940s, when people fought a war, there were not many guns. Each group had a few guns and the rest just carried sticks, knives, and axes. Now it was a time with different types of weapons used in the war between Laos and Vietnam. The new artillery barrels were as big as the size of human thighs. The bullets were the same size as banana blossoms. One shot would be as loud as thunder roaring. The small rifles soldiers used to have, had the barrels as big as their finger tips and the bullets were as small as hot chili peppers, they were no longer effective to deter their enemies. Thus, fearing the future destructive war which would affect our lives and Father's safety, our journey began. Finally, one day in early 1965, Father abandoned our century-old home in Tham Thao village in the Nong Het (ໜອງແຮດ) area. Father fled to get away from the trouble in the village to hide further to the west in the central area of the province, hoping that god would shed light on him. He also hoped that this was the way to escape the conflict between the two political systems.

A few days before his departure, Father whispered to his close relatives that he must leave the area. Soon the rumors spread on to other villagers. Many people wanted to leave with Father, too. If he was going to move, he wanted to take his animals with him, but this was impossible. The trip would take three days and three nights before we could reach central Xieng Khouang. With his request, the *taseng* gave a gesture allowing Father to leave the village. But he warned that he allowed only my father's family to move. Somehow, he secretly ordered his body guards to block all the routes that my father could use to get out. Thus, with limited exits, Father hired a Lao Theung man, who lived with them for a long time, to carry his back basket full of tools and supplies, pretending he was going to the farm, but carried it to another village far in the west. Then Father snuck out to the woods, crossing mountains and valleys to meet the Lao Theung man in that village. Early the next morning my entire family of ten with packs on their backs and 15 animals moved out of the village. Once we got to the edge of the village, we met many bodyguards waiting there. They asked for my father. My family told the bodyguards that Father was still in the village greeting and comforting his relatives because many people were sad about him leaving. At the end of the day he would leave the village to catch up to his family. The bodyguards then allowed us to pass, but they waited for my father who they believed was still behind. In truth, Father was already far ahead of us the day before. Maybe that day the bodyguards waited all day long to catch Father. However, he never showed up at the end of the day. After three days, Father was in central Xieng Khouang.

One thing Father told me in my early life was that neither side won anything during or after the war. Those Hmong who sided with the French in Xieng Khouang had to crawl like wild cats crouching while hunting prey when they wanted to ask the French for help. During the time the French colonized Laos, the big legal issues within the villages must always be brought up to the French officials in central Xieng Khouang to settle them. Whenever there was a dispute in the village or anyone was accused of anything, it was always difficult to request a meeting with them to resolve the issue. One-time Father with a group of people went to see the Hmong and French officials in Xieng Khouang. Before entering the building, they had to walk on their knees up the stairs and squat kangaroo style, moving sideways inside the building with their backs against the wall. Some people who did not crawl appropriately, the guards kicked on their butts. It was very degrading. The French were like the masters, while the Hmong were the humiliated slaves. On the other side, those Hmong who sided with the Pathet Lao and Vietnam were happy that the French were gone. They earned nothing but served the Pathet Lao for 30 years without benefits. They called themselves *Neo Lao*, meaning like seeds of Lao, while they called the French allies *Sak Tu*, meaning, enemy.

When we were in our new place of Sala, Father met two Vietnamese tourists who spoke fluent Lao. They told Father that they were happy that the French were gone because tax was the main issue. Father told them that many poor Hmong families had to sell their children to the rich families to get silver coins to pay tax. Later, if they had the money, they could repay their debts and bring their children back. Some families never were able to make payments to get their children back again. Some of Father's cousins had adopted a few children from the poor families because they helped pay the tax to the French before the system ended. The widows were waived from paying taxes. My grandma was a widow. When the tax collectors came to their village, they also came to collect tax from grandma. She refused to pay the tax. She walked on foot for two days to Phak Khae to complain to Lyfoung because he was related to her in some way in the extended family. Lyfoung had the power to stop people and told grandma to go back home and tell the tax collectors if they needed money from her, they should go to see him. He would pay them. In truth, no one ever went from grandma's house to Lyfoung's house for tax money after grandma told them this.

2

THE FIRST JUNGLE HOME

*"Thaum Hmoob tej zej zog raug luag **tua**, Hmoob thiaj coj tej niam tub mus nkaum qhov **tsua**. Peb Hmoob nyob txom nyem **ntsuav** los vim yog raug ob tog yeeb ncuab muab peb lub neej **rhuav**."*

In 1965, we settled and farmed in a small village which people called Phuv Thav, close to the city of Phonsavanh. I do not have any memory of this place. In 1966, we moved to Sala village. In 1966 we had our rice and corn fields south of the village up on the top of the highest mountain, which was called Green Hmong Mountain. Our cornfield was in the valley below the rice field, further down south. Up in the rice field, we could see our Sala village in the deep valley at the bottom of the foot of the mountain. I remember that during the rice harvesting, we had a lot of people working in the fields with my family. In those days we called this an exchange of labor, *pauv zog*. When your rice was not ready to be harvested yet, you helped the neighbors harvest theirs. When your rice was ready, you called all those people who you had helped to come work with you. For instance, you had two people help one family for one day before, then you could ask them for two people to come to help you for one day.

Father planted a lot of bananas alongside the cornfield. When the bananas were ripe on the trees, Father cut them down and carried them home on horseback. There was no market in the small village to sell those bananas and other goods. Also, every family grew enough of their own to feed their family. Every year there were a lot of porcupines, wild pigs, and brown bears to knock down the stalks and eat the corn. Father made traps, but never caught one. Above the cornfield, Mother planted sugarcane in one area as wide as a few houses together. It grew very well. There was another kind of wild animal that looked like a red fox, *nees daj duav,* that cut down and chewed the sugarcane too. At the end of each year, Mother and older sister cut down the sugarcane, peeled off the hard-outer skin, chopped and pounded it in the sturdy seesaw mill and pressed the juice to boil to make molasses and hard sugar loaves. Mother used the molasses to mix with crispy rice every New Year. There were also acres of wild passion fruit. When the fruits were ripened, they turned purple and fell to the ground. Father picked them into his basket and brought them home. I loved the smell and the taste of the sweet yellow juice very much. It was tasty.

In 1967, we also cleared another farmland in the north of our village to grow more corn to feed our pigs and chickens. The territory on this side was much flatter. At the end of corn harvesting, we could transport it easily on horseback home. Below the cornfield was a very large flat area with very fertile soil. Father reserved this area for Mother to plant hemp *(maj)* for making clothes. The plants grew up to eight feet tall. Its leaves looked similar to marijuana leaves. The stalks were about the size of fingers and hallow inside. When it dried, it was very light. Living in a place far from the city with the difficult traveling situation, it was not possible to go buy clothes. We had to make our own clothes from this plant. Usually in September or October, Mother and Father cut down all the *maj* and dried them in the hot sun for a couple days before taking them home. Sometime if the weather did not permit, we just bundled them up and carried them home to dry in the attic, which we called *nthab.* After a few days we would sit down together to peel off the thin bark. We wove it into yarn and Mother boiled it with ashes in the big wok. After a little while its color turned grey. Mother took them out again to wash in the cold water. Then it turned to be super white. Mother spun the fibers into thread and then wove them into cloth.

Our first home built in 1966 was up in the high hills. In 1968, Father and my brothers built a better home for us in the flat area at the bottom of the village, where two streams met. One was coming from the southside of the foot of the high mountain and one was cutting through the middle of the village. They built a very spacious house with five bedrooms and one guest bedroom. With wooden shingles and wooden walls, they hoped it would last for a long time. This time we had three uncles, who were Father's cousins, along with a few nephews, of my generation, who moved from our former Tham Thao village in Nong Het to live with us. That same year we also moved to clear a different land on the north side of the village, about thirty minutes walk, to grow rice. After two years, the soil of our old rice field in the high mountain had become depleted. Our cornfield still existed there. The corn was still growing very well. A portion of the field was cultivated each year for opium poppies. Opium was the main product to be traded for Chinese silver bars and old French silver coins at the time. In 1969, we had to clear a different field again to grow rice. This time we had it in the east of our village, which was across the stream next to our home. It was close to home, so everything seemed more convenient. But, a few families who had lived there a few years before we moved in, even had a better life than we did. They had many water buffaloes. They had constructed good rice paddies and used water buffaloes to plow their terraces every year. They did not have to clear forest each year for a new rice field like we did.

In this place the peach and guava trees bore very good organic fruit without any larvae inside. Father planted many peach trees, but they did not bear fruit yet. Along the stream on the foot of the high mountain next to the village were a lot of wild berries. One kind bore purple fruit, and another bore yellow fruit. Both were very ripe in the month of June.

On hot days my brothers went there to pick them and returned with big bowls of yellow or purple berries separately, but some mixed them together in a bowl. They made a sour juice and delicious.

Soon the peaceful time was over. When we were in this new home, we were not aware of other things. Suddenly, the Pathet Lao soldiers were everywhere, conquering our home village as they advanced their troops further into the central area. We had nowhere to go other than stay where we were. The decision Father had made a few years ago to move from Nong Het to the central area did not get us away from the conflict for very long. We saw both sides, the Pathet Lao and Vang Pao's armies, patrolling by our village often. While ruling our village, the Pathet Lao forced villagers to attend their monthly seminars, called *samana*. Everywhere Father went, he always took me with him. As I remember being with him in those days at the *samana*, each session was usually held in the woods rather than in buildings in the village. It was not fun at all for the attendees because this was not our traditional way of life. In our way we would meet in someone's house to discuss issues, not in the woods. It was more like punishment.

During each session the attendees had to sit crossed-leg on the ground in a circle for many hours before lunch break and afterwards until the *samana* was over in the afternoon. The Pathet Lao soldier, who conducted the training, would stand in the middle and turn around 360 degrees to watch his attendees while he was talking. The topics were more anti-capitalism and praise for their system. Whether it was interesting or boring, no one should ever lose their concentration. Otherwise, people would be criticized at the end of the day for not being interested in the subject, or for disliking the communist system. If anyone failed to be an active listener or fell asleep, that person would vanish from the group to a re-education camp. They never handcuffed anybody for wrong doing. What they did was to call the person who made the mistake to go to re-education camp. If family members asked why the person had to go and where he had to be, the response was that the person needed to learn more in order to increase his knowledge. If the person had been gone for a few months without returning home, the Pathet Lao would tell the family that their family member was far away and studying very hard. Someday he would return home to be a good leader. However, by that time the person either was in prison or more likely dead. We called it, "The bones already decomposed", *pob txha qob tag lawm.* As time passed by, the person never returned. This was what Father told us about the communist system.

There were two young men in our village accused of spying, but with no specific proof. After they were sent to re-education camp for months, people asked the Pathet Lao about their status. Their response was that the two men were studying far away. A year later, someone told the families they had been dead a long time already. This sort to punishment made everyday life devastating, as we were sleeping with the enemy.

Another thing about Communism was that everything belonged to everyone. They used the Lao words *luam mou,* meaning everything together for everyone. If you owned one cow, for example, it belongs to you, to your fellow villagers, and to the government, too. You could not kill an animal for food unless you lied to them that it was killed for a kind of ceremony. The communist did not like business or rich people, either. Those who tried to do business to become rich, very soon would disappear. My father often told his nephews and cousins, "Don't even think about or try it." In their store they used meters for measurement instead of yards. Each family was allowed to buy two meters of fabric per person for the whole year. Whether you had money to buy more or not, they would not sell more than that to you. It was not a free market in those days under the communist system.

One day in 1968, a group of Kong Pachai soldiers, the Hmong army battalion serving under the Pathet Lao, came to our village. Their general, Paser Yang, had a good character, a very loud voice, was a good talker, and was very well liked by his subordinates, as I noticed. They came to our village to kill a water buffalo for a celebration. The buffalo belonged to a Yang family that had fled to Long Cheng a few months earlier. This family and the general were cousins, except each family believed in a different political system. That's why the general joined the communists while his cousins fled to join Vang Pao in Viang Chan. They invited most of the officials and many villagers, especially men, to join their happiness celebration. They prepared to serve lunch in the courtyard of the elementary school. At the party were many dogs running around in search of food, so the soldiers had to set the benches for serving food up as high as four feet above the ground to prevent the dogs from sharing their food. Obviously, the soldiers were more numerous than the civilians at the ceremony. Most of the mess cooks were not carrying guns. Other soldiers were walking and checking their activities with their AK-47s by their sides all the time.

Before the lunch was served, the general made a speech wishing everyone good health. In the speech he hoped one day they would be able to chase away the enemies, meaning Vang Pao and the Americans. Since there were no Lao soldiers with them at the time, he spoke only Hmong. When the lunch was served, I was next to Father, hugging one of his legs under the bench because it was too high above me. He grabbed a ball of sticky rice, a piece of meat, and handed them to me under the bench. Other fathers did the same for their children. Right after the lunch was over, the soldiers along with the general sang a song together. They put their arms across each other's shoulders while they were singing. To make the sound of music, they put dried corn kernels inside some empty cans and shook them. As a little boy who knew nothing other than he needed food, I thought it was a very fun day. It seemed to be a good lunch for the soldiers and everyone around the benches. For Father, it was just a show of appreciation or to save face because we were under their control. Later, Father said if they invited villagers to join them, but they did not show up, the Pathet Lao would think they disliked their system. Everyone must be careful when doing anything. "It seemed trouble was there all the time," Father said.

The area behind our second home in Sala was as big as a soccer field. One day later in the year, the Kong Pachai general, along with some of his fellow soldiers visited our village again. The village chief, Shong Ger Moua, did not have anything to show them for entertainment. He decided to have a bullfight as a traditional entertainment for them to see. The village chief had one bull, we had one bull, and other villagers had theirs, too. The village chief was the host, so he was going to have his bull fight against any bull in the village. However, the others refused to have their bulls fight and wanted to have our young grey bull fight with the chief's black bull. My father was reluctant to have his bull fight because it was only five years old. It was big and strong but was still considered to be young and not ready for fighting yet. The chief's bull was about eight or nine years old and had many fights in the past. Once other people heard that Father did not want his bull to fight, they complained about many things in front of him. Maybe they thought Father was a delegate to the village chief, so Father should have his bull fight the village chief's bull instead of someone else's bull. They said it was not about which bull would win the fight. It was about how to save face for the village chief and show some fun to the soldiers who we had no choice but to live with now. It would be just a gift for them. After the fight was over, they would leave the area. Father then had no choice because many people were waiting in the field behind our house. The village chief's bull was there snorting and pawing the ground, ready to fight in front of everyone.

Since our bull was very aggressive, my father opened the outer gate of the fence first and then the stall door to let him out. Once the door was opened, it ran out as fast as it could to the field and attacked the village chief's bull. It was a moment that appeased everyone's hunger for a bullfight. Everyone surrounding the field was cheering for the fight. Our bull was young and strong. He pushed his opponent around the field for about 15 minutes. Finally, his opponent could not resist any more and ran off the field. Our bull was too tired to chase after his opponent, so he just stood where they stopped. My brother ran to grab his nose ring and took him back inside the fence. The soldiers gave a big applause for the victory. After a while they left our place to go back to where they came from. After the fight, our bull was very tired. He did not eat very much for about a week and urinated a dark brown color. My father said the bull was seriously hurt internally from the fight. Since then Father reminded me that in real life some people would push you all the way to the limit like the moment they forced him to have his bull fight. Sometimes if you are being too polite, others would think you were weak, either mentally or physically. Then they tried to take advantage of you. He was too polite that day. That's why they were able to force him to have his bull fight.

One night very soon after this bullfight event, ten Lao soldiers, including the leader, came to our house. Mother and brothers told me to stay away from them and let only Father greet them. Father spoke to them with a very heavy accented Lao language. He did not know very much Lao language but was just able to communicate with them. I knew Father had a heavy accent because when I grew up and learned Lao, he said something that I did not even have a clue what it was. That evening I leaned forward against Father's back when he was sitting on a low stool talking to them. I asked him who they were. He told me they were the white hat *(kaus mom dawb)* people instead of telling me they were the Pathet Lao soldiers. After that question, I wondered why I was so dumb at the time for asking Father such a question. Later in life I learned that some villagers called them the white hats because their green uniforms faded as they were exposed more to the sunlight. Their hats turned from greenish to light grey. They used the slang term, so the Pathet Lao would not know it.

In our house we had a bowl hanging from the roof down about four feet above the floor and a couple of feet away from the wall. We burned pine wood in it every evening to give light during mealtime because there was no electricity. We had eaten our dinner before the soldiers came with four chickens which they bought from our neighbors. At our house they killed the chickens to cook for dinner. While the soldiers helping each other soaking the chicken in the hot water in the big bowl and pulling off the feathers, Father told one of my brothers to keep throwing the little pieces of pine woods into the bowl to give continuous light. We had to pretend that we really liked them, enjoyed them, and welcomed them at the moment. This way they would not think that we had something against them. I watched them clean everything off the chickens before cooking. They also cleaned and cooked the chicken's crops. I turned to Mother and asked her why they also cooked that piece because Mother always took it out and threw it in the garbage. She said maybe it was their way of cooking chicken. When their chickens were cooked and served on our table, they invited everyone to join them. Since we had our dinner, we did not join them. Father ate with them to show appreciation for their invitation and to save face. After dinner it was late, so they left and said goodbye. Every young soldier called my father his father in Lao Language. I heard a young soldier kept calling Father in our language *(txiv)*. Later Father said before leaving our house, that soldier told Father that if Father heard that he was dead then Father should be happy for his death *(Yog txiv hnov tub tuag no txiv pab zoo siab)*. I asked Father why he said that. Father said maybe he was tired of being a soldier, or maybe he did not want to go to fight the war, but his government forced him to go.

Even though the hope was to get away from the conflict in Nong Het, we soon faced the new era of airplanes dropping bombs on Xieng Khouang. The nightmare never ended because the fighting never stopped, and we never settled down in one place. It was the era when T-28s and jets were used to fight the air war. The Pathet Lao and Vietnamese advanced more of their troops into our area. Our new place, which was considered a safe haven and would not be affected by the war, was later shattered by bombs as the war went on. It seemed in those days any village close to the Lao-Vietnamese border was considered an enemy target. Whether it was a village or a genuine enemy target, bombs were often dropped on it. Besides the villages, high cliffs must be bombed because sometimes the enemies were hiding in caves underneath. Those were good hiding places for the Pathet Lao and Vietnamese. The bombs they dropped did not get rid of the enemies.

Instead, they made civilians angry. By judging the physical damage to the beautiful nature in the regions, the people started to wonder who their good friends were. Maybe the ideological influence of the Pathet Lao was better because they only struck their enemy's sites. There were no indiscriminate communist bombs dropped from the sky on them as their Lao right-wing friends did. Some seemed to have open arms to welcome the Pathet Lao if they reached their territory.

I was told by Mother that we would no longer be able to live in our place in Sala. Some days we saw a big airplane fly over our village. Father said maybe it was the one they called a B-52 plane. I had not seen one bomb in my life, but one day my brother said each bomb was the same size as a grenade. When the bombs were dropped, they spread in the sky and fell down to earth like horse manure. Besides the big plane, there were T-28s and jets. They flew very fast and made a loud noise. Father told us those planes also went to drop bombs on the Lao-Vietnam border. Some day we heard the bomb explosions, (boom, boom, boom, boom…), very close to where we lived because our home was still very close to the enemy targets. This was the time the war was again brought directly to our homes. As they continued to bomb the region in the middle of 1969, our second home village of Sala was bombed and destroyed completely. We had nowhere to go but seek refuge in the jungles to protect ourselves when our village became a ghost town.

As more bombs were dropped, many creatures and humans died from the man-made explosive materials which shattered them, or the odor and fumes they breathed in cause them to slowly die from illness. The lucky ones like us were able to escape, to hide in a safer place, and lived longer to tell our stories to the next generations to come. It was not a generation of death by natural causes, but rather a period of human-caused death. The unlucky ones who had died, their blood soaked the soil, and their flesh decomposed or was eaten by other creatures. Some of their bones would remain on the spot for as long as they could. Hopefully, their souls would travel through their long journey to heaven and to another more peaceful life. It was the same for us. We moved from place to place, valleys to mountains and mountains to valleys, just to find a peaceful life.

Near our cornfield to the east a few miles away, there was an army camp on top of a long narrow hill, stretching from south to north. We did not know whether the Viet Cong or Vang Pao's Army had built the camp first. One day when we were at our farm, there were three or four planes bombed the camp with many flights throughout the day. As we watched, the T-28s dropped bombs on it and the helicopters tried to land afterwards, but more gunfire continued from the ground. So, the helicopters flew away again. The T-28s repeated the bombing for four or five flights before sunset. By the time the sun went down over the mountain and its shadow was cast over the camp, we heard the loud speaker say something for a few minutes and then stop. My father said it was the soldiers in the camp announcing to their fellows to abandon their camp. Finally, the helicopters (Chinooks) attempted to land again and there were no more gunshots. Father told us that the Vietnamese might have abandoned the camp by then.

My oldest sister got married in the late 1962 before I was born and while my family was still in Tham Thao. I never saw what she looked like. In 1968, my second oldest sister got married to a Kong Pachai soldier when we were in Sala village. In the middle of 1969, both of their families were forced by the Pathet Lao to move from their homes in Xieng Khouang to Hanoi, Vietnam, to get away from the war zone. This region was a bombing target for days and nights at the time. After my sisters and families left Laos, we did not have any contact. When the Pathet Lao took over Laos in 1975, they returned from Hanoi to live in Xieng Khouang again. Even after they had come back to Laos, I did not have a chance to see them because we lived in Viang Chan (ວຽງຈັນ) Province at the time. Shortly after the Pathet Lao took over Laos, there was a hostile situation which divided families into two sides. Our region was transformed as Chao Fa fought another war against the Pathet Lao government. It kept my two sisters even further apart from us until today.

I have very little of this in my memory because I was told it was the middle of 1969. Airplanes flew to the east over our village more than ever before and later they returned again. The war was being fought everywhere all year long by ground troops and by airplanes dropping bombs. Just as a precaution, my parents would take us with them to the fields every day instead of leaving us at home.

This year our rice field was on the east side of the village. When our rice was about a foot high, maybe in July, our parents took my fourth brother, Chia, my little sister Chee, and me to stay in the hut in the rice field. The rest went to the cornfield to clear weeds. One day at about 3 PM, the planes started to bomb somewhere near our village. While they were still in the field, Father feared that the three of us might not know where to escape to if the planes ever bombed close to us. He left the cornfield to find us in the rice field near our village. Suddenly, before he arrived at the rice field, we heard the roaring of the jet coming from the east. It was an unusual flight because every day they just came from the west. My brother carried our little sister on his back and dragged me by the hand, running to hide under a huge tree trunk next to the hut for protection. The second we got under the tree trunk, we heard bullets hitting at our hut and all the way to our village on the other side of the stream. In a few more seconds the loud noise was gone. We looked up and saw the smoke of burning houses in the village. Some were in flames and shattered. The cows, horses, pigs, and goats were running like they had lost their heads. The jet made only one flight and never returned. We hid under the tree trunk for about 30 minutes until there were no more planes coming again. My brother took us back to the hut. We saw some small bullet holes in the ground next to the hut. We checked around the hut and there were no bullet holes anywhere. We thought it was just lucky.

About 30 minutes later, my father arrived at the hut. He was running fast to see us. He was happy that we were safe. However, we anticipated that the T-28s would be coming again. My father decided to take us to a valley further to the east, where there was a better place to hide in case the planes bombed our place again in the late afternoon. In fact, they did come to bomb our village and everything surrounding it. In the valley, many other families joined us, too. About the time we left our rice field, my remaining family members left the cornfield to join us in the valley as my father had instructed them before he left. After a while, we were re-united with all my family members, except my mother. They told Father that when they were on the way coming toward us, the planes dropped many bombs on them. They ran in every direction to hide from the bombs. My mother was separated from them at that time. It was such bad news for us because we were not sure of the whereabouts of our mother. Father separated us from the other villagers and took us to a farmhouse not very far from there. Next to the little house, the farmer had built a trench for his family's protection, but they were not there that afternoon. In the little house, we just waited and waited until dark. We did not see Mother come. We started to worry but hoped that Mother was fine and would find us in the night or next morning. It was not only Mother who was missing, but we also did not have any food to eat that night. In the farmhouse, the owner piled up a heap of ripened cucumbers and dried corn. We were hungry. My father peeled cucumbers and sliced them for us for dinner. It was all we had for the night. It was cold during the night, too. My little sister was still a baby and had no milk throughout the night. I thought it was going to be very difficult without Mother by her side.

Early the next morning, Mother found us in the farmhouse. The night before she met a young lady who had also escaped the bombs at the same time. This young lady was from the Yang clan and lived in our village. They had slept throughout the night in a trench dug by villagers very close to where we stayed.

Once Mother found us, Father and one brother returned to visit our home. In about a half hour they came back with the bad news that we could not go back home anymore. It had been all shattered by the bombs from the day before. Our house had not burned because it was built with wooden shingles and wooden walls. Some of the houses built with thatch roofs had all been burned down. It looked like the entire village had been destroyed, so villagers did not have their homes to return to any more. They also believed that the planes would come back to drop bombs again soon. Father and brother brought with them a back basket of rice. Then, he decided to take us to our cornfield which was farther north of the village. It would be a better place to stay since there was a very high cliff above the field. If the planes ever bombed the area, it would be a better protected place for us. So, that morning we walked to our cornfield with nothing because almost everything was still in the house. Father said if it was quiet without air strikes during the day, they would consider going back later to get whatever was left in the house.

Later in the day, my parents returned home to gather some more of the household items. The lively village of about 50 houses scattered throughout the valley and around many small hills became cold. In some houses there were animals looking for their owners to feed them. The animals would soon become ownerless and wild after no human contact. Sadly enough, the place became a ghost town where weeds and trees soon started to grow. As my parents returned to our farm in the late afternoon, they said our future home would never be in the same place again. We might one day end up in the jungles if both sides of enemies prolonged the war. We stayed under the cliff above our cornfield for two days without a home. Mother and Father went to cook food for us in the farmhouse early in the morning and late in the evening. This way the airplanes would not see the smoke, so we would not be bombed again.

Uncle Tong Pao, who was Father's cousin, came to see us during the day while we were in the cornfield. His family hid in the woods between our farm and the village. He expressed concerns about the situation of each family hiding individually in the jungle. We had to find a place big enough for more families to live together to have better security, so we did not have so much fear of everything. The best way would be to move with the Yang cousins to a place adjacent to the former Lee village, the Nam Phai area, which they had abandoned a year earlier. It was a place far away from the route the Viet Cong traveled so often. It had water in the stream and was a good place to hide because there were a few close caves tucked in the narrow valley. However, they thought to move there it would be better to travel at night to minimize the danger from air strikes. Father and uncle agreed to the decision because we really had no other place to go.

That same evening after Uncle Tong Pao went back to his family, my family packed and moved, gathering together with our cousins at their place closer to our homes. Moving was very difficult for us. The rain was pouring down in the late afternoon and throughout the evening. The flooded water was everywhere as we walked down the path with mud under our feet and rain pouring on our heads. We could not use a flashlight or oil lamp while walking either. The only thing was to use the moonlight, but it was not bright enough because most of the time the path was under the thick forest. On the path we could not see whether snakes, scorpions, frogs or other creatures were under our feet. All we did was follow close behind other people in the dark. There were many children that cried of hunger or because they were soaked with the rain. We, the children, did not know how far our destination was. We just kept walking with our parents. Finally, sometime about midnight, we reached a place where farmland had been. In this area we saw the moon very clearly above our heads. It was good this region was not hit by the rain. We stopped there for the night. Everyone just laid down on the weeds. We were very tired and fell asleep very quickly. It was a sad night without a bed to sleep in but looking at thousands of stars flashing in the sky was like heaven was existing.

The next morning before sunrise we moved down to the deep narrow valley of jungles below, a place Father and Uncle Tong Pao expected to be. Together in this place, we were a few families of our Thao cousins along with a few Yang families. The hope was to stay there until the war was over and then return to our old home village. In this new place, nature provided a thick jungle of trees, wild bananas, and many other plants. They thought it was a well-protected place to hide where we might be able to sustain ourselves during the long war. We built a little house with a banana leaf roof and bamboo walls. With the protection of the thick jungle, we did not fear very much the planes bombing us again. However, even though we were under the thick jungle, we only cooked before dawn and late in the evening, so the airplanes would not detect the smoke. If smoke rose up into the air, airplanes would bomb us, assuming we were the Viet Cong. It was the rainy season, so the water dripped from the trees, and poured on us almost every day. Even after the rain had stopped, all day and night, water was still dripping from trees onto us. Both during the day and night, there were plenty of mosquitoes sucking our blood. Soon legs, arms, and any uncovered parts of our bodies, especially children's bodies, were filled with mosquito bites. Life was so sad without a home. The adults had no farm work to do or crops to harvest while the children had no good food to eat or hope for their future.

Even after we moved to hide in the jungle, the planes continuing bombing our Sala village. Everything was shattered or burned. Our rice at home had been burned. What we had left was the corn we had stored in the farmhouse. Therefore, from July to November our meals were corn instead of rice. The men went back home and transported the stone mill to the valley. Every day we had to grind the corn from the stone mill to make flour before it could be cooked. Beside the stone mill, they also installed a seesaw rice mill in the jungle for pounding rice. It was a very difficult situation, but still we had nowhere to go. From November to December we could not harvest our rice in the field due to the planes bombing during the daytime. Most of the people went to pick up rice at night by using the moonlight. Villagers feared that if they used a flashlight, the spy plane would see them. Every night they just pulled off the heads into the basket *(zaws nplej)* and took them back to our home in the jungle before dawn. It usually took a few hours to walk from where we lived to the field.

In this place whenever we heard the noise of airplanes, everyone rushed to the cave for protection. One day, a lady dried her clothes in the sun where they were exposed to the sky. We heard the spy plane fly in circles above us two times before going away. We rushed to the cave, assuming that the bombers would come soon. The woman grabbed her clothes and ran too. After just a few minutes, the T-28s came. They bombed us very heavily. Everything inside the cave shook as though it were going to fall on us. Rocks and dirt fell on top of our heads. In the dark, children cried and screamed in fear of death. It was lucky that the bombs missed their target. After the planes left, we came out of the dark cave and found five craters a few yards aways from the cave. The bushes had been cleared away. Banana trees were left with only stumps. If the bombs hit right above us, we could all be dead because the rocks on top were not very thick. On that day people learned their lessons, but they also blamed each other for the trouble. Since then no more clothes were to be displayed in the areas that would be exposed to the sky.

Although it was hard to hide in the jungle, we continued to stay until December of 1969. We did not have a New Year celebration. Every year Mother had steamed sticky rice and dried it. The day before the New Year she would deep fry it and mix it with molasses to make sweet crispy rice for us to eat during the New Year. It was so sad that this year for the first time we were in the jungle without molasses and sticky rice. So, we did not have the traditional crispy rice served on our table.

While living in this jungle place, my third brother Yeng, took me with him to see the former Lee village on a sunny morning with heavy dew on the weeds. We went there to gather some wild vegetables because we were far away from our old farm in Sala. The place was in the steep narrow valley further south where houses were built on both sides of the slopes. In the previous few years, I had gone there with Father whenever our Lee cousins needed Father to do shaman rituals. Before my brother and I got there that morning, we knew the place would be different since no one lived there now. As we arrived and observed, most of the houses were burned to the ground. These areas grew a lot of pumpkin vines because the villagers kept seeds at home. Other places grew mostly weeds around some posts that were still standing. It was also a scary moment because we feared being seen by airplanes. Anything we did must be done fast, and then go back to the woods. There were a lot of young squashes, so my brother gathered them quickly into his basket to fill it about half full and we returned to the cave.

One afternoon Mother took my fourth brother, Chia, with her to gather vegetables in an old farm tucked in a little valley close to the mountainside not very far from where we lived. While she was picking vegetables, unaware of anything, two soldiers came out from the woods to arrest her and my brother. After the soldiers captured them, they told Mother to return home to tell the men that all the villagers must abandon this place and go with them within 24 hours. They were there to get as many people as they could to go to Vang Pao's side in Viang Chan (ວຽງຈັນ). One soldier was from the Thao clan. His name was Ying Thao. He told Mother he was Nai Sai Ying Thao, which meant he was the communication operator. He assured my Mother that things would be okay before letting her return home. She asked them to let her son go, too. They refused. One reason was they feared if both went home together, more likely she would not inform the men in our hiding place to surrender to them. We might rather pack and go to Vietnam instead. It was difficult enough for them to get in touch with us since the Vietnamese soldiers were patrolling everywhere. They not only kept my brother with them over night, but the man said he also wanted my father to go to see him early the next morning in a cave up on the high cliff. If Father did not show up and all the families did not move with them by late afternoon the next day, they would just take my brother with them to the army camp, and ultimately, to Long Cheng. With no choice at the moment, Mother promised Ying Thao she would make sure Father went to see him the next morning, and make sure every family hidden in the jungle packed and went to surrender to them the next day, too. Mother came back, but her son was with them over night.

Once she returned home in the late afternoon without her son, she was depressed. She whispered to Father that Vang Pao's army captured them in the vegetable field. They released her to come back home to tell everybody to go with the soldiers. She said there was nothing else they could do to get my brother back. The only choice was to comply with them by doing what she had promised. The man who led the group, Nai Sai Ying Thao, wanted to talk to Father early the next morning in the cave where they were hiding. She was told that if we continued to live in this place between the Viet Cong and Vang Pao armies, one day the two sides might be fighting here. By then it would affect our hiding status.

After Mother told Father about the soldiers' demands, he was very anxious. Certainly, he was worried because his son was kept by the soldiers. He thought the information must be shared with Shong Ger Moua, our former Sala village chief. Then Father walked to his hut right above where we lived, about a quarter mile away. At the meeting, Father told Shong Ger Moua that the soldiers had captured his wife and son that afternoon. They released his wife, but they kept his son with them in a cave on the mountain. The soldiers also wanted him to go see them the next morning to discuss the matter. Then Shong Ger Moua told Father that he had attempted to reach Vang Pao's army for about five days already, but he was not very successful due to the interfering of too many Vietnamese soldiers patrolling the area. He agreed with Father that if the army really wanted us to leave with them, then we must go. He knew one of our future problems would be food. We might not be able to grow any more crops to feed our families the next year. Also, the planes miscalculated their targets so often. If the planes spotted anything in an area, whether it was civilians or Vietnamese positions, they just bombed it. They believed that the planes could not tell the difference between enemy targets and the hidden civilians. That's why they bombed our home village and the hiding place in the jungle, too. Also, it was impossible for us to walk through the jungle by crossing so many mountains and valleys to get to Lard Saen (ລາດແສນ) or anywhere else on Vang Pao's side. Therefore, they thought it was a good opportunity to go to Vang Pao's side while his soldiers were waiting there. We would be protected by the soldiers on the trip. So that evening my father and Shong Ger Moua told every family to get things ready to go the next day.

Unfortunately, in the same evening Uncle Tong Pao's mother, who we also called our grandma, died. She was about 70 years old and became very weak since we moved to this place. She had told her children before that she was too old to go anywhere. She did not want to move anymore. After she died, the villagers had to do a funeral for her first. Father told Shong Ger Moua that the death of grandma would delay us and would not be able to come the next day as the soldiers expected. He suggested to Father to negotiate with the soldiers when he met them the next day. Otherwise, they might think we did not want to comply with what Mother had promised them.

Throughout the night Mother seemed not to go to sleep at all. We, the children, knew for sure that Mother missed and was very concerned about our brother, Chia, in the cave. If anything went wrong and we could not be re-united with him, it could mean we would be separated from him for our whole lives. It became another longest night for Mother until the sun finally rose again to begin the new day. Then it was about time for Father to go see Nai Sai Ying Thao. Their only hope was that after the meeting, things would change, and Mother would see her son again.

Early that morning, as Mother had promised the soldiers, Father went to see Nai Sai Ying Thao in the cave up in the mountain. At their discussion, Father told Ying Thao that he had two things he needed them to do for him. First, his cousin's mother had just died last night, so they wanted to bury her that same afternoon in the mountain between where we lived and our previous Sala village. However, sometimes there were many Viet Cong, we called them red ants *(ntsaum liab)*, patrolling the area day and night. With communication problems, sometimes the Viet Cong caused trouble for the villagers, too. The Vietnamese did not want the civilians to do too much activity in the area. We really needed to do the funeral and bury the grandma during that day. Second, he had a bull he really wanted to take with him. There must be a way to take his bull with him. If he left the place without the bull, he had nothing left in life and his children would be crushed. In responding to Father's requests, Ying Thao promised Father that before noon he would call Long Cheng to order the planes to bomb the area where they wished to bury grandma, so the Vietnamese would not patrol there. It was also his intention to keep the Vietnamese away from the area and we could travel on the path in the late afternoon to the army camp. He gave signals to Father when and how the planes would bomb and stop. After the planes stopped bombing, they could bury the dead grandma. In the meantime, every family must pack everything to get ready. So right after the funeral, every family must leave the place to meet the soldiers up in the mountain to go to the army camp. Along with my Father's first request, he would like to see how the bull behaved when we met them in the afternoon. When they concluded their discussion, Father returned home to help our other uncles with the funeral for grandma.

At noon the T-28s started pounding the mountaintop area where they wanted to bury grandma. There was a route the villagers used and the Vietnamese traveled frequently by day and night. They flew one flight after another as though they wanted to crush the entire earth. For our safety, we were put in the cave while the parents were working on the funeral. As the bombs were dropped on the mountain, it shook all the way down to the valley where we stayed. We heard the sporadic sound of bomb explosions that felt like they were exploding on our backyard. After a few flights of bombing, we knew it was finished as Ying Thao had instructed Father. It became very quiet again. Then they quickly took grandma to bury in the mountain. Two hours after the burial, the shadow of the sun had fallen over the valley where we lived. The Viet Cong had not begun patrolling the route yet. All the men returned home, and Father, along with Shong Ger Moua, said it was time to leave. We must abandon this place.

The moment we were supposed to leave Mother did not have much to say but was even sadder. She was thinking about all our animals we had to leave behind. The one bull, which hopefully we might be able to take with us, while a few fat pigs were kept in the sties. At home we had two horses, more than 10 cows, and many pigs and chickens that ran into the woods. There was no time to butcher any animal for food. She was sad because over the year we ate only cornmeal with vegetables and no meat. We did not consider butchering a pig or cow for food. Now everything would be abandoned within minutes because of this war. The place where we used to live would be left behind and maybe no chance to return to see it again. The planes bombed the region so much, so we assumed that some of our animals might be dead by then while others would be running wild in the woods. A few days before our departure, they had already seen a few dead cows in the village when they went to pick rice. When we were about to leave, Mother went to open the sty door for the few fat pigs to get out. She cried because we lost our permanent home in Sala before, but this time we would have to leave our jungle home completely. Our future was uncertain. Where would we be? There were no other choices than to comply with what she had promised the soldiers the day before which was to go with them and to be re-united with my brother as soon as possible. I did not know much about what was going on. What I remember was that one brother did not come home for the night. I was told not to talk out loud while on the way up to the mountain to meet the soldiers. There might be Vietnamese hiding somewhere and would hear our conversation. Then they might approach us about our movement.

 We did not carry many things at all. Most families had blankets, some food for the night, and some uncooked rice in case we did not make it to the army camp. At the time I did not know how big I was and maybe very skinny. On the way I had to carry a small back basket with plates, bowls, and spoons in it. My youngest sister was the only one not carrying anything. There were a few Yang families and our Thao uncles with us on the way, maybe over 100 people. My oldest brother, Lauj, and his wife lived with other Yang and our Thao cousins in another cave in the mountain not very far from us. Once we left our place, they were supposed to leave theirs, but go on their own route to another army camp in the same area. We walked on a little path up to the mountain for a while and came to a sugarcane field. It belonged to one of those families in Nam Phai who left their village a year earlier. We were tired already once we got to the field. The countryside, the sky, and everything seemed quiet now, but in the trees were so many different kinds of birds singing. Some families dropped their belongings on the ground and rested. Others just kept going. As we rested for a while, Father cut a few links of sugarcane, peeled off the hard-outer skin, and gave my two sisters and me one piece each to chew on and feed our thirst. Both Mother and Father told us that we must chew the cane there and not be allowed to carry any with us. In about ten minutes we were told to finish chewing whatever was in our hands and mouths. It was time to move on. I threw my half-foot-long piece away. My fourth sister, Ying, finished hers to the last bite before we proceeded. My little sister refused to get rid of hers and chewed it on the way. Mother and Father did not want to stop her because she might scream very loudly and not be controlled. We walked up for a few minutes then cut across the slope of the mountain toward a little valley tucked into the high mountain. After a while we reached the field where the soldiers had captured my mom and brother. There was a little fallen hut on the side of the field. When we got close, the soldiers came out, holding my brother's hand and released him. At this time some families had already gone ahead of us to the camp.

When we met the soldiers, our bull started acting aggressively because he saw a group of strange people. Ying Thao said they might not be able to transport the bull to Lard Saen (ລາດແສນ) because it was too aggressive. He told Father to cut off the nose ring to let it go back to be united with the herd in the village. He promised Father that in the next few months if they were able to push the enemy back further to the east, then he would call Father to come back to get the bull again. At the time we were in an intensive war zone. Everyone had to be flown from the camps to Lard Saen instead of walking on foot. Then Father had no choice other than to cut the nose ring and the bell from its neck. The bull just ran directly back to where we had come. My second brother, Qhua, had tears running from his eyes as he watched the bull run away. It seemed the promise of Ying Thao was not a real one that could be kept, and we knew for sure we never had a second chance to return to get what we had left behind. Besides that, my father learned from his life experiences not to return to an old place after it had been abandoned. He saw many people die in their old homes because they returned to get something they had left behind. He said whatever happens next, just forget about the bull along with other things if Ying Thao could not carry them with us now. Life and family were the most important things on this earth. It was true, more and more Pathet Lao were advancing into the area after we left. Vang Pao's army could not even push them back to the Nong Het area as they wanted to. The bull, cows, pigs, and chickens ran into the woods and became wild. It was the end. Ten years later, Father met a soldier from that group in KM52 in Viang Chan Province. His name was Zeb Thoj. He told Father that they had killed our bull a couple weeks later for food. Father did not say much but told him that Father was happy they had killed it for food. It was better than the Vietnamese soldiers had.

When we arrived in the army camp, the shadow of the sun had covered the deep valley below us. The camp was on a very flat land on top of a high mountain. A coiled barbed wire fence surrounded the outer camp. Next was a ditch right before we entered the inner area. In front of the ditch were a few square holes about waist deep for soldiers to sit in for lookout. Next to the ditch inside the camp were red, white, green, and blue nylon lines stretched about half a foot above the ground to trap the enemy feet if they attacked and ran through the camp at night. The middle area was the place for activities such as cooking, dining, mustering the soldiers, and doing other things. Further to the south side of the camp were trenches where soldiers slept at night. They slept on the dirt like animals. The south side was very steep, so we could see very far down below. Looking to the west, the sky was very clear all the way to the horizon, with the orange colored clouds above and the glowing sun going down. The dusky lumps of clouds were beautiful.

When we arrived, the soldiers had not had their dinner yet. Once we dropped our stuff in the unoccupied area, a big tall man with a green uniform and a pistol on his waist told every family that we had to stay there overnight. We did not know his name. No one bothered to get his name either. He said the army would prepare the helicopters to fly us to Lard Saen early the next morning. The elders just nodded their heads like they all understood what he said, or maybe they did not even care as long as he could get them out of there as soon as possible. That would be for the best and the most desirable to get away from this camp. It would be better than being torn apart by grenades and rocket propellers if the enemies attacked. He asked if anyone had food for dinner because he did not want people to stay hungry for the night. They had enough rice to distribute to people if we did not have any. However, the people seemed to have carried enough rice to feed their families for a couple of days. It was a moment of being generous to offer rice to us.

While stirring rice in the big pot set on top of the fireplace, the mess cook, who was called in Lao language *Ai Liang*, held a piece of cooked beef, about a couple inches long, in one hand while chewing some in his mouth. He waved the meat to the people and asked if anyone would like to eat the piece of beef in his hand. One guy said he wanted it. Maybe he did not really want it, but pretended he wanted to eat it. Then he walked toward the mess cook to grab the piece of meat. When he got closer, about a yard away, the cook dropped the beef on the ground and stepped on it before the man could grab it. It looked like he was only teasing the other guy. Then he said he was going to kick the cook in the butt and then turned away again. The *Ai Liang* just smiled.

Soon it was the end of the day and the night came to take over again. We did not have tents to sleep in during the night. At dark we were ordered to put out all the fires. The sky was clear. The weather was dry. Our life without a home in the camp was different because everyone just laid on the ground and covered themselves with blankets.

Since there was no water, then no bath either. It was the second quarter of the moon, so for a while we had moonlight shine on us. Early in the evening some children cried, but none later or throughout the night. During the night, soldiers were on the lookout and roving all night long. That was how a soldier's life was, I guess. They walked past us many times to check on people to make sure we were okay. We had a peaceful night since the enemy did not follow us to the camp. However, some adults felt like hell in the camp. It was too long for them before a new day came. Imagine that all those civilian lives were in those soldiers' hands over the night. The soldiers could not wait until the new day had come either. If the enemy had followed us, we did not know how many bullets would penetrate each body. Some would have been torn apart by grenades, B-40s, or mortar explosions, with flesh and blood stains everywhere. We might all have perished, and my story would have ended unwritten here.

At dawn while it was still very dark in the woods, the same tall man from the day before, came around again. He told people to get up to cook breakfast for the children and eat as much as they could before the helicopters arrived. We did not have water for cooking, so they had to give us some. For a while my mother steamed the rice in a pot on top of the fireplace. The grass was very wet from the heavy dew of the night. Very soon we saw the sunrays strike the mountain in the west, but the sun did not get to us yet because it was still blocked by the high mountain to the east. After a moment, the guy came back again to tell us that Long Cheng had sent him a message that the helicopters were on their way. There were ten of them. It sounded very powerful. Everyone must be fast. Father asked Mother if the rice was ready yet. She then pulled the pot out from the side of the fireplace, opened it, and shoveled each one of us a scoop of hot rice into a little bowl. It was damn hot. It was such a rushed moment for us to swallow the hot rice. She poured water on it to cool it off, so we could just eat it with a spoon.

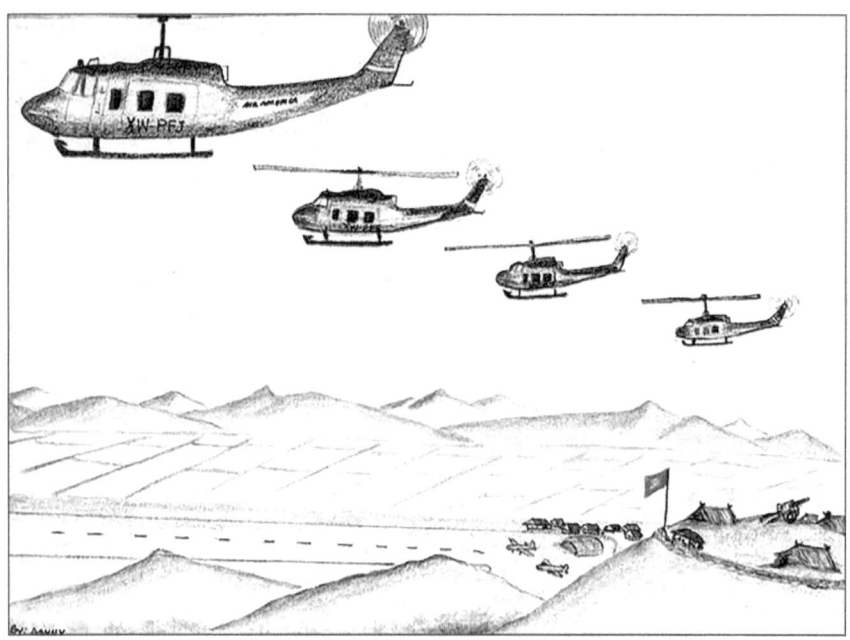

Flying Helicopters by Danny Yang Xaiphia

A few minutes later the sound of the helicopters came from the south, but we had not seen them yet. The tall man yelled very loud that every family must get things ready because that was the sound of the helicopters coming to get us. The noise grew louder and closer. It echoed from the high mountain in the east, too. We were looking at the mountaintop in the east where the noise was coming from. As the noise got closer and closer, the echo was gone. Then we heard the real noise, "ter, ter, ter….and turned bler, bler, bler…." as they got closer from the west. Finally, there were one, two, three, and four helicopters, the UH-1B kind, coming toward us and the sound of rotors sounded, "bler, bler, bler…." instead. There were not ten as we were told. Maybe the soldier just wanted to impress us. They all had the shape of tadpoles, so later we called them the tadpole helicopters. The tall guy screamed very loud for everyone to get ready. A few minutes later they were close enough to touch on the ground. The tails were swinging from side to side. The wind blew so hard. Some gusts filled the air with dust, leaves, and other flying objects like bumblebees. The grass laid flat for a while before they landed but rose up again once the heavy wind calmed down a bit. The tadpoles were on the ground. The loud noise became softer.

The soldiers rushed to push the families boarding the helicopters. Some soldiers were also watching and making hand salutes as we were boarding. Maybe they wished they could go home with us to see their mamas, too. Instead of loading one family per helicopter, they just pushed as many people as possible to fit inside the stomach of each one. I was too young, and it was also a hurried moment, so I did not remember how many people were in one helicopter when flying from the camp to Lard Saen. My family was getting in one of those in the first flight.

Once we all were inside, everyone turned around to see who was there, but my father and two brothers were not with us. The door just slid shut with a "boom." Then we felt the helicopter tip forward on the ground, but we also felt it lift off and up. For a few seconds, the motion went up and down, up and down. Some people started to feel nausea. A woman with a little girl was crowded in with us. She wiped her tears off her face with her green silk scarf. She said that we would be gone forever this time and never be back to see our village again *(Mus tas ib sim neej yuav tsis rov los pom peb tej zej zog ntxiv lawm)*. It sounded very sad like it was the end of the world. We held tight to each other. The children panicked that they were going to fall down as the helicopter descended to Lard Saen in the lower altitude. After a while it descended, making the loud noise again. Then we felt a couple of bumps as though it was going to tip over again before it settled down completely. The guy sitting next to the door popped it open. He pushed everyone out onto the large brown dried grassy area. The people coming out of the helos, especially the females, tried to walk against the heavy wind that blew their hair, sashes, and scarves everywhere. Mothers held their crying babies very tight to their chests. The packages inside the helicopters were tossed out on the ground. People grabbed them as fast as they could and tossed them to an area further away before the tadpoles lifted off again. The elders assured their youngsters that we had arrived in Lard Saen safely.

Once we got outside to look around, we saw they were landing one, two, three, and four tadpoles not very far from each other. Only a few minutes after everything was tossed out, the men shut the doors again. Their tails lifted up one after another, and the bodies tilted up to fly away.

We could hardly wait until the next flight came back to see if Father and brothers would come out from one of those tadpoles when they landed. All we did was just keep watching to the North, and maybe other families who had members left behind would do the same thing. When the second flight landed, Father and brothers came out from one of them. Our worries were over. The flights kept going and coming all day. More and more people were unloaded on the field. The population from the large families in a village of about 50 houses doubled when the second group from a different camp came at the end of the day. The total number of people was 400 or 500, or even more gathered in this new place. Both groups of people from the two different camps were almost equal in numbers.

Finally, my oldest brother, who lived up in the mountain with the Yang families, arrived at noon with his wife and son. Based on what he told us, it seemed the day before they had arrived in their army camp earlier than we had. As his story went on, he told us that when they arrived in the camp, a soldier grabbed a girl and told her parents he wanted to marry her. The parents could not say much, but they gave up their daughter to him. The next morning before the helicopters arrived at the camp, he told them he would fly her to Long Cheng instead of letting her go with them to Lard Saen. She was sad at hearing this. My brother mentioned the family's name, but it was too long ago for me to remember.

In the afternoon when we arrived in Lard Saen, some officials came to visit us. They registered people in their handbooks. Soon after the registration, they distributed one kilo of sticky rice per person to each family. Along with the rice, they also provided some utensils and some yards of plastic sheets for families to set up tents to cover their heads.

For people like us who used to live in the mountainous villages, Lard Saen was unusual. It was a very large flat grassy area. The nature and environment were very different from what we knew. There were a few Hmong families who lived in the area already. There was also a small Lao village on one side of the plain. Some people were confused and could not tell the directions of which way was east or west. One day a group of women went to the woods to gather firewood. Once they got into the thick jungle, they did not stay together. One woman got lost and could not manage to return home in the afternoon. She stayed in the woods until the next morning when the sun rose, so she knew which direction to head back to the place we lived. When she got home, she told people that she was not able to get back to where she started. Any direction she went, she seemed to keep moving into the thick jungle. Finally, she found no way to come back home and stayed in the cold place all night long.

The new living conditions, food, and other things were also very different for us. The tents were set up one next to the other. The plastic sheets replaced our temporary banana leaf huts in the jungle or the solid wooden-roof houses we had in our villages. The water was pumped or pulled up in buckets from the well instead of from the small, clear stream. Even our sleeping place was on the ground rather than in beds. Crowds of children came to see and play with each other while we had been strangers to one another before. The tasteless sticky rice smelled bad like mold which was different from the mountain rice we used to eat at home, and some children refused to eat it. Adults were talking about how this was the way a people lost their country. We never would have the homes, farm animals, and fields we used to have. We never would have the food we used to eat. Children became agitated or aggressive toward their parents when asking for this and for that, but they did not get the kind of food they asked for. They used the proverb, *muaj tsiv pluag, pluag tsiv tuag,* for short. This means you are rich, but if you keep moving, you will become poor. If you are poor and you keep moving, then you will all die. First you lost all your household items plus your livestock, and you were able to carry with you only one or two pairs of clothes and, at best, a little money. Next you would spend all your money for food or other things. Finally, you have nothing left, and if disease strikes, you die. This was the way the refugee life started.

The day before we arrived from the army camp, Joua Yia Moua, who was our aunt's son-in-law, was already in Lard Saen waiting for us. My father also called him son-in-law. He escaped to Long Cheng a couple years earlier. With him were *Nai Kong* (ນາຍກອງ) Chue Ker Moua, who people considered an important figure, and other officials. They came there to register some men to go to Pha Khao (ຜາຂາວ, White Rocky Cliff) for an interview and also to get people organized to live in a certain place. My father was not sure how many new men the officials registered because it was an anonymous decision of who should go and who should not. On the third day in the afternoon, they just called my father, Uncle Wa Toua, and Joua Pao Xiong to get on the small plane and fly to Pha Khao. Before my father left the area with the others, he told my oldest brother, Lauj, to watch over everyone while he was gone. As I was watching, Father was wearing black clothes, a silver necklace around his neck as usual, and walked with the other people to the plane. In his right hand, he carried an extra set of clothes in a small bag. It was very sad to the point my tears dropped to see him leave because I thought they were taking the three of them to jail. When we lived with the communist if someone was taken away by the officials, it was to be sent to prison, or what they called "Education Camp." I thought, what if Father never would be allowed to return, what would happen to us then? However, Joua Yia Moua was his close son-in-law, so if the officials took them for a bad reason, he should have told Father already. They did not know what to expect by going there either, but hoped not to be sent to jail. What kind of information did the officials need from these mountain farmers anyway? He did not say in how many days he would return to Lard Saen because the officials only told them that the trip would be for a few days.

Upon arriving in Pha Khao, they were asked some unspecific questions, such as had they seen any enemy sites, and when the planes bombed the enemy, did they ever hit their targets. Other questions were about how the Viet Cong advanced their troops on the Ho Chi Minh Trail, or even further into Laos. Obviously, as Father said, they had never seen what the trail was like, so how could they tell the officials such thing.

Lard Saen was a plain with some marshes and small streams in some parts. There were some bomb craters close to the area where we stayed. Even though it was not a hiding place for the enemy, many bombs had been dropped on this area before. Some of the craters close to the stream were half filled with water during the rainy season and had a lot of fish in them. On the third day after my father had gone to Pha Khao, we walked around to see what damage the bombs had done. On the tour we saw a group of six or seven Lao people shoveling the water out of one of the craters, so they could catch the fish after they had emptied it. They filled water into bowls, small buckets, and pails to toss out. It was the first time I heard Lao people talk in their language. While the adults were shoveling the water out from the crater, some children already went down inside and tried to catch the fish. Some were topless and stained with brown mud, while others wore loose pants and were careless about getting dirty. While we were watching, a lady yelled out loud at the children. I asked my third brother, Yeng, what she meant. My brother said he guessed the lady told the children to stop doing that until the water was gone and then they would catch the fish together. It looked like the children were having fun in the mud.

On the fifth day, my father and his two companions were sent to see a man named Pacher Yang, who was supposed to order the plane for them to fly back to Lard Saen because they were done with the interview. When they got to Pacher Yang's house, he told them there should be a plane to take them back to their families in Lard Saen the next day. They had to stay for one more night. They returned to where they stayed before. On the sixth day at about 10 o'clock, they went up to see the man again. The small single engine plane landed on the airstrip. Pacher Yang told them it had to fly two flights, sending ammunitions to two other sites before it could fly them to Lard Saen. They waited there for two more hours and finished chopping a heap of firewood for Pacher. Suddenly, the bird arrived again. He rushed them on board the plane. On the plane were the pilot, a monk, Father, Uncle Wa Toua, and Joua Pao Xiong. At one time in the air when they flew across the rocky mountain next to Pha Khao, the pilot just wanted to scare them off. He flew the plane very high and then let it go into a steep dive down to the rocky cliffs as though it were falling down. Without any seat belts on, they all slid back and forth inside the plane and hit their heads many times against the walls. They thought maybe something was wrong with the plane. Once it had descended and almost hit the cliff, the pilot accelerated to go up again. It did not hit anything. They were scared to death and turned blue or pale. The pilot turned back and smiled at them. Then they knew he was making fun of them. With his big stature which was almost six feet tall, Uncle Wa Toua took no jokes or insults from anyone in life. He called the pilot, "The damn horny man who was needing females."

While we were in this strange place, the Lao people took the opportunity to do business with the refugees by selling their noodles, called *khao poun*. Each day a few ladies carried noodles in one bucket and the broth in the other bucket to sell around to the newcomers in the area. Some children were hungry, crying, and begging their mothers to buy the noodles for them. The problem was that most families had only silver coins. In this place they had no currency exchange for people yet. A little bowl of soup cost five cents *(tsib npib)* of old French Indochinese coins. Thus, the parents did not want to waste their silver. Some parents told their children that the broth was nasty because it was made with dung beetles *(kab quav nyuj)*. It was not made with fish or other meat such as what we used to have at home. This kind of trick made some children not want to ask their parents for noodles again.

After my father returned from Pha Khao, most of the men decided not to stay in Lard Saen anymore because they feared one day the enemy might attack the village. If this happened, we might end up in Pathet Lao hands again. The T-28s flew over us one or two flights each day. No one knew what their purpose was, but assumed they continued to drop bombs on Vietnam or the Ho Chi Minh Trail. By judging the craters in the fields where we stayed, the men thought one day bombs might be dropped on us. The best choice was to move to Sam Thong by ourselves. Besides that, the Lao villagers prohibited the new refugees from getting firewood in the forest. They imposed a new rule that they were not responsible for anyone's life while people were out in the woods. Some of their sons also had joined the Pathet Lao army. Thus, in this village we were still sleeping with the enemy.

On the tenth day, we packed and moved westward to Sam Thong, the place where we hoped to live for a long time. The trip was long, tiring, and painful on our feet. We walked all day up and down on the bumpy mountain path. By noon on the first day, we had reached a very high mountain, which was called Penis Mountain *(roob txua qau)*. It was named that because a long time ago a Lao Theung girl died there due to her love affair with a man. When he left her, she chased him on a long journey until she got to this mountain, but she could not catch him. She was exhausted, collapsed, and died. This was what we were told at the time. After her death, the people decided to remember her with a ceremony, so each male traveler was to make a wooden penis for her with a bless. For children and females, each one just gave her a little tree branch. The blessing was often meant to ask her to boost their energy, strengthening their health, protected them from evil. They also blessed her for a brighter life when she was re-incarnated, and may god give her a better lover in her next life. Then she would not have to repeat her same mistake. Everyone had to do this each time they passed this mountain. If someone did not do anything and later had some leg pain or other body part pain, it would be said that the dead girl was punishing that person. It was unbelievable that this ceremony had been going for so many years, and thus, the heap of wooden penis and tree branches was about three feet high and a couple of yards wide. While Father was making a little wooden penis from a twig and threw it on top of the heap, I just picked a little branch tip with three leaves and threw it on.

On our trip, there was a young lady married to a man who used to be in the army. The man quit the army before he married the young girl. His young wife gave birth to a set of triplets in the jungle a few days before we came to the army camp. She had two girls and one boy. On the trip she carried a little pack on her back with one baby on her chest. Her husband carried one while her mother, who was a widow, carried the third one. It was amazing that she delivered three babies without a hospital or even a midwife. The three babies were born with no immunizations or medical care. And above all, they all survived. The mother was fine, too.

Late in the afternoon of our first day, we arrived in a valley with thick wild banana trees. Everyone was tired. We stopped there before the sun went down to build a hut for the night. The place was a very deep, cool valley with less sun exposure. Soon it was very dark. Each family would have a fireplace burning to give light in the tent. Some children would still sit around the fire before they fall sleep. Throughout the night we heard many kinds of noise of creatures and owls. It was another peaceful night since we no longer feared the bombs dropped by the planes as before.

The next morning before we started our journey again, people started to make noise by chopping firewood to start the cooking fires. Children cried. After a while smoke rose everywhere to the sky, but soon disappeared once it reached up into the trees. There was a heavy dew on the grass and banana leaves. Without realizing it was only dew, my little sister and I asked Mother and Father why it had rained that night, but we had not heard it. My second brother, Qhua, told us it was only dew. We did not have much to eat before leaving this place for the day. We each had a couple spoons of the tasteless sticky rice from Lard Saen and a little piece of dried salty beef for breakfast. The day started again with walking, resting, but without knowing our destination.

After three days walking, we finally got to Sam Thong. It was a dusty place where a few roads came together. The place was larger than I imagined, but the conditions were worse than what I had thought. When a car drove down the road, an orange cloud rose up following it, and then slowly the air cleared again.

On the first day in Sam Thong, Uncle Wa Toua's little daughter was very sick. Always, he looked up to my father for help because his father and my father's father were brothers. His older brothers escaped from Xieng Khouang to another village, Pha Daeng (ເຜາແດງ), a few years before. They left him with my father. He was more attached to my father than to his own brothers. His first wife died a year before we left Sala, and he remarried another woman, but the daughter was from his first wife. In the late afternoon before the sun went down, they called a shaman to perform a ritual, but it did not help. As soon as the man was done performing his rituals, the child died. Uncle Wa Toua did not have any more children left. We were very poor. We were in a bad luck situation.

Once we arrived in Sam Thong (ຊໍາທອງ), the people who came along with us all disappeared. They went to settle with their relatives scattered in the village. I really do not have much memory of this place because we spent so little time in it. Besides that, I did not pay much attention to the surrounding environment. Three of our uncles, Tong Pao, Chia Fong, and Walee, stayed with us in a group of houses next to each other on the side of the dirt road where vehicles passed by a couple times a day. We stayed with a family related to our Uncle Walee's wife, but I did not even know their names. They had a big house. This family had five children ranging from ages 3 to 13. One little girl of about five or six years hated us children very much. Whenever she came close to us, she blinked her eyes very fast, or closed them very tight to show us that she really hated us. There was also another younger boy who often tried to intimidate us. One time when we went out to their backyard, he held a stick about a yard long. He swung very hard toward me like he really wanted to hit me. When the stick got very close to me, he held it back. It made my body feel a tingle and it felt like the stick touched my skin already. I came back inside the house. After that day I did not follow them anymore. As a refugee, I thought that was the beginning of my suffering. A few days later before we moved out, he came to persuade me to go outside with them to catch butterflies. I refused and told my little sister, Chee, not to go either. I was so glad that we did not spend many days with them.

On the fourth morning in Sam Thong, my parents took me to the market with them. My brothers, Qhua and Chia, went to the market very early before we did. By the time we almost got there, my brothers were already returning. They said they did not find anything to buy. My second brother had some dried crunchy buffalo skin strips in one hand and was eating one strip from the other hand. He handed me one and told me that it was buffalo skin. They were fried just like pork rinds. He asked me to take it and return home with them because there was not much going on in the market. I refused to take the buffalo skin because I did not feel like I wanted to eat it. I also wanted to go to the market with my parents badly. So, we went to the market while they returned home. Int the market, the vendors sold goods in an open space like a flea market. The clothes were hanging high inside the house. The meats were on the tables. But vegetables and many other dried items were displayed on the ground with mats underneath. Since we had just come from the village and were never exposed to any market place before, I thought people in Sam Thong were very civilized.

According to Father, a few days after we arrived in Sam Thong, the officials wanted to send us back to Lard Saen. They set up three meetings three days apart for each to meet and negotiate with the officials to send us back. Then Shong Ger Moua, our former village chief of Sala, was disappointed with the news. He argued that when Vang Pao's army came to Sala, he secretly killed cows and sent beef to feed the soldiers. When the Pathet Lao asked him why he killed the cows, he lied to them that he killed the cows to do some ceremony to ask for gods and mother earth's help to protect his own villagers. The truth was he sent beef to feed their soldiers hidden in the jungles. He did everything he could to keep the soldiers safe from being killed. The officials should not turn their backs on him and the rest. If they really wanted to send us back to Lard Saen, why not just let us stay hiding in the caves in Nam Phai? We had been through all those dangerous routes to Sam Thong, but finally they wanted to send us back to face our former enemies. He did not care whether we died or stayed alive by hiding in the cave. He did not see the reason why they wanted to send us back to feed the enemies. Ironically, that had been a better place to live than bringing us to Sam Thong. It was a betrayal and punishment to the newly arrived villagers. If we were sent back to Lard Saen, we would just be a target to be bombed. If we returned there and the enemy captured us again, the men would be accused of treason, and we all could be killed. As the debate went on, the officials finally listened to his point and let us stay in Sam Thong.

In a week, the new people decided to move to a place not very far from Sam Thong village. My father took us there with them, too. It was farmland in which people had stopped planting crops for a year already. In this place, only a few families had lived for a couple of years. In our new group, about half from Sala, Yang, Moua, Xiong, and Thao families came together to settle with the original families. Once every family arrived, they used their plastic sheets from Lard Saen to set up their little houses as temporary shelters. We did not receive much assistance except some tasteless sticky rice.

Soon after we moved into this place, the Mayors and *nai kongs* imposed a new idea by dividing Sam Thong into three sections. Each one of them used their people within their section to watch for the enemy. If anyone had information about the Pathet Lao coming close to the area, they must report to the officials and get ready for the battle if anything should happen. My father, along with other men, thought it was such a lousy idea. It would not be possible for the civilians to defend

Sam Thong if the enemy marched there with cannons and tanks. This neither made sense, nor was the village defensible. The men did not like it because they had enough already of military tactics in Xieng Khouang before they came here. In the past month before we moved there, people already saw Pathet Lao soldiers scouting in the mountains, but they could not tell exactly from what units and how many soldiers. It seemed likely that one day the Pathet Lao might invade the territory. After a month in the small village, Father thought we must move to Pha Daeng where his cousins lived. He told Chue Ker Moua, the man who was related to our village chief Shong Ger Moua, that he declined to accept their rice assistance. He wanted to move to Pha Daeng, where was remote from the enemy target. Whatever would happen to his family, he would not bother the officials for help. Upon arriving there, he would seek help from his relatives rather than waiting for assistance from the refugee program. Then not only Father wanted to move out, but most of the newcomers wanted to leave this place to settle with their relatives elsewhere as well. After a month in this new place, we moved again. The day we were leaving, there were many families moving with us.

It was early 1970. A few days before we moved out from the place near Sam Thong, Uncle Blia Cha Thao came to visit us in full army uniform. He was in the army at the time. Father told me he was our Uncle Blia Cha. Uncle's dad and Father's dad were brothers. I wondered, "Why he had a very narrow face, slender body, and was very tall. He looked very handsome, too. He must be a leader of something with that kind of uniform." The purpose of his visit was to recruit more soldiers to fight the war in Laos. He was serving under the Lao right-wing army, in the 21st Battalion, which was supported by the American CIA. At that time my second brother, Qhua, was still too young, not ready to be a soldier yet. Thus, Uncle Blia Cha decided to take my oldest brother, Lauj, who was already married, and our young Uncle Walee, who was also married at the time. My brother and Uncle Walee each had a child already. My father, Uncle Blia Cha, and Uncle Walee were very close cousins because their fathers were brothers. He promised Father that he would keep my brother and his cousin Walee in the army for only two years. Father had no choice and did not want to upset Uncle Blia Cha, so he let uncle take my brother and Uncle Walee with him to the army. My father also had a fear that the officials were arresting men everywhere at the time to become soldiers. Sometime the young men had to go hide in the woods if there were some officials who showed up in the village with soldiers. There was a very big demand for soldiers at the time. So, my father thought if he let my brother and Uncle Walee join Uncle Blia Cha's command, it would be a better choice than if they joined with someone else. He hoped that uncle would keep his promise, and, besides that, he might treat them well while they were under his supervision. Since we were going to move again, my father told Uncle Blia Cha to postpone taking Uncle Walee and brother Lauj until we completed our move to Pha Daeng. Once we all completed the move, my brother and uncle would just pack up to go with him.

Our lives were unsettled because of moving from one place to another. The hope was that when we got to Pha Daeng, it would be our permanent home. When we were ready to move, we just took off the plastic sheet from our temporary shelter, packed, and abandoned our small home. Even though we were little children, from the jungles to the army camp and from there to this place, each one of us always had to carry a small pack of clothes, blankets, or a small back basket with something in it. The trip was up mountains and down into the valleys again, with much steeper elevations, until we reached our destination.

The trip was three nights and four days. Our second night was on the bank of the Nam Ngeum. We arrived there by noon. It was the first time we saw the river, and it was huge. Moreover, there were so many people and only two bamboo rafts in the water. Each time only two or three people could get on a raft to cross the river. Also, there were only three or four people able to paddle or steer the rafts. Most of the men were too afraid to do it because they did not have any swimming skills. They feared tipping over the raft and drowning. Therefore, those men who were able to steer the raft were over-worked. They became exhausted after so many trips crossing the river. My father and I were the last two people on the last trip. Once we got all across the river, it was getting dark already. Thus, most of the families stayed very close to the river overnight, so they could use water from the river. Instead of setting up the tents, people just put their plastic sheets on the sand to sleep over night. Every time when I woke up during the night, all I heard was flowing water. Even though the water level stayed the same, I was very scared that the river might flow over us while we were sleeping.

Along the way to Pha Daeng, a Yang family who had lived with us in Sala, had a newborn baby. The mother died soon after giving birth while we were still hiding in the cave in Nam Phai more than a month earlier. During the trip the baby was sick and did not get enough nutrition. On our third day when we got to Ha Ee and Phou Kang (ຜູ ກາງ) villages, his grandmother said he was weaker and had very shallow breath during the day. Late that afternoon just before sundown, the dusky sky above us was beautiful while we were in the long narrow mountain village. The cool breeze was welcomed by the healthy people. However, the tiny motherless baby was very sick. While his grandma held him to her chest, wrapped with a thin white blanket, and sat on a stump in a flat area by the side of the path, he stopped breathing and closed his eyes. I saw his face was still pink and pale while I walked by, but his grandma said it was the end. I do not remember having seen his father and siblings with grandma and grandpa at the time. It seemed that the baby's siblings took a different route, or they were still behind us. I stopped for a while, watching him. I heard his grandma say a few words that she loved him very much. Her tears dropped from her face. She had a lump in her throat and wailed. I walked quickly again to catch up with my siblings after seeing the baby. Father was behind me. He stopped and talked with the grandma and grandpa for a few words. After that, before it got dark, we moved to some empty houses which people had recently abandoned. We spent the night in that village, but I did not remember what they did with the dead baby.

The next morning was our third day of the journey. We left Phou Karng for Pha Daeng, which we thought was not far away, so we should be there by sundown. However, we were too tired, especially the children who had sore feet, so the walking was not very fast. By sundown we got to a village very close to Pha Daeng. It was called Guava Fruit Village, *zos txiv cuab thoj*. Some families continued to walk ahead by going up the hill, but Father decided to stop the trip. We moved to the side of the village to set up our tent for the night. Two of our uncles' families and some of the Yang families stayed with us there. It was not a good place at all, except the weather was very dry. I thought if we could make it to our Pha Daeng, it would be a better night. We burned a big fire, and many children sat around it. We listened to the elders recite some scary folktale stories. Soon children just dropped to the ground asleep. It was the end of another day.

On the fourth morning we left at dawn without breakfast. We kept walking and hoped we would get there soon. By late morning, maybe at ten o'clock, we got to Pha Daeng (ຜາແດງ), a place just as I had imagined it. But, yet it was not exactly what I thought. The village was built on top of a very long narrow mountain that ran from east to west. This place had many empty houses because those people had moved elsewhere. We moved into a house next to Mother's oldest brother Tong Pao Yang's house. There were a lot of uncles from both Father's and Mother's sides, who I had never seen before. The families living in this village were mostly Yang and Thao. There was also another village in the lower land, which was comprised mostly of the Lee and Moua clans. It was a quiet and better place to live because we heard no more bomb explosions from the airplanes. The nightmare of sleeping with the noise of planes flying over us was over. We hoped it would be our permanent place.

3

SHORT YEAR IN PHA DAENG

*"Zej zog nyob saum **roob**, thiaj nyob kaj siab lug li lub neej **hmoob**"*

It seemed as refugees we had too many problems along the way. A few days after we arrived in Pha Daeng (the Red Cliff Village), Uncle Wa Toua and his wife had a fight. He was very depressed due to the loss of his first wife and his two daughters. Besides that, his brothers who left Xieng Khouang two years earlier, scolded him for being separated from them. In the evening after the fight, he took some quinine medicine to end his life. When my father was called and arrived at Uncle Blia Cha's house, where uncle stayed, my father was not able to communicate with him anymore. All he did was to yell very loud at Uncle Wa Toua a few words to find out what had happened. By then it was too late. He did not get a response. Suddenly, Uncle Wa Toua involuntarily jumped up and blood spilled from his mouth and nose. He became limp, dropped into their arms, and stopped breathing. It was the end.

In Pha Daeng there were many children younger than I was, who already attended school. Some mornings, older siblings had to drag their crying younger siblings to school because they did not want to go. We had just arrived in the village and our parents did not want to send us to school yet. Those days in Laos there were no preschools for children in this small village. When a child was ready for school then he or she would just go directly to first grade. The test for readiness was for the child to reach up over his head with one arm to touch his ear on the other side of his head. Even some older children, who should have attended second or third grade, still had to attend first grade if they had never been in school before. Some children spent two or three years in one grade if they did not pass the final exam at the end of the year. In the afternoon when those children returned from school, I had a chance to play with some of them. They spoke a mixed language with both Lao and Hmong words. Sometimes I raised my eyebrows and wondered what the hell they were talking about when they spoke with some Lao and Hmong words together in the same sentence. For instance, when they said, "We go to the farm", they would use the Lao word *pai* for *go*, to replace the Hmong word *mus* which cut me off from understanding the whole thing.

There were also many children who did not attend school at all. I did not have much to do, except some days I accompanied my parents to the fields. Some days when I was home, I played outside in the dirt yard or went to the woods with those children to pick sour buds *(pos teev taum)* and eat them with salt and hot pepper. Usually, at noon we would go back to our homes to have lunch and then come back to play until dark. We had so much fun those days. There was nothing to worry about in this homogeneous society because one people spoke one language. No such kidnapping or abducting by strangers, except we were scared of ghosts in the dark. Some evenings we lined up in teams, it did not matter if girls or boys were together, to kick each other until one team gave up. It was a different style of youth culture in a different era. Some children got bruised or hurt badly on their knees or lower legs from the game. One day a girl who lived very close to us walked like a crippled person because she got hurt the night before from this kicking game. Her grandma scolded her very loudly, to demand answers what was wrong with her that morning. She replied that she tripped on a bump and hurt her shin the night before. Her grandma insisted that maybe she must be hurt from the kicking game. She continued to say it was not so. Even though she was hurt, she was told to move faster like an uninjured person while doing her house chores.

During my childhood I was treated badly by the stronger ones for no reason or at least very little reason. They looked down on me, and sometimes, they thought I was too weak and could be insulted. Some children even used bad language on me, but most of the time I never retaliated. I made some friends while we were in Pha Daeng since it was my first place to be exposed to children other than my close cousins. I usually tried to befriend the weaker ones because I believed that they would not take advantage of me. Sometimes the friends of my friends were also my enemies. If there were any conflicts between us, my close friends would approach their friends who were my enemies to resolve the problem. Between the ages of six and 12, we had a lot of fights due to someone who was rude enough just to kick others for no reason. Later in my youth, fortunately, I made more friends than I encountered enemies.

In those years, I lived together with so many cousins from Mother's and Father's sides in the same village, but I never hung around with them. I rather befriended children other than those close cousins. The reason for that was that not very long after we arrived, I followed a few of my second cousins to the valley to pick wild star fruits *(txiv xwm leej)*. They told me if sliced and soaked in sugar, star fruit tasted good. They promised me they would climb up the tree to pick the fruit and, once they came down, they would be willing to share some with me. Thus, I believed in them enough to follow their butts to the valley. Once we got there, I could not climb the tree to pick fruit, so I was told to wait for them on the ground. When they came down with a lot of fruits, they gave me two little ones. I thought it was okay since I did not climb up the tree to get them. When we returned about half way home, one of my second cousins yelled that a ghost was chasing us. As a child growing up in the jungles of Laos who heard many adults talk about ghost in the woods, I was scared to death. These cousins were bigger, stronger, and ran faster. I did not have shoes and I feared thorns would jab my feet. So, I just walked as fast as I could. After a while the four of them had disappeared. I slowly managed to get myself back to the light in the village where I believed there would be no more ghosts. By the time I got home, two of them were sitting right at their porch next to their father. That uncle smiled at me but said nothing. My thinking was maybe because they got home first, they told their father that they had scared the hell out of me so badly while we were in the woods. Since then I never had any attachment to those second cousins. One time the parents of the cousin who scared me in the woods killed a pig for a ceremony in the late evening. The next morning their mother came to our house inviting us to join them for the breakfast. I refused to go. I pretended not to be hungry and being shy. The truth was I did not feel like I wanted to approach the children who had done bad things to me in the woods. Another reason I thought that maybe I was not born to be a likable child, so I should not be with them. I took it as a lesson to learn and be myself. In my life when I had done some good thing or some good thing happened to me, I remembered it only for a few days. When some bad thing happened to me, I remember it for life.

Another day not very long after the first incident, these cousins persuaded me to go with them to the other side of the village to pick guava fruit *(txiv cuab thoj)*. I was dumb enough to believe them again. I thought I would just try to go with them one more time to see what happened. When we got there, his nephew went the other direction and did not come back. The same boy who had scared me the last time, kept calling his nephew very loudly in front of us. I did not realize that he might get angry if I just asked him. Thus, all I did was ask him why he had to call so loudly, because, reason number one, the boy might not be lost anyway, and, reason number two, he might just be playing a trick on us by hiding somewhere nearby. Then he stopped calling the nephew and turned on me. At that moment I thought I was in big trouble for sure. He yelled very loudly directly in my face to tell me to shut the hell up because he just tried to find his nephew. Without saying a word, I just stood there like I was frozen. That was the end. I never played with them anymore.

In the same year of 1970 while we were still in Pha Daeng, the epidemic of red diarrhea *(zawv plab liab)* struck heavily on the people in the village. It was named "red diarrhea" because the form of stool was bloody with sticky mucus. I was infected with this disease. Every time when I was having a stomach cramp, I felt like something was tearing inside my bowels (which we called "twitching or twisting"), then it was time to go pass stool, but it was not very much either. During the first week when I was still strong enough to endure the pain, I thought I might get better soon. After five days as the symptoms continued, I became physically weak. I just laid flat in bed, waiting to die. I thought one day I might just close my eyes. There was a small public pharmacy in the village with a male Hmong nurse managing it, but I did not remember if we ever obtained any medicines to treat my diarrhea. Often Father boiled tree bark and distilled its juice for me to drink. The juice was a purple color. Its taste was like the taste of banana skin. Once a day he also inserted a little ball of opium, about the size of a sesame seed, inside a piece of garlic. He baked it until it was cooked and then gave it to me to chew and swallow very quickly afterwards. It did not taste very good, but at least it helped to sooth the pain for a few hours. Fearing overdose, Father never increased the amount to be bigger than a sesame seed. Many of the young children, especially those who were younger than five, died from this illness. There were two things going on every day. The sound of the drumbeats of the funeral ceremony for the dead people was non-stop and the noisy sound of gongs was made by the shaman performing rituals to treat the sick people. The diarrhea led people to believe that it was caused by evil spirits rather than by bacteria. The truth was there was no sanitation in the area to prevent the spreading of the disease. The weather was hot, with flies everywhere. The villagers used mostly herbal medicines and shamanism to treat the illness, but they were the wrong methods. The disease was not contained. After a few months when the disease was finally gone, many children had disappeared. At last I recovered from the illness and hoped that I would live. I felt my body was so light. I looked at my arms and legs and they seemed to be very long. The fact was that I was too skinny, even skinnier than when we came from Sala.

Soon after I recovered, my oldest brother's two-year-old son became sick with the symptoms of diarrhea and croup. He died shortly thereafter. The diarrhea, along with the high fever, caused him to lose too much water in his body, and could not be replaced. The croup blocked his airway and made him unable to breathe. Before he stopped breathing and closed his eyes, he made a lot of couching noise like the sea lion's barking. No one was able to get medicines to treat the illness while everyone was watching him struggle with the pain in his body. At the time, I wished he could say a few words to his mother and father that the disease was too strong, and his body could not fight it off anymore. But this was only my wish for him. He suffered so much. He was too little to tell us about his pain. So, he had to leave his parents on this earth. He departed this world forever and we never saw him again. Life was very sad thereafter because we were poor. After his son's death, my brother took his wife with him to Long Cheng where the main army station was.

In April of 1970, it was about time to plant crops, but we did not have any fields. There was a man, Tong Khue Yang, who was from my mother's clan, offered his old farm to us for growing rice. He was very attached to my father and he also called my father an uncle. He was a man who did things like an important person. In 1971 when we moved to Pha Hoi, he also moved with us. He liked to dress in Western Khaki clothes, carried a manual Lao typewriter like a secretary, and went to work in Phak Khae. Once a month he came home to see his wife and children in Pha Hoi. Each time he returned home, in the area next to his front door, elders would sit surrounding him to chat like he was an important guest. He said he had an important job to do.

Father had a lot of good friends and relatives whom he had helped with marriage medium *(mej koob)* and shaman perform ritual while living in Nong Het and Xieng Khouang. Once we arrived in this village, those old friends and relatives who moved here two years earlier gave us lots of their good rice while we still received a small portion of the tasteless rice from the refugee program. The small Dakota plane dropped sacks of rice each month in the airstrip in the lower Pha Daeng village. The helicopters, H-34 or UH-34, which we called grasshoppers *(kooj tshuab)*, landed and unloaded cans of beef stew. When we heard the sound of the helicopter, everyone rushed there to watch it land. Living in the mountains like us, we were very happy just to see the helicopters landing. It felt as good as if we got gold and silver. Whether it was true or not, my second brother, Qhua, told me that the rice was from Thailand and Burma. The cans of beef were from America, a country that was on the other side of the vast ocean.

In 1970 it was peaceful in this village. Our Uncle Blia Cha came home for the New Year celebration. During the New Year days, he was in full army uniform with a red beret. While walking to see young people tossing ball, he was holding a walkie talkie chatting with his pals in the front line in the Plain of Jars and Bouam Loung. He seemed to still have work to do while was on leave. He was home for only a few days and left again.

One year in Pha Daeng was like time flying. Soon everything had changed within the village as the new year arrived. The place we hoped to be our permanent home once again we had to abandon. The relatives, friends, children, and school were divided, leaving some to go and some to stay. In 1971, the *taseng* (ຕາແສງ), Nor Yeng Yang, asked Father to move with his Yang cousins to Hoy Quinine, a place close to Pha Khao and Long Cheng. All those Yang families were also Mother's brothers and cousins. As a *taseng*, he ordered many of them with their families or without families to spend two days walking to Hoy Quinine. The purpose of the move was to help Tzong Lee Yang *(Ntxoov Lis Yaj)* build the temple for worship. They also planned to build schools for Hmong children to learn the Yang Shong Lue script.

When they arrived in Hoy Quinine, the *taseng* sent most of his men to help the people there to carve a statue, which would be erected next to the temple for worship. Then he took Father with him to meet *taseng* Chia Xa Yang *(Txiaj Xab Yaj)* of Hoy Quinine to discuss future plans. At the discussion table, Chia Xa Yang told them that it would not be good for them to build the temple because the place was going to be bombed very soon by the army. There were a lot of people against the idea of establishing the temple. Upon hearing this, it seemed their quest for a different future belief was ended at the meeting. Therefore, after the meeting with Chia Xa Yang, our *taseng* took his men back. He wanted to move them back to settle in Pha Hoi (ຜາຫອຍ), a place which was closer to Pha Daeng. However, one-third of the men who had their families with them at the time refused to come back. It was difficult enough for them to get there and they did not see the reason why they had to come back just a few days later. Whether they stayed in Hoy Quinine or came back to Pha Hoi, they believed it made no difference. Thus, those who did not want to return stayed there with Tzong Lee Yang or scattered around in the area.

Since he was a delegate for the *taseng*, Father had to come back with him to settle in Pha Hoi. When they returned to Pha Hoi, Father decided not to reside with the *taseng* in the same place. Instead, he and one of his cousins built their houses in another place tucked into the narrow valley further southwest. This village was comprised mostly of Green Hmong with Christian beliefs. To make his people happy and due to the shortage of future food for the families, the *taseng* ordered the government to use helicopters to transport all our rice from Pha Daeng to Pha Hoi village.

Airplane dropped sacks of rice by Danny Yang Xaiphia

From Nong Het to Pha Hoi, Father was always appointed to the *nai ban* position. In Tham Thao, he was appointed by Tsa Jer Yang and later worked under Neng Vang. In Sala, he was appointed by Shong Ger Moua to work from 1965 to 1969. From 1970 to 1975, he was appointed to work under *taseng* Nor Yeng Yang in Pha Hoi, until the day the Chao Fa fought the war against the Pathet Lao. In those years as a *nai ban*, who was working on the farm to feed his family and at the same time was working for the *taseng*, Father was doing too much work without pay. In 1973, he along with other *nai bans* received their first annual salary. They had to take the songthaews from Pha Hoi (ຜາຫອຍ) to Viang Chan (ວຽງຈັນ) to get their money. When the group returned home, Father said the money he spent on the round trip, including hospitality, was more than the annual salary he received.

Nevertheless, my father thought maybe it would not happen as they were told by *Taseng* Chia Xa Yang that the army would bomb the temple. After pulling back from Hoy Quinine to live in Pha Hoi, Father still sent my second oldest brother back to attend school there to learn the Yang Shong Lue script. He believed there was nothing wrong in learning the Hmong script. So, my brother continued to live there until one day when the army opened fire on the temple while he and other people were inside. A piece of shrapnel, about a quarter inch long, hit straight into his left temple near the eyebrow. He must have been very lucky because if it had struck about a half inch lower, he would have lost his eye. Two days after the attack, my parents received a message that he was hurt. Then Mother took one of my sisters with her to go on foot to see him. When they got close to the village of Hoy Quinine, they met my brother who had already packed and left the place to come home. They all returned home from there. He was hurt, but fine. Since the shrapnel had been removed right after the injury, the wound was not infected very badly. When he got home, Mother applied some herbal medicine to it for a few days until the wound had healed completely. The temple in Hoy Quinine was burned down. Many people were killed. My brother came back to live in Pha Hoi permanently. And the Hmong heritage, the future hope of a new direction for Hmong children, disappeared.

While living in this narrow valley village, we often went to visit some of our Yang cousins in the real Pha Hoi village. One hot sunny day in 1971, Father took me to visit them because Shong Ger Moua, our former village chief of Sala, was visiting them and the *taseng*, too. Once we arrived, Father took me straight to see the former Sala village chief. In the large dirt yard at the front door of *Taseng* Nor Yeng Yang's house, a large group of guests were sitting on chairs and standing in a circle. Shong Ger Moua, a soft-spoken man, mentioned that a Hmong pilot fell into the enemy territory in Xieng Khouang province because his bird was shot down. I did not remember exactly who the pilot was. He was worried that the army might not be able to rescue the pilot again. He said there were only a few Hmong pilots. If one was killed, it was hard to get another one to replace him. Whenever one was shot down and killed, it also shook the entire village. When one pilot was killed, all the people in the village grieved and were depressed. The moment he ended these words, some men in the circle had tears and blew their noses as they heard the bad news. It was the last time I saw Shong Ger Moua. When we arrived in KM52 in late 1979, he was there, but I did not have a chance to see him. A couple weeks after we arrived, a Pathet Lao soldier, they believed, disguised himself as a civilian and came to ask Shong Ger Moua to fix his knife because Shong Ger was also a blacksmith. While he was pounding the piece of red-hot metal, the Pathet Lao pulled out his pistol from his pocket and shot him in the guts. After the shooting, the Pathet Lao escaped into the woods. Shong Ger Moua died shortly afterwards. After his funeral, the city came to play a black and white film movie to show their empathy to the family.

In the same year, 1971, there were two Lao men who came to stay with our Yang cousin, Mother's nephew Fai Dang Yang, in our narrow valley village. The two Lao men were very good friends of our cousin. They came from Viang Chan (ວຽງຈັນ) to work in Phak Khae by sawing wood for sale. In my cousin's house there were not enough rooms for them to sleep at night. So, they came to sleep in our house, where we had one extra bed. All the time when they returned from their work, they had body aches. They asked my little sister and me to walk back and forth on their backs while they were laying down on their tummies. Even though we did not speak their language, they used body gestures, asking for help. We were not even sure whether it relieved their pain or not, but they kept asking for us to walk on them.

My brother was in the army for two years. At the end of their contracts, the army did not discharge him and Uncle Walee either. They needed more soldiers because after ten years of fighting the war, no more people wanted to join the army. Each time when they came home, brother, Uncle Walee, and cousin's brother-in-law were crying because of each battle they fought. Whether they won and maintained their camp or lost and abandoned it, their arms were sore for many days because each battle one soldier had to finish throwing three to five cases of grenades, just to rip off the mighty enemies. The Viet Cong soldiers came outnumbered of Vang Pao soldiers as many as ten to one. It did not matter how many hundreds of enemies were killed, wounded, and fell to the ground, the alive ones kept crawling over those fallen bodies to blanket their camp like the army of ants. Those horror battles haunted them every night in their sleep. My father thought that Uncle Blia Cha did not keep his promise that he needed them for only two years. Father thought between Uncle Blia Cha and him, they would not solve the problem of getting his son and Uncle Walee home. Instead, Father went directly to Colonel Neng Chue Thao (Neej Tswb Thoj), the man above Uncle Blia Cha. Neng Chue was their nephew. Up there, face to face, Father blasted at Colonel Neng Chue that their contracts were ended, so the two young men should be released. Father told him that it was not their war. It was the king's war. When Uncle Walee got injured from the battle, they did not monitor him closely in the hospital to get good treatment. Thinking about this made Father's temperature rise high, too. Besides that, their wives suffered from a hardship life with little support. If the government wanted more soldiers to fight the war, they should go get them from other countries. Between uncle and nephew, Neng Chue could not say much because he feared of losing the relationship. Losing two soldiers was better than losing the relationship in the clan. Therefore, Colonel Neng Chue released my brother and Uncle Walee from the army.

In 1972 my father decided to farm down on the lower bank very close to the Nam Ngeum, which was next to Pha Daeng, our former village. They had to clear up forest and burn the brush before it could be planted in corn and rice. Our cornfield was on the side of a steep mountain facing Pha Daeng to the north. The rice field was on the lower flat land next to the river below. The distance between the two fields was about 45 minutes walking. Because women have to do more house chores when men have to do farm work, Father took me to the farm with the rest of my brothers. Mother and three sisters were at home. It was a scary year for me. We were very busy between the two fields after they had been burned and cleared, ready for planting crops.

We had a lot of chickens in the cornfield. Thus, they went to the rice field early in the morning and left me alone with a little dog in the cornfield to watch the chickens. This dog was my only partner and it made me feel confident enough to stay in the field every day. We did not have much to eat, so my family cooked a pot of rice for me. Sometimes they left me a can of beef which was from the refugee assistance. From April to June the field was almost bare ground with corn sprouts. It was easy to see everywhere. My job each day was to feed the chickens. Before sundown, I had to steam a pot of rice, so when they returned from the rice field, the steamed rice was ready for dinner. This time of the year the weather was getting very hot. There were many tree trunks fallen across each other in the field. During the day I walked with my dog to tour around the field by jumping from one to another while the breeze was blowing. I also trained my dog to walk with me on top of the tree trunks. Sometimes when we got to the limb that hung up too high above others, he turned back and jumped to the ground.

Early in the same year, they offered vaccinations to people in Nam Yorne. My parents took the entire family to walk along with other families for one hour to be there to get the shots. It was the first time we got the immunizations. In the clinic the nurses gave us sugar cubes with one side stained with purple color to chew and swallow. We were told that the purple area was the polio medicine. After we chewed the sugar cubes, the nurse used a sharp needle to scratch many times two spots on our upper arms and then applied some medicine to them. The day after I got the shots, my father took me with him back to the farm. For the first two days and nights, the spots on my arm were very sore. I had a fever and did not want to eat anything. During the nights when the fever came, I had nightmares that tigers or brown bears were chasing me. Within two weeks, the two spots became red, swollen, oozing, and draining a little. Since they were busy with the farm work, they did not check with me very much. Thus, I had to endure the pain by myself. After a long month, the spots healed but left a longer scar in the lower spot. I was the only person who got a big scar on the arm.

The rest of my family was fine, even my little sister did not have to bear the soreness like I did.

Living alone on the farm and looking at Pha Daeng village on the top of the mountain on the other side of the river, I imagined there would be a lot of kids playing as we had done two years earlier. I wondered why I was by myself in this quiet farm. The only noise I heard was the rooster crowing, or when my little dog barked. I could see houses on the other side standing on the brown dirt not very far away. But the deep steep valley made the distance greater than by looking through the air. In the morning or during the day I could see the smoke rose up there when people burned something. I was the loner on the farm and had no one to play with other than watching chicks hatch. I went to check on them almost every thirty minutes to see how they came out. I saw their beaks cracked through the shells first. Soon they came out with wet furry bodies and nodding heads because they had just come out into this world and had weak necks, I guessed.

There were many small planes flying along the Nam Ngeum from Viang Chan to Long Cheng each day. They were helicopters, the H-34 or UH-34, Dakotas, C-130, Sky Cranes, Tadpoles, and other small ones. We called the H-34s, grasshoppers *(kooj tshuab);* the C-130s, opened bottoms *(tshau qab);* and the Skycranes, smoke pipes *(yeeb nkab).* For each one that flew past, I would break a little stick to pile up together to see how many planes had flown by in a day. Some days I got about eight or nine sticks, not including the ones that returned from Long Cheng.

In this farm I had the chance to go take a bath in the river once every four or five days. I remember one time in April or May my hair was long. It was itching so much on my head to the point that I could not stop scratching. I told my father about the itching problem. One afternoon he and Mother came to stay with me. Mother search in my hair and told Father that I had too many lice and nits. My father pulled out a pair of old black scissors and cut me bald. After he did the cutting, I was still able to pinch off some nits stuck to my hair. It was the nastiest thing I ever had. The next day he took me with him to the river to wash off. It was such a poor and suffering life.

After June, however, the corn grew taller each day. Our little house disappeared in the middle of the field of tall corn. The sky turned cloudy or foggy, with showers almost every day. Life was boring sometimes because my dog and I spent most of the day in the house. I was very scared from day to day when I could not see very much outside anymore. Occasionally, my dog was barking constantly toward the woods. I thought it must be thieves out there spying on us. When some strange thing like that happened, I shut the door, jumped into bed, and covered myself with the blanket for a while. As a little boy having no other things to protect me, I psychologically believed that the blankets would help to protect me from danger. Each day in that little house I kept thinking that if some bad people came and shot me dead and took all the chickens with them, there would be no one to tell my family what had happened. Sometimes when Father and my brothers returned from the rice field really late, I was tired, and went to bed and was asleep already. By the time dinner was ready, they woke me up, but I did not get up to join them at all.

There was a scary thing that happened on the farm which I saw with my own eyes and remember clearly for the longest time. One afternoon in July, my father and oldest brother, Lauj, stayed with me in the cornfield. They went to clear weeds in the field while I was in the house with my cute little brownie dog. They were in the field for about an hour, but came back with my brother's elbow bleeding badly. While he was clearing the weeds in the field, his elbow hit against a dead bent stalk of bamboo with a sharp edge at the crooked part. The sharp edge cut his shirt and penetrated to the skin and then went on to cut a blood vessel on the elbow. The blood was shooting out like pumping water out from a syringe. It was so bad that we did not know how to apply any medical techniques such as pressure points to stop the bleeding. When they were back in the house for a few minutes, the blood continued to flow without clotting. At the time the sun was about ten yards above the horizon in the late afternoon. Father used one apron *(daim sev)* to wrap around the wound and decided to let me walk with brother to our home in Pha Hoi village to get help. Father predicted that we should get home before dark without realizing what would happen next if brother ever passed out on the way. After he completed the wrapping, brother and I walked home for a distance of about two hours, up and down hills.

After we walked for about 30 minutes, the blood soaked through the apron. It started dripping on the way home. His arm became heavier. Then he took off his shirt to wrap around it for an extra layer. We tried to walk faster than normal. However, it seemed that the faster we walked the more blood pumped out from the wound. In about 30 more minutes, the blood soaked through the secondlayer of his wrappings. Then I took off my shirt to wrap around it for another layer. We were shirtless now. It was just to protect the blood dropping on the way, but it did not help to stop the bleeding. On the way home, we did not meet any people walking along the way either. By sundown when the wild creatures in the woods started to sing, we got to the split path where one was going to our house further in the south and one was going to Uncle Blia Cha's house in the east, which was about fifteen minutes away. Then we decided to go to Uncle Blia Cha's house because it was closer. Now the blood already had soaked through the third layer of my shirt. He was pale and weak already while we still had to continue walking. I was ahead of him and hoping that he would be able to follow me all the way to the village.

Fifteen minutes later, when we arrived in Uncle Blia Cha's house, they put him to rest in the guest bed. Aunty was at home with the children, but uncle was still in the army. She called a Hmong healer, who was a third-grade teacher, living a few houses away, to do the magic healing to stop the bleeding. When he arrived, they started to peel off the wrapped clothes from around brother's elbow, layer by layer. The blood clots in between each big layer and in the small sections, were about a quarter inch thick. The bloody clothes dropped to the floor in a pile, weighing a few kilos. When they finished unwrapping, brother was ready to faint. The blood continued spurting out like it had when we were on the farm. The healer did his magic by blowing air at the wounded site three times, but it continued to bleed. He suggested we go get further help by calling another healer, a second grader teacher, who lived very close. The teacher was a Lao Theung whom people believed had healing magic more powerful than the Hmong man's magic. Aunty had her son run there very fast about five minutes away and he returned with the Lao Theung healer. My brother was limp and laid flat in bed, not able to communicate anymore. No one had applied any direct pressure to the wound. The surrounding neighbors started to flow into the house, maybe about ten people, to evaluate the bleeding if they could do something to help. Aunty Blia Cha asked two men to go get my mother and my sister-in-law at our home to come to see brother Lauj. If they could not stop the bleeding, he might die. Fearing she would pass out from the news, aunty told the two men not to scare Mother and sister-in-law when they got there by saying something was so serious. They just were to tell Mother and sister-in-law that brother got a cut with some bleeding.

We were fortunate. The Lao Theung healer asked that a duck be killed for him to suck on the blood and blow it onto the wound site. This was his healing technique. With the elbow straighten, the blood was still flowing steadily onto the floor. We did not have a duck at hand. Auntie ran to the next-door neighbor to get a duck from them. Within five minutes or so, she returned with one in her hands. Then the healer sang his healing magic and one cousin cut the duck on the back of its neck after the healer completed his first singing. In a moment the duck's neck was bleeding as much as my brother's elbow. The healer sucked the blood from the duck's neck and blew it at the bleeding wound from a distance of 18 inches away. It was amazing that after the third blow of the duck blood on the bleeding wound, the dripping blood was slowed to one drop at a time. Within minutes the wound was clotted with thick blood on it. The healer told everyone to help keep the elbow straight for a moment before they wrapped it up again. My brother was pale and went completely limp in the bed with his slow heartbeat. I believe there were many reasons to cause the bleeding to stop. One was maybe the magic healing was working so well to stop it. Two, my brother did not have very much blood left in his body to pump out as he had before. Thirdly, he was lying down and calm now, which did not cause the blood to flow as strongly as when we were walking on the way. About one hour later when mother and brother's wife arrived in the dark of the night, he was able to open his eyes to see people and tell them how he felt. It was a big appreciation that we would never be able to pay back to the healer. In these days, I reflected on this old memory and thought we should have stopped the bleeding in the first place by using one of the simple techniques. If we knew how to use the pressure point or direct pressure at the time, my brother would not have lost so much blood when we were in this panicky situation. It was lucky that some little tricks saved his life. It was not just a bad life experience, but it was rather a great lesson to learn in my life.

In October 1972, brothers and Father built a crib about three yards wide and four yards long to hold the corn. They built it about two blocks away, above our house. In the end of October, we harvested the corn cobs into the crib. Then came the strangest thing I ever saw in my life. In the end of November, Father and I came to check the corn and saw that the rats had eaten so much of the corn so on the top were only cobs. Assuming there must be a lot of them, so he said we must do something to save the corn, or we would not have enough corn to feed our chickens and pigs. He went back to the rice field that day. The next day two brothers and one nephew came to stay with me in the corn field. Father was not coming with them. In that first day they chopped down a whole bunch of corn stalks in the field and had us haul them to make a fence around the corn crib. We built the fence with the stalks about three feet high, so we could kill the rats inside during the night. We kept the space about three yards wide in between the crib and the fence for maneuvering when we chased and hit the rats. On the second day by late afternoon, we completed the fence and were ready to kill the rats that night. I was too little and skinny at the time and probably was very weak too, compared to other kids at my age. My third brother taught me that evening the swing technique when you hit the rats you had to sweep from the center against the fence. This way you would have a better chance of hitting them because that moment the rats would run against the fence as they were searching for ways to get out. If you hit them vertically, you would not hit them in the way you wished. Besides that, we had to tie our pants cuffs, so the rats would not crawl up our legs. I had no clues whatsoever because I had never experienced this situation before. Not even in my wildest imagination could I think what it would be like when the rats began coming out of the crib. I thought maybe there would just be a few rats running around for us to chase. I did not think it could be as true as what he had said. His words had not impressed me that much.

Before dark, we chopped dried bamboo into small sticks and bundled them up in the size of our arms. We would burn them to give us light when we went to chase the rats inside the fence in the dark night. That evening we stayed until 9 PM and then burned our bundles of bamboo sticks and ran fast upward on the steep path to the crib. I was behind them. When I was about ten yards away from the fence, the three of them already slammed, yelled, and laughed so hard inside. I thought it must be a very exciting thing to do. I ran fast to climb up the two-foot high gate to put myself inside with them. I was stuck for a moment and could not get in. I tried to lift myself up harder and dropped inside. The moment I stepped inside with my bare feet, catching my breath, I was freaked out not knowing where to put my feet by seeing those numerous running rats. They ran in both directions along the foot of the fence to find their way out like swarms of piglets. Not only the alive ones, but also those that got hit, either dead or crippled, slid from the higher ground toward me. When they came into the crib, they climbed up the fence in an easy and slow way and most peacefully. When they were chased by us, they did not have a chance to think and climb up the fence again. My brother yelled at me, "Hit them! They are getting away!" I swatted one stroke and hit a couple of them. They did not die. They still were dragging their legs slowly behind the fast ones. I repeated a more hits and hurt just a few more which ran slowly toward brothers and nephew. It seemed they continued to have fun slamming the rats while I was watching some climbing up on the fence. Now I could hit vertically from the top to make them fall back down again to the ground. For a moment, there were no more running rats because there were no more left in the crib. All I saw were the dead ones laying everywhere and piling up in the lower area next to the fence. My heart was still pumping fast. They were laughing very hard about what they did to the rats. Then older brother said that it was time to gather them and go back home. My brothers and nephew grabbed them by the tails to drop into the basket and carried down to the house. I was too scared to touch them. When we got back to the house and counted them, we got close to 50 of them. That first night we made four trips to the stall. The first trip was at 9 PM. The second trip was at 10 PM. The third trip was at 11 PM, and the fourth trip was at 12 midnight. As the night went by, each trip we got less and less. Maybe they came to eat more in the early evening.

The next morning, we counted over 130 dead rats. We chose ten big ones, burned them on the fireplace, peeled off the skin, and smoked them for food. They were very fat under the skin. After a half day smoking them dry above the fireplace, we baked them on top of the hot charcoal. The fat was sizzling. The meat was delicious, too.

At dawn, one brother and the nephew carried them to sell to the Lao Theung people in the village next to our village of Pha Hoi. They like to eat them very much. Brother and nephew walked for three hours to reach the Lao Theung village. In those days they sold three for one hundred kip of the old king's currency. They sold them all and returned to the farm by late afternoon. During the one week of school break when they stayed with me on the farm, we killed almost all the rats. After the third night, we made a few trips and got only four or five of them.

In the field Mother planted many things such as *yuca (tapioca)* trees to harvest their roots, yams, sugarcane, and papayas. During the months of December to March in the next year, we had plenty to eat. The papayas were ripening on the trees. The sugarcane was ready for Mother to press the juice, boil, and make molasses or many brown sugar loaves for us to share during meal times. During these years of 1972 and 1973, Mother stayed at home in Pha Hoi with my two younger sisters and my fourth brother, Chia, while he was attending school. Mother came to the farm once a month to bring some sweet rice cakes and sweet rice alcohol for us. When she came to the farm, she went to pick ripe papayas and boiled them to make sweet soup for me for lunch or dinner.

Papaya tree

One day her older sister, who lived in Turtle Hill village *(roob vaub kib)* next to Phak Khae, died. Father and Mother both went to attend the funeral for one day. The next day she came to the farm. I asked her for more details why her sister died. She told me that her sister had suffered headaches for many years before she passed away.

She stayed only one day and one night in the field. On the afternoon of the second day, she gathered papayas, yams, yuca roots, and sugarcane into her back basket. Once she got everything she needed into the basket, she put it on her back, told me not to be afraid of anything, and be good before she left. I was going to ask her if she allowed me to go home, but I just could not speak up. One thing I knew for sure if I asked her, she would say "No" to me because no one would watch the chickens. Without people making noise and my dog barking, the little wild cats *(plis)*, hawks *(liaj)*, and eagles *(dav)* would come and eat all the chickens. We would hang a two-foot long bamboo tube and hit it with a stick very often to scare the wild creatures which would harm our chickens. As she was leaving, my dog and I watched her walk slowly on the narrow dirt path with the basket on her back until she disappeared at the end of the field. Then we went back to the house. In my thoughts I wondered why it must be me to stay in the field to take care of those chickens. With my dog beside me inside the little house, I was thinking about the story of an orphan boy whose parents died when he was an infant. After their deaths, his uncle and aunt adopted and raised him, and later sent him to stay on the farm to take care of their animals. He was very lonely, just as I was, until the day he was old enough to have his own family, then he separated from them. Then I sat on the bed, leaned my back against the wall for a while, and counted how many more years before I would be old enough to be on my own. My tears came down on my chin while my little dog was wagging his long skinny tail in front of me, slicking his nose with his tongue like he wanted to kiss me. I figured that it would be a long time before I got to the adult stage. For my dog, "You are such a good friend and such a good protector of me." The worst thing I ever feared was that one day I might be robbed and killed in the farm before I could go on my own way. It was very sad and emotionally painful which I could not reveal. These days I have my own children. I hardly ever want to leave them for anyone else to take care of because I remember back to my childhood being without parents was painful. I understand how important it is that a child needs parents to be with them and how painfully a child suffers when there are no parents around. Even these days the anger, the pain, and the fear still linger in my memory because I have been through such periods of negligence and lacking supervision.

One day a man with a young boy came to our house from hunting. They asked for permission to cook their lunch there. I allowed them to go ahead to cook their meal. They asked me where my parents were, so I told them that they were out there in the field, clearing the weeds. Then I told them that I would walk my dog with me to see my parents in the field. In fact, they were in another place about 45 minutes away. I just wanted to lie to them that my parents were there too, so they would not do any harm to me. I called my dog up. We ran to the thick cornfield to hide for about one hour. When we returned home again, they were gone, too.

Soon some bad things happened. One late afternoon in early August of 1972, my dog ran down to the road. I tried to call him many times, but he never returned. Maybe when he got to the road, he met some dogs down there and escaped to look for friends because he was too lonely. My life became even more devastated afterwards without him. I was upset that I did not tie him up. I put some of my father's dry tobacco hanging on the wall in his water bong and lit it. I inhaled a big one. I got too much smoke into my lungs. I then coughed many times and had lots of tears too. I knew it did not release my anger but caused me more suffering. I laid flat in the bed and fell sleep for a while. It was the first and last time I ever tried tobacco. Some six months later my parents found my dog with another family which lived in the village very close to our home in Pha Hoi. They brought him back to me again.

Because of growing up in a large family as the second to the last child, anything I said was never taken into consideration from my childhood to adulthood, whether it was right or wrong. In our family role and culture whoever was born first, that person had been eating more food already, so that person had more ideas or knew more. That was our belief. It was that younger children should keep quiet when older children talked. What the older said was always more important than what the younger ones said. Never interfere with older siblings when they had conversations because it would not do any good. Being the youngest son in the family, I should just eat when the food was ready on the table and should not argue with anything, whether I liked it or not. This continued until the day I reached my adulthood, then it was time for me to ignore this myth in my family. I realized that talking would not work, but action does prove that something can be done. Thus, it was a time that conflicts were taking place within the family because I chose a different path to go in my life.

One night in this stilt farm house, my father, my fourth brother Chia, and I were sleeping inside, and our dog was barking furiously toward the road. Sometimes he also jumped back and forth like something was out there. Father looked for a while, but he did not spot anything. He finally shot the carbine rifle twice in that direction. Then the dog stopped barking. Maybe the gunshots scared the ghost away.

During this time Nhia Her Lor, who lived in Nam Yorne, raised a herd of American white pigs. Every year he distributed one of his female pigs to each member under him. In 1972 my father got one white pig from him, too. He raised it, and once it produced babies, he gave one to each of his members as well. It was the first time I saw a white pig. These pigs were bigger than our black pigs, but they also had to be raised in a better environment. If not, they would not grow as well as expected. For instance, without feeding them powdered cow's milk, they did not grow very well. It became a chain of distribution to help people get on their feet for a while before the country fell to the communists. At the same time, he had a very large Hawaiian brand of pineapples, which we called green pineapples. When we traveled on the road close to his farm, we could see the big green circle garden in a flat field in the huge valley. If we had lived longer in Laos, he might have distributed his pineapples to people to grow too, since he had already given away his pigs. Unfortunately, we did not stay long enough for the changes.

Close to our home in Pha Hoi was a Lao Theung village where the people really needed hot chili pepper. From November 1972 to February of 1973 our peppers were ripening on the plants on the farm. While they were busy in the rice field, Father told me to pick them every day and dry them in the sun, so we could sell them to the Lao Theung people. Since I was only a little boy with a little dog staying there, I did not have much motivation to pick the chilis. Each day I got only about 1 or 2 kilos. The juice of the pepper stained my hands and they burned for a long time. What had been picked was about one-third of what the birds ate or fell on the ground. So, we did not have very much to sell to the demanding Lao Theung people.

One day in April of 1973, my third brother Yeng and third sister Mai, left me alone in the farmhouse while they went to get water in the valley. I was inside the house, and it was very quiet after they left. After a while I heard the chickens make strange noises under our stilt house. Then I thought I should just go check to see what was down there. When I went to see, I found a big green snake already half inside our house and half hanging below. It came through the corner and was going up to the roof. The body was as big as my thighs. I was so scared, but I decided to use a stick about a yard long, took a deep breath, and hit the half of the body hanging below. When I hit it one time, the body just kept pushing upward faster inside the house. I hit it a second time, and it pushed almost its entire body inside. Then I stopped and went to stand on a big tree trunk next to the house. I kept crying and calling for my brother and sister for about an hour. Finally, they were very close to the farm and heard my voice. They were rushing up the side of the steep mountain to look for me in the house because they thought I was being kidnapped. When they arrived, I told them there was a big green snake went inside the house. We checked around for a moment, but still did not see it anywhere. We went to look up on the roof. It had pulled its body out at the ridge with its tongue flickering all the time. My brother aimed his carbine rifle at it from the higher ground level above the house and shot many rounds. It was like he was fighting a war. The bullets blew up and shattered the long bamboo shingles, piece by piece. Usually a snake would turn around to another direction and move quickly. For this one, even though the bullets struck the shingles next to it one after another, it just kept moving slowly to the gutter toward us. Brother kept shooting until two shots hit the snake's neck. It slid down and dropped dead on the ground. It was huge, scary, and shining green. Now it was even bigger than my thigh when it was dead.

Due to our fear of robbery, in September or October of 1973, Father decided to move from our farm to live with a Vang family up in the hill about 20 minutes walk away from where we lived. The father's name was Joua Vang. He was Father's cousin's brother-in-law. Father called him brother-in-law *(dab laug)* as well because his cousin married this Vang's sister. He had a daughter married to a Vue man. They built their long side-by-side house on the side of the hill. This Vang couple, who had four grown sons and one daughter, lived in one side while their oldest daughter and son-in-law lived in the other. We called their children cousins and called their brother-in-law our brother-in-law, too. It was the way in our culture that you can call your cousins' in-laws in the way you call your own in-laws. Their house was on the side of the hill, facing north. The top of the hill was very flat. They let us build our house up there. While living in this place, we all got along well and helped each other very much. It was a very nice place where we could see Pha Daeng village in the north on the other side of the Nam Ngeum. Life was peaceful. I no longer had the fear of being robbed by bad people as I had feared on our own farm. This was a very enjoyable period, living with many farm animals. Every day helicopters flew along the river from Viang Chan in the south going to Long Cheng in the northeast. The Vang father also really liked my father. Some evenings, when they were not busy, especially when they had done their farm work and spent more time at home, he came to our house and talked for a long time until midnight or until they were tired. Then he went home.

Their third unmarried son Pao, who was in his teenager years, was very nice. He was a very good talker with good manners. He came from their home in Phak Khae every summer when he was off school. He also had a younger brother named Ger, who was about my age, but did not attend school yet. Pao Vang loved to show me how to practice karate because in those days people knew more about this type of martial art than the Chinese Kung Fu. He was very passionate about learning everything. In 1975 when we were completely out of school and had no hope of going back again, he started to learn how to play qeej, the mouth pipe organ. After he learned some basic notes from his father, he climbed up to the roof on any nice day and played the qeej. He was successfully completing his lessons in early 1977 when we moved to Meuang Orm.

In December 1973, Father thought I was old enough to be in school. I was sent home to enroll in first grade. It was like hell in the classroom because I was sent there at the wrong time. I should have started in September. On my first day in school when I looked around the room, there were some smaller children, but others were bigger than I was. About one-third of those bigger kids were those who had failed the test to go to second grade. They had to be there for one more year until they passed the final exam the next June. It was really a bad year for me. Bad things happened to me from the beginning to the end. My second day before class started, a boy threw his pen and hit my right eye, which hurt so badly. It was good that I blinked fast enough, so the pen did not hit my eyeball. I was crying so loud for help. My fourth brother attended third grade, but I did not know where he was at the time. The third-grade teacher came to ask me in Lao language what had happened. It was only my second day, so I spoke only Hmong and understood no Lao yet. He asked me to speak Lao to him, but I could not say a word. Maybe he did not know that I was new in the classroom. Some of the children were laughing at me. One boy who had been there for two years already, laughed at me and said in Hmong that I was such a stupid child. It hurt my feelings badly. I promised to myself that I had to work hard to be at their level or higher some day in the future. That boy was advanced to second grade in the school year of 1974 to 1975, while I failed the test in June because I spent only two-thirds of the year in class. Every day each student was called to go to the blackboard on the wall to solve a math problem. One day in early 1975, the boy could not do his second-grade math. His teacher came to our classroom looking for a student to go show him how to solve the math problem. Many students in my room pointed their fingers to me. The teacher pulled me out from my classroom to go with him to his classroom. When I got there, I scratched quickly to get the answer. A whole bunch of students in the room yelled, praised, and cheered for me for the good work while that boy stood silent next to me. I tapped the chalk dust off from my hands and stepped out of the room.

My life was always unhappy during the school year of 1973 to 1974. From December to January, it was very cold with frost on the grass every morning. I had to walk without shoes, sandals or even flip-flops, for one hour to school each morning with my brother who cared nothing about me. The road from our narrow valley village to school went along the deep valley which did not get sunlight until 9 or 10 o'clock at this time of the year. It was so cold that by the time I got to school my toes were red, sore, and all numb. The good thing was that the school was situated where it was exposed directly to the early morning sun. Some children who lived close to the school came there early to start a fire for other children who lived far away to join them before class started. Sometime if I got there15 minutes early or so, I had the chance to heat my feet up at the fireplace before I went to class. At 8 o'clock the temperature was warm enough in the room. Then there was no one shivering in class.

Every day in class I was sad and depressed. So were some other children. In those days teachers were there to teach, but also to punish students as well. The teachers expected every student to learn at the same pace. If a student could not learn, they did not bother to find out what was the problem. What they did do was punish the students by forcing them to kneel down or hit them with the yardstick. I remember back in Pha Daeng in 1970, a teacher used the edge of his clipboard to hit one of my Yang cousin's head and cut a line about two inches long.

It bled a lot, but the parents did not have the right to say anything, or maybe they thought it was their child's fault. Some people called this type of punishment "French Rule", but no one ever knew for sure if the French people actually did that or not. Because I started late in the year, they had already taught beyond the beginning part of the lesson such as all the Lao letters and the Arabic numbers. When I got to the class what I saw was the blackboard full of sentences from a story. The teacher told me to read, but I could not read because I did not even know all the 33 consonants plus over 38 vowels. During the mathematics hour, there were all problems of addition, subtraction, division, and multiplication. For the math problems I did not even know the numbers one to ten. So how could I solve the math problems? Besides that, twice a week we had to each individually recite two poems while standing in front of the class. It was difficult to memorize them because they were one or two pages long. Some pupils just went to stand there without saying anything because they were clueless. I was so sad. I was not able to keep up with others. I could copy what was on the board, but I could not read or understand what the hell they were talking about. All the teacher did was punished me if I could not read or do the math problems. He did not realize I started school late in the year. Many times, the teacher made us students who could not do our math problems or recited a poem in front of the class to use our palms to rub back and forth on each other's ears. By the time he told us to stop, our ears were red, sore, and close to torn off. It was not that the students failed to learn, but it was a stupid failure system and inability to teach of teachers. In ten years or even 20, our education did not move up one inch further. That's why we kissed the Western butt for an educational system.

 In the classroom when a student wanted to go potty, the student had to go bow in front of the teacher and ask for permission to leave the room. When you asked permission, you had to tell the teacher whether you went for light or heavy. If you went for light, meant you went for urinating. If heavy, then passing stool. One day a boy asked the teacher one time, but the teacher told him to hold on for a while. Then he came back to his seat. A few minutes later he asked the teacher again. He allowed the boy to leave the room. He had gone for longer than usual. The teacher told another bigger boy to go check on him to see what happened to him or where he was. He also told that second boy to hit the boy who went to potty with his knuckles if he found him. The teacher thought maybe the boy was just playing outside, not wanting to come back to the classroom. The second boy, the messenger, left the room for a few minutes and returned and told the teacher softly that he brought the boy back to the yard, but he did not look good. He got some heavy thing in his pants. He accidentally pooped and urinated in his pants. It was the teacher's fault. He made the student wait too long so he did not make it to the toilet on time. Another bigger boy in the room was laughing and saying that the dam ruptured. The teacher told us to be quiet. I heard him say, "Go get him back here for me to see him!" When they got back to the door, the teacher told him to turn around. His pants bottom was wet and really heavy. Many younger students were surprised. It was too late and too bad. He gave a really good message for the teacher. Then he was sent home.

Every day when I returned home from school, my parents kept scolding me for being stupid. They did not realize that without knowing all the letters, I did not even know what was in the book. They asked why I went to school but was not able to read. They expected me to be able to read and tell them about the story. My parents were saying that they sent me to school by mistake. They never thought I could be that stupid, but I was stupid. At the end of school year in June 1974, I failed the final exam and was not advanced to second grade. My brothers were very displeased, as though I did some big thing wrong against them. In September of 1974, I started fresh from the beginning again. It was not that difficult. At the beginning of 1975, I was able to read second grade level books, something not very many students could do. My second oldest brother was surprised when I read the thick second grade book. My family's attitude toward me was better. They did not have to teach me how to read again. Late in 1984, I met a man who lived in Saint

Paul, Minnesota, who said he had the same problem that I did when he went to school in Laos. His brother was illiterate, but he told him to read the book every night. He just pretended he was reading a page for a while then flipped to the next page to appease his brother's desire. In fact, he had no clue what was in the book.

In 1973, my second brother, Qhua, left to join the army. While he was leaving, Mother was not very happy that Father had sent him to attend school in Hoy Quinine and got hurt from the attack. This time Father still let him join the army. Mother said he was mature in the mind, but his physical appearance was just like a thirteen-year-old boy. The war was going on every day along the frontier. He would not be able to carry the big army bag, the gun, and the grenades on his waist. Those who joined the army were mostly poor children while the children who were from rich families had the luxury of going to school or hanging around in the village. Mother asked why must it be her poor son to be in the army? If he had to go to fight a battle and got killed, it would be too bad. But, Father told her that everywhere in the world, sometimes we have to participate when there was a war going on. It was the way to protect the country. Then she could not say much except kept on crying. He liked to hunt. Every afternoon while he was on the farm, he hunted for squirrels. With his carbine rifle, he always brought home something from the woods. If he did not hunt, he netted fish in the huge Ngeum River. Now her hunting son just disappeared from the house.

One day in January of 1974, I fell down while I was playing in school. I got two big scratches on my lower and upper right leg. This year Mother was staying more on the farm doing the farm work. Because the lack of proper care, they became infected. Every day they were oozing pus. It took about a month to heal. I never told anybody about the pain.

In February 1974, *Taseng* Nor Yeng wanted Father to move to live close to him in his Pha Hoi village. Father also thought it would be a good place to live, and my brother and I would not have to walk a long distance every day to school. Unlike our village in the narrow valley, this village was in the lower altitude. It was not as cold as our previous home because it was where the early morning sun rays hit directly from the horizon. We moved again to build a new house on the little long hill very close to our Uncle Blia Cha's house. Our front door was facing the east. The other end of the house pointed toward the west where our school was. Below our house was a large pond. On the back of our yard going up to the foot of the cliff were more houses. The cliff in the north was beautiful in the morning sun every day. It was not just a cliff, but rather it was a warm sacred place for the villagers. A place where people felt they belonged to because its high cliff symbolized a statue for them. The meaning of Pha Hoi was snail cliff. It was named so because the tip of the cliff twisted a few levels, which looked like a snail shell.

Now, the routine work in the family changed. Mother and all three sisters went to work in the field. They left me alone with my fourth brother to attend school at home. Occasionally, my brother did not get up to cook breakfast for us in the morning. I had to get up to boil the rice and steam it. After pouring the rice into the hot boiling water in the huge wok, I was too little to reach down there to stir the rice. I had to climb up on a small stool, so I could reach and stir down in the bottom. The edge of the wok was too hot and burned my elbow and under my upper arm often. Even while I suffered all this, I never told my parents.

After school in the afternoon, while my brother was playing soccer in the field, he told me to come home right away to carry water from the valley to add to the big wooden barrel inside the house. There were two big girls in the village who came to get water in the same place. I met them so often on weekday afternoons and some mornings on the weekends. They asked me where my brother was and why he did not come to help me carry water. I told them he was busy playing soccer in the field with his friends and the teachers. When they asked me these questions, I missed my parents very much, but they never knew about what I was going through. Even if I told them sometimes about what happened at home while they were gone, they ignored it. The one thing I hoped was that one-day I would be a grown man and become independent.

Sometimes we ran out of rice in the house. I had to pound the rice for us because our parents had not returned from the farm for months. The rice mill was a sturdy seesaw eight feet long, with a three feet long pedal at one end from the fulcrum, and on the other end a mallet that hit the rice grains in a big wooden bowl underneath. After I put the rice in the bowl, I had to put some heavy things in my back basket and carry it on my back to give me some extra weight. With the extra weight on my back when I climbed on the foot pedal, the mallet end would rise to pound the hulls loose to get the rice grains. After finished pounding a bowl, I was very tired because of the heavy basket on my back. Even though I was very tired at the time, I had to winnow the grains in a big flat basket *(lub vab)* to get rid of the husks. It was a heavy job I had to do.

One afternoon in April after school I told my brother that I was going to the farm. He did not say much other than, "If you go, then watch out." I put the little woven bamboo basket on my back then started to run. One of my flip-flop straps was broken, so I just ran with bare feet. The path went down a few valleys, up a few mountains, and some part of it cut through the side of the steep mountains. Some parts of the path were through farmland while others passed under thick jungles. It was so thick you could not see through to the sky. I was scared of ghosts or dead people, monsters, and bad people who might kill me. But since I was too hungry and wished to go see Mother and sisters on the farm to cook me a good meal, I just kept running. When the path was going uphill, I walked. When it was going downhill and straight across on the side of the steep slope, I kept running all the time. There was an area before our farmhouse in Uncle Vang's farm that was very dark. There were two very high cliffs on each side of the path. The thick jungles from each side of the high cliffs tunneled the path underneath, and it was dark like the sun had gone down already. Before I got to that area I slowed down to catch my breath and gain some strength. Once I got close to the dark jungle tunnel, I felt my hair rise, my skin moving like insects crawling over it. But I had made the decision to come and no matter what I had to pass through. In my thoughts, "It was very close to the farm, so I should not return home just because I was scared of that dark path." I knew it did not take very long to walk through that distance to get to the other side. If I ran fast, in about two minutes I should get through the dark tunnel to other bright side where there was farmland again. Without stopping, I forced myself to go. The moment I was under the trees, I heard no sound of any scary creatures, except some birds sang. Before I got tired again, I was on the farmland and the path was a zig zag going downhill to the valley. I kept hopping down the path while my fears settled down. Soon I got to Uncle Vang's farm where our house was up on the high hill. At our farmhouse my two older sisters were there taking care of the pigs and chickens. I did not go up there. I relaxed a bit and kept going straight. I felt like I heard human voices somewhere again. After passing this place and ten more minutes of running, our cornfield was right above the path. Then to our ricefield was still another distance which would take me about twenty minutes by running, too. I decided not going to our farmhouse because I thought there must be some one in the ricefield, close to the river. If I went straight to the rice field and no one was there, I could come back again since the sun was still up in the sky. I kept running and running, mostly going down, and hoping that someone would be there. There was another area right after passing our cornfield that had a mixture of wild palm trees, bananas, and huge trees. The path passed through a narrow valley with a high mountain lying down from our cornfield above and another high mountain stood on the north side, extending to the river. Once you got in there, the temperature was very cool. There were more rocks on each side of the path. It always smelled like skunk odor. In the dry season I liked the fresh smell of nature. I kept running and hopping tirelessly.

    Finally, I got to the house and there were only Mother and little sister. They were surprised to see me. Mother asked me why I came by myself. I did not say much but told her that I missed them and did not want to be at home for so long. But inside my liver, (in our culture we don't say heart), I was crying because there was no peace. It was stressful at home. Being on the farm, the nature, the cliffs, the bluffs, were all beautiful and peaceful. The sound of the big Ngeum River flowing was harmonious. It was more peaceful indeed. Since we also kept a lot of chickens on this farm, I asked Mother to kill a young rooster for dinner. After dinner, I went to sleep quietly because of the long walk. I woke up in the middle of the night hearing the owl hooting in the banana trees around the yard. On Saturday afternoon, we went to the river. I liked to jump from one big rock to the other with my bare feet. It was fun when skipping flat rock on the surface of water. It bounced many times before it stopped bouncing and then sank down. The water was cool. It was so clear with the hot sun above. When I submerged my head in the water near the big rock, I saw schools of small fish. I wondered why the fish have a peaceful life. I stayed in the ricefield until late Sunday afternoon, then Mother sent me home with some of the Yang relatives who farmed next to us. Mother told me not to come again unless an older person accompanied me. My answer was, "Yes, mother." But in my mind was that, "Mom, don't you know that I have no peace at home at all." Sometimes I wished I had never been born on this earth. I was just angry with myself because I had something to say, but could not express what I wanted to say. I was very angry that I could not speak up intellectually to Mother. But sometimes I said something to Mother, she seemed ignored me, too. My last thought was, "Forget it, I'll just go home."

At home I had to learn how to take care of myself. This was the time I had to teach myself how to sew. It was another life skill I needed to learn as a little boy. I was a boy who had parents and yet lived a life worse than an orphan. When my shirt buttons fell off or the seams under the armpit or any other place broke, I had to sew the stitches back in because Mother was not at home. Since I had seen Mother do a lot of sewing clothes and embroideries, I was able to stitch the torn seams back in, to hold temporary until she returned home. Every other day I had to run down to the stream to wash myself and wash my clothes and bring them back to dry on the clothes line to be ready for the next day. Mother often said that you need your clothes and yourself to be clean and smell pleasant. Whenever we ran out of soap detergent that we bought in a bigger village market, I just washed my clothes without it. It was how mountain life was without my parents in the house.

We got off school to have lunch break from 11:30 AM to 1 PM. One day in the spring of 1974, my brother was asked by the teacher to go with a group of students to deliver some things to another village during lunch time. I do not remember what the things were. After my brother left with the group, I broke off from class as usual to have lunch at home. Early that morning when we took off to school, brother put a two-yard long log diagonal against the door. After lunch I locked the door again and put the log back into the position it was before. I went back to school thirty minutes early to play with other students in school which was the routine we liked to do during break time. Before class started, he came back home checking, and the log was still in the same position from that morning. Maybe he assumed that I just played with those students the whole time and never went home for lunch. The three of us were playing tossing rocks. He came with a stick about a yard long, walking toward me. I saw he was coming, so I stood up. He hit me twice on my butt in front of my friends and said "Why did you not go check on the house and have lunch at all. You must have spent the whole time playing here." I was very angry but looked down to the ground and told him that I did go home and had lunch while he was gone. But he did not believe me because he saw the door was still locked in the same way he had done that morning. I did not say anything to argue with him further because I knew for a fact that it would cause more pain to me. It was very emotional pain. The way he walked toward me, the impression I got from him at the moment, and what he said to me, stayed in my head until these days.

Of the five boys in my family, I thought I was the dullest. In another way, I thought I should be the ugly darling and loved as the last one in the family. But, I was not that one. I always was feeling hurt.

When I grew up and more mature, I thought maybe life was more like a competition. I have to work to earn the love and care. If my brothers earned a bronze or silver medal, I should try to work harder to earn the gold one. This was the only way I could eclipse my dullness image and bring myself to the bright side. But life was not always as easy as what I thought.

From May to November 1974, the large pond below our house was full of water like a small lake. Every day during lunchtime, students liked to go swimming down there. One afternoon in 1974, before class started, one student drowned while he was swimming in the pond. When a student stumbled on the dead body in the water, he alarmed everybody. They pulled him out from the water and called the teachers to see him. He was Teng Yang *(Teeb Yaj)*, our class leader, who used to live in our old village in the narrow valley. They could not tell when he had drowned. At the same time, we could not believe that the water could cause his death because it was only about three or four feet deep. Some students said maybe he had a seizure, while others said maybe the dragon took him away, meaning pulled his feet down and took away his souls. Our teacher, Paoze Lee, came to see him when he was carried back to the frontyard of the school. The teacher pulled out the notebooks from his backpack and cried. He flipped the pages and told us that the writing was his handwriting. It seemed that what he left behind was beautiful. He knew Teng Yang's family very well. Bad things happened to the family one after another. Before his death, some people stole all his family's money, including paper money, silver coins, and silver bars. They never caught the thieves. Our teacher knew that it was going to be very difficult for the parents to deal with the death of Teng Yang. The teachers just had the students wrap him up and arranged for many students to carry him home that afternoon. We cancelled classes. Everyone was sad. Since that day, nobody wanted to go swimming there again because they feared Teng Yang's ghost was there. Later in the year they cut through the dam to drain the pond completely dry.

After Teng Yang's death, I was assigned to lead the class from September 1974 to June 1975. In the classroom there were some bigger students who should have been the leader, but they skipped class too much. Thus, the teacher rather chose me to lead the class based on my good record. Soon after I was assigned to lead the class, our teacher Lee was transferred back to his home school. I called him the army boots teacher. Every day he came to teach in class with shiny boots tied up high just like soldiers. When he was gone, we had another Vang teacher replaced him. He was better than Lee in terms of everything, but very mean. He spoke the green dialect while most of the students spoke the white dialect. He was smart, skillful in teaching, energetic, and had a stronger voice. When he led us to sing a few times in class, he had a very loud crystal voice. While I was leading, everything went well until one day in April of 1975, when we had an accident. Before class started, there were four students in our class who wanted to play bullfighting. To play that game, everyone had to crawl on hands and knees. On the grassy area behind the building they wanted me to be the neutral person as a referee to watch over them. Then they used their heads to push against each other like bulls fighting. I should also pretend to be the owner of the bulls. After they fought for a couple minutes, a student's head hit against another student's ear, and it hurt very much. The ear became red, and he cried so loudly. The teacher happened to be there just at the time when the boy was crying, too. I was in deep trouble. Everyone pointed fingers at me that it was my idea to play the game. This, as a class leader, I could not deny, but just accepted the fault, took the blame and responsibility for the accident. The teacher went inside the classroom for a few seconds and came out with the yardstick. He hit me four or five times on my legs and butt. It was painful, but that was fine, an expected punishment.

About ten minutes later when class started, the teacher pulled me out to stand in front of everybody in the classroom. He said I was a person who did not care for or love my classmates. After he said it, he asked the class to repeat what he had said. He repeated these five times before letting me go back to my seat. Definitely, it was not justified to punish me twice for one mistake. He held me guilty on every count. Some students in the class who did not see the incident had no clue what the hell was going on. After the class was over, some of my friends asked me what happened. I told them about the incident. They empathized about what I had been put through, but it was too late to say something about it. It was an emotionally painful event. Since then I learned my lesson from this mistake and kept my eyes open for everything that could happen. He was a great teacher in every aspect, and I learned a lot from him as a young boy. On the other hand, I was not happy about the punishment he charged against me because it was too heavy. Instead, he should have done a thorough investigation before he punished me. I felt it was not a punishment, but rather it was an insulting and humiliating treatment. Soon the country fell to the communists, our school was closed after May 1975, and I never met him again. What I heard was that he went back to his home village of Hoy Kablarng.

In 1982 when I arrived in Ban Vinai Refugee Camp in Thailand and attended a free English class, I saw the boy who got his ear hurt in 1975. I went to the class for a week, but stopped because I was sick. In 1999, when I was working at Lao Family Community of Minnesota, Inc., a nonprofit organization in Saint Paul, I met the boy again in the parking lot. We now were men. He begged me for some money to make a phone call to his family because his car had died in the alley behind the Burger King Restaurant on University Avenue. He knelt down to beg me for the money. He even called me, *"me kwv ntxawg"*, which means "Darling younger brother." He may not have recognized me at all, but I did recognize him very well. We had lived in the same village for quite a few years. I knew who his family was. At the moment he was asking me, I did not know what to do. I pulled out $5 from my right pocket for him because I believed what he told me was a true story. A few months later in the summer, he approached me again while I was driving out of the parking lot to Maryland Avenue in Saint Paul, after I had been to Walgreens store to get medicine for my children. The moment my car was crossing the sidewalk waiting for traffic to clear, then he ran to put his hands on my car's open window. He told me that his car ran out of gas and was dead at the next corner of the road behind those houses. So, he needed some money to buy gas. I told him I was sorry to hear the bad news, but I could not help him at this time. He stepped back. I drove off. We never met each other again. Later in the year I heard the Hmong radio on Channel KFAI 90.3 broadcast that a man in the Twin Cities area kept doing that kind of trick on people. Based on the description I got from the radio, it was him, the man who asked me for money in the parking lot.

In school in those days the students were always in uniforms. The boys would wear white shirts and blue or black pants. The girls would wear white shirts and black or blue skirts as well. Youth culture often changed from decade to decade. What I had seen was that the third grade to sixth grade boys started to wear bellbottom pants, which was the most popular style. Some teenage students started to sew two pieces, either white, black or blue to their bottom pants legs, which made it open bigger. They thought it was a cool style. It became more and more popular until the late 1980s or even to the early 1990s. It was contagious.

Another thing about the school system in Laos in those days, it was a pyramidal shape. In the elementary levels were more schools, so almost every child could attend. Once we moved up to junior and senior high, there were less and less students who could get through because they had fewer schools in the upper levels. It was not just a challenge, but rather it was a screening matter. By the time students got to college, there were only the children from the rich families and, especially the children of the high-ranking officers and city officials, who could be there. Even though during the school year the poor and the smart kids were always at the top of the class, after the final exam, only the rich kids passed the tests. It made the poor parents wonder what happened to their kids who the teachers often reported to be the top ranking. This gave us one clue that their parents paid money for their children to pass the exam to go to the next level. My brother stayed in third grade for two years, but I did not ask him if he ever passed his exam in 1975 to go to fourth grade or not. For many reasons as the world turned, the country fell, economics and politics changed, and we all fled to resettle in countries other than Laos. Some of the rich children, who attended higher education in Laos, became successful while others had nothing to do but raised cocks for fighting. It seemed their education had been washed away by the Mekong River when they crossed it. So, many students from the poor families have tried their best and succeeded when the opportunity of higher education came. In the current day we see the true colors of the smart kids from the poor families surging up to be on top in academics or even become prominent stars in the new generation when the doors are opened to them.

AFTER THE COUNTRY FELL

*"Nyob rau Xeev Khuam ces yog qhov chaw ua rog **loj**, mab dawb thiaj tuaj muab Pov Vaj tsa ua tus **coj**. Qhov tseeb tiag yog npua tshom rau dev **noj**. Thaum mab dawb rov qab mus **tsev**, Hmoob raug ua nyab laj liab tus thawj **qhev**. Hmoob tsis muaj lub chaw **ntsaub**, los koom haum ntiaj teb tseem tsis nrog lees **paub**."*

After the negotiating was done and the Hmong army laid down their weapons, it appeared that we were in a time of peace again. There was no more rice assistance from the government to feed the refugees. We no longer saw many kinds of airplanes, flying along the Nam Ngeum from Viang Chan to Long Cheng. What we heard from the elders in the village was that *Lao luam Lao* (ລາວລວມລາວ), which meant Lao surrendered to Lao, or Lao people came together. The Hmong soldiers returned home to be with their families and became jobless with no compensation. Even though hundreds or thousands of them had no more jobs to do, their concern was not the money or food to feed their families. Instead, their next concern was survival. If there was no place to hide or no way to go, they soon would be facing their foes, the Pathet Lao, who they had fought bitterly for one and a half decades. One day, they believed, they would be pushed all the way to their limits by the Pathet Lao. They had no hope of reconciliation with the Pathet Lao. Some of them would be slashed in the throat or sent to a muddy prison hole of about four by four feet wide. Their American friends, who once had helped them and who they had helped, disappeared instantly after the planes took off from Lao soil. They were scared to death when they heard not only the Vietnamese had come to Laos, but also the Red Chinese. They remembered so well their history of escaping from China when their ancestors were chased out of the country to hide in the mountains and valleys. They said the Hmong who moved to Indochina were those able to escape from death. The Chinese threatened to kill every single male who had two bean-sized testicles in between his thighs. They still believed if the Vietnamese and Chinese arrived in Laos, they might kill every single male as they had tried to do in China many years earlier. I was trembling when the elders were talking about these things. Every day I listened very closely to those elder villagers talking about what they should do before it was too late. In my thoughts, "They are going to kill me because I am a male?" Would anybody be scared if the enemies were going to cut off his nuts? Absolutely.

The end of the path had arrived. It was such a desperate situation that people were running without feeling hungry. The day they started airlifting Hmong out of Long Cheng, our Mayor Xor Chia Thao *(Xov Txiab Thoj)*, did not want to leave the country. According to the informant, he was concerned that if he left Laos, all his relatives who stayed behind might not be able to cross to Thailand to be re-united with him in the future. But in the meantime, General Vang Pao wanted him to leave the country. Then the mayor was given some amount of paper money to pay for transportation to take all his relatives to Long Cheng to be flown to Thailand. Without knowing what was going to happen next, he thought they would take more days to fly the Hmong to Thailand. In the minutes before he flew out of the country, he gave the wad of money to another man to rent at least ten trucks to transport his relatives to the airstrip as he wished. However, after the mayor took off, the man who received the money did not make a move until the third day. By the time the message was sent to my father and his cousins in the remote Pha Hoi village that their cousin mayor had left the country and he found someone who would send the trucks to bring them up to Long Cheng, it was already too late. They closed the airstrip sooner than the mayor anticipated. Our mayor, who expected someone to get his Thao relatives to the airstrip, including my father and his cousins, got nothing after all. He was separated from his cousins, leaving them to live with the communists while he was in Thailand on the other side of the Mekong River, watching the wind blowing through the coconut trees in Laos. The wad of money he gave to someone before he left Laos had been washed down the drain. The old sad joke, "The bridge has been cut off."

I was on the farm early in the month of May 1975, because our school had been postponed a week before airlifting people to Thailand. We did not even anticipate that they would arrange for planes to fly Hmong people to Thailand either. One late afternoon in early May, Father mentioned that he received a message that our Mayor Xor Chia Thao had left Laos. In Long Cheng, the planes flew the Hmong for three days, but stopped on the fourth day. The message had also included that many people were marching west on foot, going in taxis, and the pick-up *songthaews* (ສອງແຖວ) to Ban Sorne. Late that same evening Father and my brothers had a secret discussion of what to do without letting me know before I went to bed.

At about 3 a.m. the next morning, my second brother Qhua, who recently came back from the army, woke me up to eat chicken and eggs. Without knowing what was going on, I asked him why he woke me up so early. He told me that overnight while I was asleep, they had killed many chickens. We had to eat and go to Thailand because the Vietnamese were coming to Laos. At that moment I wondered what was wrong with them because I already heard them say the country was now at peace. Why were the Vietnamese coming? I rubbed my eyes and looked around the house. Fire was burning in the fireplace. On the wall was the dim oil lamp's little glowing flame giving extra light. On the dining table, I saw a heap of chicken bones left over after the meat was sliced off. My brother said they chopped the meat to fry dry and pack for our meals on the journey to Thailand. This way, the chicken meat could be kept for months without rotting. I was not clear yet about what he was saying to me. Then I went sort of, "What?" In my thoughts were, "Don't tell me you have killed my rooster!" To me, it was too sad that many of those chickens were killed at one time, but it was even sadder if the Vietnamese were definitely coming to our place.

Because Father and brothers had heard of the closing of Long Cheng airstrip, Father thought we must find a way to go on foot. He was anxious while he spoke softly to us in the dark morning that we may have to leave soon after we packed. As a very quiet child who did not want to disturb them much, I was wondering what would happen to our animals after we left. We had many pigs, chickens, and dogs waiting for us to feed them. In the meantime, he also expressed some concern after we left our home for our journey to Thailand. We might end up not having enough food for ourselves. The trip would also be costly. Beyond that, the weather in Viang Chan and Thailand was too hot for us. We always feared hot weather in the lowlands. We might become sick because we could not get used to the hot climate. In those days Hmong people who lived in the higher elevation believed if we went to the lowlands, we were going to die. Father still had the bad memory that our grandpa died seven days after he returned from a trip to the lowlands, near the Lao-Vietnam border. We feared both equally, the hot weather and the Pathet Lao. However, no matter what would happen, we were taking the risk at this time. We had to follow the flow of other people if we were to get away from the communists. Father said we must escape because he knew the communists so well and he was really tired of their system since we lived in Xieng Khouang back in the sixties.

At dawn that same morning, Father also said that before we left, at least, he should inform his four cousins, our Uncle Tong Pao, Uncle

Walee, Uncle Joua Vang, and Uncle Pa Xao. They lived in Pha Daeng, a village on the other side of the Ngeum River. He did not want to leave them behind without telling them what was going on because he was the oldest within the immediate clan. Everyone looked up to him because he knew everything about the clan religion. However, this contact would take half a day by walking on foot and crossing the river by raft. A few hours later when the sun rose, he let my second brother, Qhua, go to Pha Daeng to inform our uncles that we were going to Thailand. They should pack immediately and come with him. Once they all arrived in our farm, we could just get on the road to go to Viang Chan. The whole day my brother was gone, but he did not come back in the evening as he was expected. Instead, he stayed over that night. Father was not just worried that brother did not return. He was very mad that brother did not do exactly what he was told because Father considered it as an urgent situation.

It was easy to say, but in reality, it was difficult to do. Father did not foresee the disagreement between him and those uncles on the other side of the river. At the table of discussion at their homes, brother urged them to pack and come to our place, so we could all go together as Father told him. They refused. They wanted to go back to Xieng Khouang and Nong Het (Rhino Pond), their birth place. They told him to forward their sincere message to Father that his children were grown, so it would be easy for him to live in Thailand. For them, their children were young and without education. It was difficult for them to leave the country. Besides that, their in-laws were in Nong Het at the time. If they went back there, they would be protected by their in-laws, who had lived there for a long time. The communist might not do any harm to them since they were just farmers.

The next day, brother returned to our farm with empty hands, except his American made M-16 rifle on his shoulder. There were no relatives with him, not even one. When my brother got back home without our uncles, Father was even more disappointed. We had not packed and the ten trucks Father heard that our mayor had ordered before he left the country had never been rented to pick us up. Even if it was too late for us, Father still wanted to leave the country. One of the reasons he wanted to leave was because he did not want to face his old communist foes. Secondly, to Father and his cousin Blia Cha in Pha Hoi, the story was different from their cousins in Pha Daeng. He had two sons who were in the CIA army and had guns. He always said that the communist never loved you. His cousin also was in the 21st Battalion. Even though it was a little too late, we would listen to the news of how the situation was first and then slowly move us to Viang Chan without his cousins living on the other side of the river.

Within a week, a crazy rumor spread to people in our village. We heard people say that once the Hmong people arrived in Thailand, Vang Pao was going to buy a piece of land in Burma for the Hmong to settle on. The Hmong, traditionally, liked to plant crops such as rice to feed their families and corn to feed their livestock, such as pigs and chickens. Burma is a country where the land is very fertile and would be suitable for the Hmong to earn their living without much trouble. However, this idea of Vang Pao buying a piece of land in Burma was just from someone in the village who created the rumor. It was the speculation of a panicky people who were desperated for peace. Their imagination was bigger than in reality. The old used to say, "Your ears heard of it, but your eyes have not seen it yet." *(Pob ntseg hnov xwb, tab sis qhov muag tsis tau pom)*. The villagers did not understand or know that their leader was in exile. They still thought he was in Thailand with his full army uniform. Therefore, he was going to do two things for the Hmong people. First, he was going to buy a piece of land in Burma for the refugees in Thailand to settle on. Second, he would prepare his troops to fly back to Laos to fight the communists. They waited for him to return to Laos just like a child who waited for his daddy to return from the farm at sundown.

After two weeks and we had not begun our journey yet, the bad news was echoing around us that the Pathet Lao had ordered soldiers to shoot at the marching civilians in Hin Herb, a checkpoint on the

Nam Lik bridge. It was sad that every possible path has been closed for us. First, the airstrip was closed before we made it there. Now the road to Viang Chan has been cut off, too.

Leng Yang, who was a student at the time, walked with the crowd to Hin Herb. As he observed, the Pathet Lao forced the taxis and other vehicles coming from the Viang Chan side to transport the Hmong people back to Ban Sorne without pay, whether the drivers wanted to or not. Once the people were forced back to Ban Sorne, they divided into many groups. They scattered around in the area. One main group moved to the Phou Bia area where they later in the year transformed into Chao Fa. There was a portion of these people settled down in Ban Sorne.

Pathet Lao continued surveillance of the people in their homes. They saw soldiers standing at the corners of their houses every night. A couple months later those who remained in Ban Sorne, were stressed by their nerves. They could not take the pressure of the activities the Pathet Lao were doing around them. One early morning they pulled out their weapons to attack the Pathet Lao Army units. After the first attack, they escaped and moved to many places such as Phou Bia, Phou Sae, Pha Hoi, and Vang Vieng as well.

At last when every route had been cut off, Father thought we should postpone our trip for a while. Father also had a little hope that if we could not get out to Thailand at all, there were some Hmong leaders such as Lor Fai Dang and Lor Nhia Vue working with the Pathet Lao. There was also still Touby Lyfoung living in Laos as well. These important Hmong figures might negotiate to establish peace for the Hmong who lived everywhere in the country. It was only Father's hope. On the other hand, some elders in our village already doubted Touby's safety. The villagers, especially ladies, gathered in houses and whispered nervously to each other that they distrusted the Pathet Lao. The frustraction was spreading everywhere, like people catching germs. They did not want to plant their crops for the year. Whether the new system was good or bad, people who lived to the east of us kept moving westward, passing our home almost every day. It was an indication to us that the country was not at peace.

Soon, the fate of both groups of Hmong leaders whose villagers hoped would establish peace for the Hmong in the country had faded. By the time we were aware that trouble might come to us, many of the former high-ranking Hmong soldiers and civilian officials were already sent to re-education camps. There were many more who were still hiding, not yet caught by the Pathet Lao. What I heard from the elders in our village was that they were not scared of anything more than the disappearing of these men. In the village, one man who just moved in and spoke softly and slowly, mentioned that the Hmong made the mistake of helping the Lao right wing to fight the war. He said in his expression that they wasted their fat and blood to defend the country for nothing *(Nkim roj ntshav pua teb chaws)*. The battles they fought for 15 years and the titles they earned, finally turned against them. They were like the hard work hunting dogs now being kept in the tight cages after their owners left them behind. Those who had not been caught yet, were trembling and searching for a place to hide. Now it was like the wind blowing on the glowing flame, scorching their butts, and the swords were pressing against their throats. Father, along with his relatives in the village, thought maybe they made a mistake by not trying hard enough to find a way out of the country. The few lucky ones were those who were able to board the planes in Long Cheng and now were in the crowded refugee camp in Thailand. Even though they were in the crowded refugee camps, they did not suffer from physical and political pain like those who were still in Laos under the Pathet Lao.

Later in the year, when the Pathet Lao had already penetrated our village, rumors spread out to villagers about bad torture of prisoners. They said prisoners were used to pull the plows to plow land for farming just like farmers had used water buffaloes. Some ladies came to our house very often to share their concerns with my mother. They wondered what if the Pathet Lao arrested every man in the village and did the same thing to them. Whether this was a true story or not, people in the village believed this routine abuse went on and on until some of them were dead. There was a middle-age lady from Mother's side who said that the communist way of torturing prisoners was very deep, bitter, and painful. It was painful and was like putting red hot charcoal on your raw liver while you were still alive.

The end of May 1975, I returned from the farm to take the final exam. It was determined that we should continue school in September as usual since most of the villagers had nowhere to go. I took the exam and passed it with little hope of continuing to the second grade in September. Two of my sisters, Mother, and I were in Pha Hoi village. At home people were still talking about the Vietnamese and Red Chinese coming. Our living situation was still unstable because some people were always searching for ways to go to Thailand.

One morning in early June 1975, the *nai kong*, who was also a shaman, was concerned about the ruling of the new government. If things happened the way people believed, it would affect his people severely. Therefore, he thought he should do some ritual asking the earth spirits *(tim tswv teb chaws)* and gods *(tswv ntuj)* for guidance whether his villagers should continue to stay, or should they go to Thailand. Behind his cousin's house, an area where people routinely passed through by day and night, he instructed a man holding two young chickens, one rooster and one hen, in his hands. Surrounding them in the area were many children and adults, watching them. The shaman held a bunch of burning incense with glowing smoke and the gong in his left hand. In his right hand was the gong stick with his split buffalo horns. On top of his head he wore his red shaman hood. On the ground, two little tree branches were staked in the ground standing up like soccer field goal posts, from north to south. A white cotton string was tied from one branch to the other, symbolizing the division between east and west in the sky. On the ground he also drew a line on the surface beneath the string from north to south, dividing between east and west on earth as well. The east side represented the side where the communists were coming from Xieng Khouang in the east. The west side represented the side where the Hmong were going to Thailand. He chanted and asked the spirits to come and tell him if the communists would treat the Hmong well when they arrived, then after he killed the chickens and dropped them on the ground, the chickens should finish their jumping and die on the east side of the line. This would show him that his villagers should be safe to stay in Laos after the communists arrived. If the communists would harm his villagers when they arrived, then when he killed the chickens they would jump and die on the west side of the line. This would indicate that all his villagers should escape to Thailand because it was not safe for them to stay. During the ritual process of calling the spirits to come, he said a few words and hit the gong one time. Then he said a few words and hit the gong again one time. He kept doing this for a while then tossed his split buffalo horns on the ground to show if the spirits were coming to the scene to respond to his requests. At last, he dropped his buffalo horns in the ground. Both sides faced up, indicating that the spirits were coming to the scene for his request. He then told the man who was holding the chickens to cut their necks and drop them on the line he had drawn on the ground. As we watched after they were killed, the chickens jumped back and forth for a couple minutes. Then they finally dropped dead completely. The hen died right on the line and the rooster died further on the west side of the line. The shaman suggested with sadness that the death of the chickens had shown him that the Hmong had to leave Laos because the communists absolutely were going to harm the Hmong when they arrived in the village. The spectators did not have anything to respond to the shaman but were despondent and anxious about leaving the village. Some of them shook their heads, not knowing what to do because it was difficult to travel with many children. Slowly, they scattered from the area and returned to their homes. How many villagers left this village after they saw what the shaman did? No one.

By the middle of June Father took me back to the farm. We had already planted rice and corn in the field. Our Vang cousins, who we had moved to live with a few years earlier, abandoned their home. They were going to Viang Chan on foot while Father was stuck with almost everything. After our Vang cousins left, Father then wanted to go without the rest of his cousins. It was a devastating situation for us in the farm. But at the same time, Father also feared not getting to Thailand because the road had been blocked. Once our Vang cousins left their house, we felt like the farm was empty. It was very quiet and cold. At dawn and dusk there was no smoke coming out of their rooftop like before. I felt cold and not even wanted to go close to their house for fear a ghost was inside. They had pigs, dogs, and chickens on the farm, but no one fed them. Life was not only sad for us, but for the animals, too. Father and brother would just shovel corn for their pigs every other day to keep them alive. The Vang cousins were gone for approximately a half month, but they returned home again because the road was difficult to pass through as it was blocked by the Pathet Lao. Once we saw them return, we felt better and the place seemed warm again.

For a while, fewer people traveled on foot from one place to another. In our village people were talking about some people in other villages who had abandoned their homes, but did not know where they went. It seemed houses were emptied, and ghosts were coming to take residence. Those who decided to stay were only the people who could not afford to escape or feared being killed on the way. Soon, some houses in our village were vacant too. We also saw some new people moved from Phak Khae to take up residence. The monsoon was approaching. The weeds on the roads started to grow fast to cover every single path. The small roads from our village of Pha Hoi to other villages in the surrounding area disappeared. People did not want to travel for the reason they feared being shot or raped by the Pathet Lao soldiers. Wherever they went, it must be a big group together. Time was flying and yet there was no way for us to get out of Laos.

At the end of June, two men were killed at Nam Pha, about half the distance between our home in Pha Hoi and Phak Khae in the east. They were found dead and their suitcases were cut open to search for valuable items. The people believed it to be the Pathet Lao soldiers who killed the two men to get money. Elsewhere, such as in Hoy Kham, Meuang Cha, and Long Cheng, people were killed too. Since there was no proof, the villagers could not blame the killings on any group of people. In every small or large village, people did not feel as safe as they used to anymore.

At this time, the Hmong in the country seemed divided into a few groups. The first group surrendered and bowed to the Pathet Lao. They, finally, were forced to move back to live in Xieng Khouang like confined monkeys in cages. The second group were those who kept moving towards Viang Chan. They searched for every possible way to cross the Mekong River to Thailand. Some families did this the smart way. They pretended they were on the road to do their usual business. The mother took one or two children with her on the road to Viang Chan. Then the father did the same thing. Once they were in the city, they got together again as a family. Then they moved to Thailand. The third group stayed where they were and later in the year formed guerrilla units to fight against the Pathet Lao government. They were named "Chao Fa."

A month later, my third older brother and I were alone on the farm. One morning he went to the cornfield early before I woke up. When he returned home at about 10 AM, he complained that he was hungry. Life was going to be bad because the communists were coming closer to our place. Upon hearing he said this, I felt like the world was ending. By this time, I had let all the chickens out already. He wanted to kill a chicken for breakfast, but he could not catch them. I never thought that he would use the gun to shoot a chicken. I was inside the house while he stepped outside again with his gun. Suddenly, I heard him loaded the M-16 rifle in the front yard and fire one shot, "Bang." He shot one chicken sitting on the tree branch, about two feet above the ground. I was startled big time by the gunshot. I looked through a hole on the bamboo wall and saw the young rooster dying on the ground under the tree. It kicked its feet very fast; the wings flapped wide and then closed again. The feet dropped and stopped kicking. I thought, "It was dead." My brother walked over to pick it up and said, "Let's cook a good meal."

The end of July I returned home from the farm. The village no longer felt warm like it had before. That evening when I arrived home it was already dark, so I did not see much of anything. The next morning while Mother was cooking breakfast, I thought I should walk back to tour our school since the weather was beautiful in the early morning sun. The heavy dew on the grass was sparkling like shooting stars in the night sky. The entire village was quiet. As I stepped outside to look around the village, smoke came out of the roofs of some houses. Since I had been gone for almost two months to the farm, it felt like a new place to me. But it was not a fun new place. Instead, it was a sad old town in which later no one ever wanted to live. I walked past my cousin's house, approaching the soccer field goal posts, I turned back to look at the sun rising above the horizon behind me. It was a couple yards above the straight mountain, Pha Chon (ຜາຈອງ), next to Phak Khae with its beautiful blue sky. On my right side in the east was the high green mountain, even greener without fog and mist. To my left, the deep valley below Pha Chon Mountain, where the Nam Pha falls was with thick fog. I thought maybe the Lao Theung village down in that deep valley, where children used to come every morning to attend school, no longer existed. I had the mixed feeling of happy memories from the past school year and the sad moment in the quiet village. After a few seconds, I turned facing the school again. I then walked slowly step by step toward the soccer field, in my bare feet brushing the heavy dew on the grass. At first glance, the soccer field goals had disappeared.

When I walked further to the tin roof school building, I saw the dirt volleyball court outside the fence was only growing tall weeds. The two poles were still erected there, but no net. The place where students used to play, yell, and jump around every day now had only a little dirt spot in the center. The large field which used to be the soccer field was nothing but green grass and cow manure. It looked like not just the country had fallen to the communists, but the village had been torn as well. In my thoughts it was quite sad one early morning in a place which used to be a home for many children from the surrounding villages. The bamboo fence had too many holes punched through it. Some were big holes, and some were small, from one end to the other. But the three barbwire strands were still hanging tight onto the posts. The gate was left open. The tall bamboo flag post in the front yard inside the fence was no longer there. In front of the building were not many flowers, except a few twelve o'clocks were blooming one spot here and one spot there with many animal footprints around them. The three-classroom school building became a shelter for the cows and goats in this rainy season. The building walls were falling apart. As I observed inside the classrooms, some of the benches were still standing, but others were on the floor. They became the objects for cows and goats to scratch their itching bodies against. The divided walls in between each classroom were falling on the floor, too. Two blackboards were cracked on the floor as I walked past from one end of the building to the other. There was one blackboard with broken edges still hanging against the posts. My thought was that education was finished. I wondered who would repair the building if ever there would be classes again in September? The truth was that no one ever repaired the building because people did not want to stay. After touring the building with no future hope, I wondered where were those kids I used to play with at this moment? Maybe some of them might be in Thailand by now.

    The frustrations and fears for the villagers were increasing because about one third of them had left their homes to hide on the farms. Some of the men, who used to be in the army or held civilian positions, were gone, but left their wives and children at home. They knew trouble was coming to them. Some of those who decided not to leave their homes, like Uncle Blia Cha and my brother Qhua, changed their names, pretending to be ordinary peasants in order not to be caught by the Pathet Lao soldiers. The one thing they could do to avoid persecution, they believed, was to dress in old frayed clothes like poor opium addicts. Uncle Blia Cha who used to come home with his green army uniform, red beret, and shinny black boots, now was in loose black Hmong clothes. Like many other soldiers, he no longer had a job. One day he came to our house and my mother called him, "Nom Suav". I was wondering why Mother called him that name. Later I asked Mother why she called Uncle Blia Cha a different name. She told me that it was his new name. We should not call him the old name, so the strangers would not be able to identify him. Second thing, even if you were smart or were an important person, you had to pretend like you were unintelligent, slow, and be unwashed. If anyone could do this, he would survive in the communist system. As I listened to the villagers, especially ladies, they whispered everywhere that the Pathet Lao might draft their sons and daughters to be soldiers or even feared their daughters might be raped by the soldiers.

There was a man who committed suicide in a small village very close to Nam Yorne. I heard they said his name was Nor Cheng Thao *(Nom Cheeb Thoj)*. After the country fell, the man was very sad about the new system which came into effect that year. He did not like it but could not go anywhere either. He stabbed himself with a knife a few times below the sternum. Even though he wounded himself badly, he continued to live for a few more days before he stopped breathing. It was the most tragic and rare case I heard of in those days. It must have been a very stressful time for him before he decided to kill himself. I also thought it was such a painful wound for him to endure before he closed his eyes.

During the month of August, when I was back home in Pha Hoi, a group of people brought a herd of cows from Pha Chon to sell in our village. The villagers planned to sell their animals, so they could flee the country. They sold them at a very cheap price and customers could bargain, too. My second oldest brother, Qhua, who had been in the army, asked Mother to give him some paper money to buy one red cow. He said we needed to have some cows because we did not have one since we left Xieng Khouang in the late 1960s. We should also spend the old paper money because it soon would have no value. If we had a cow, the next few years it would produce more calves. So, soon he would have a bull like before. Even though we were planning to flee, a few days later Father went to Phak Khae and bought a horse there, too. Instead of going to Thailand, we now had the cow and horse with a whole bunch of pigs, dogs, and chickens in the farm. Our feet were tied down completely.

5

THE REBIRTH OF CHAO FA

*"Thaum Hmoob tsis muaj kev **pab**, Hmoob thiaj sawv ua rog caub **fab**. Blog liab thiaj muab hmoob hu ua cov neeg **phim npab**. Lawv sawv ua rog tua nyab laj pauj kev ntsim **siab**, thiaj raug nyab laj muab tseem khiav mus nce **phu npiab**. Yus me li ntseeb xwb los yuav mus tom **nkawj**, thaum kawg tsis yeej ces ho kwv chij ntaub dawb coj cov niam tub rov los **thawj**."*

The Hmong built a temple to worship the Lord in the Sky just as other god believers. They believed they were the children of god. There was no intention of creating hostility toward the Pathet Lao for any reason. At some point, the name was misinterpreted by their enemy, so the Hmong were portrayed as Chao Fa--King of the Sky. Therefore, this name just made them be targeted for persecution by the Pathet Lao. The truth was they were worshipers as children of god on earth.

The word *kong* (ກອງ) is a Lao word, which means group or team. The name Pachai was named after the brave Pachai, who was a Hmong warrior during the Crazy War. They believed he was the most powerful man. Thus, a Hmong battalion serving under the Pathet Lao army named itself Kong Pachai after the late warrior, hoping they would be brave and strong like him. Even though they named their battalion after Pachai, they were always ideologically and politically against Pachai and the Chao Fa.

Within Laos in late 1975, on the north side of the road from Ban Sorne to Long Cheng, the Chao Fa started their bases in Pha Hoi, Pha Daeng, Phou Kang, and Pha Ngu. On the south side of the road, the bases were established in Phou Het, Phou Sarm Phiang, Nam Mo, Meuang Orm, Phou Bia, Phou La, and Pha Phai. Without wasting any time, these regions were wrested from Pathet Lao government control soon after the country fell. This geographical region was very mountainous. The temperature was never too hot or too cold. The Hmong lived mostly on the mountaintops because they liked the mild temperature year-round. This was also a great advantage for them to defend themselves during this guerrilla war.

During the month of September 1975 while Father was in the farm and Mother was at home in Pha Hoi, she sent a message to Father to come home because their son-in-law Cheng Yang from Xieng Khouang would arrive in Phak Khae. At this time, many Yang relatives who escaped to Vietnam during the war, mostly from Mother's side, also came to visit their relatives in our village. Their son-in-law was planning to visit Father and Mother for the next few days. Along with him, there would be a few of his fellow soldiers. She told Father to bring some chickens from the farm for food. Mother also wanted to do a little ceremony for their son-in-law. One afternoon Father left the farm, carrying six chickens with him. He got home the same day their son-in-law and his group arrived. That afternoon, they killed the chickens for a little party for the group.

According to Father, at this time Uncle Blia Cha, along with the villagers had already built the Chao Fa altar for worship right at the foot of the rocky cliff, very close to the village. The same evening after the dinner at our house, Uncle Blia Cha invited their son-in-law, Cheng Yang and his fellows to join them in the celebration of the completion of the worship altar. With uncle's invitation, they could not refuse to go with him for the ceremony. After they spent a few hours at the ceremony, they returned to our home for the evening.

When they got back, Cheng Yang told Father that what he observed at the altar ceremony was a Chao Fa worship activity. He was very suspicious about everything he saw over there. Father was put on the spot and had no choice, but told his son-in-law that he had no prior knowledge regarding what he was now being told. He had left for the farm two months earlier and never come back home until that day. Besides that, he was not with them at the ceremony, so he could not answer his son-in-law's questions until he did a thorough investigation of the place to find out what was going on. It was the end of their questions and suspicion about Chao Fa activities. On this earth the only time you could deny anything as Father did was when you were not there, I guess. That's why Father was able to get away from the questions asked by his son-in-law on that late evening. On the other side of the coin, Uncle Blia Cha had invited the tiger into their glory site and made themselves targets of their enemy. He should have thought that these people were coming out of the communist's pot. It would take decades to boil them down before they could melt into the capitalist system. As a former soldier of the Lao right wing, Uncle Blia Cha should have realized that the name Chao Fa was one that the Kong Pachai searched to destroy for more than a quarter century.

Our family actually had two guns at the time. One was the M-16, which was obtained from the army when my second brother, Qhua, was serving. The second one was a carbine which Father had traded for his fishpond to another man a few years earlier. That evening after they ended the discussion of the Chao Fa activities, Father revealed to his son-in-law that he had one gun, although he had two. Father said he wanted to keep the carbine rifle in the farm for protection purposes only because there were many robberies everywhere in the country. Therefore, for Father, his son-in-law could not pressure Father to give up the gun. Instead, he bowed to Father by letting him keep the gun as he wished. Besides the two guns he had, Father did not disclose the military status of his two sons and Uncle Blia Cha to his son-in-law. Everything was normal at the time while they were staying in our house for a few days and returning to Phak Khae. After they left, Father returned to the farm again as usual.

A week later, Mother called Father to come home again because at night they saw some strange people surrounding the lower part of the village. In the morning those strange people had disappeared. The villagers discovered the footprints were from soldier's shoes. As a delegate to the *nai kong* (ນາຍກອງ), Father started to worry about the security of his people. When he received the message from Mother, he believed it must be that people had reported the Chao Fa worship activities to the Kong Pachai in Phak Khae. His first thought was certain that the Pathet Lao had made the surveillance. He knew that trouble was coming again. He remembered his life from the fifties to the sixties under communist control was not easy. Then he came home to assess the situation. When he arrived home to inspect the activities as told by Mother, they had stopped. However, he felt the clouds still up there. He considered this as a serious or even dangerous situation which must be talked through. The next day he asked his cousin Blia Neng Yang to go with him to Phak Khae to meet with Pa Lee Yang *(Paj Lis Yaj)*, one of General Paser Yang's subordinates. Father, Blia Neng, and Pa Lee Yang were related in the clan system in some way, except Pa Lee sided with the Pathet Lao while the other two joined Vang Pao. After three hours of walking, they arrived at the airstrip where Pa Lee Yang was temporarily staying. When they got there, they saw him just come out of his house. They went straight to meet him, and he invited them to go inside his house.

The purpose of their visit was to discuss the situation based on what they had seen and to persuade Pa Lee Yang that Pha Hoi village would: one, remained neutral, and two, there were no Chao Fa activities going on.

During the discussion they told him that it had been two weeks now since they had seen some strange people routinely surrounding their village. They wanted to know if the Kong Pachai Battalion had ever sent soldiers to spy on them. But the real words they expressed to Pa Lee Yang in a kindly way were, "Have ever the Kong Pachai Battalian sent some soldiers to protect the villagers in Pha Hoi." As soon as they ended their questions, Pa Lee Yang denied any involvement. He pointed out to Father and his cousin, Blia Neng, that the situation they mentioned must be *sak tu*, meaning enemy, or they were Vang Pao's soldiers. The Kong Pachai Battalian never did such things. When they heard the strong denial from Pa Lee Yang, they felt like their mouths were filled with sand, which they could not swallow. To save face, they changed the subject by asking him about the living situation at home in Xieng Khouang. How was everyone doing before he came to Phak Khae, etc. He said they had been separated for so long, but everyone was doing fine. Soon all the families that went to Vietnam would return. Since the meeting was unsuccessful, they excused themselves to get away and thanked him for the good discussion. Instead of getting a solution to their problem, they escalated the heat between the two sides and returned home with empty hands.

Soon after their trip to Phak Khae, an old lady in Pha Hoi revealed herself as a Mother Qeej, (*Niam Qeej*) a person who played the Hmong mouth pipe instrument. She played the qeej every day along with the worship activities of the Chao Fa. The way she played the qeej was to raise people up to a new clean generation to be free of evil. She also played it to call upon the mother earth and spirits to protect the villagers. According to the informant, they had no knowledge whatsoever if she had learned to play the instrument before or not. However, she played very smoothly and was an expert. This was very odd in those days because only males learned how to play the instrument. Likewise, this led villagers to believe that it must be the gods who gave her the power to play the qeej. Because she was playing the qeej amazingly well, this also made villagers confident and happy about their new Chao Fa activities in the village. They hoped that they would be able to change their course of life and be protected by gods even if they isolated themselves from the communist rule. Soon a man named Chor Lee (*Txos Lis*) also declared himself to be the god communicator or messenger (*txiv ntuj*). He told people he talked to god, and god would provide protection to the Hmong, no matter what. While these activities were going on, within weeks the villagers became even more suspicious, and completely isolated from the Kong Pachai. Instead of forming brotherhoods where the two sides came together, they were now forever enemies, the Kong Pachai and the crazy Chao Fa.

Guerrilla and Pathet Lao soldiers by Danny Yang Xaiphia

There was another old man who lived on our farm. He told people that he kept talking to god in his dreams. He said that god wanted to help the Chao Fa. His cousin, who was younger and used to work for the CIA, wondered why god never wanted to talk to the bright people. He said the old man could not perform any work, except sit next to the fireplace just to keep himself warm. He said it as a joke that we would not win a war if god kept communicating to the elders only. If there was a god who wanted to help the Chao Fa, he should communicate with those who still could perform their work and were knowledgeable about what was in the universe.

Due to the fear of future conflicts in the village, Father moved our family completely to our farm, which was on the other side of the cliff. It was a huge rocky mountain which people believed the Pathet Lao would not be able to shell or march infantry troops over to invade it easily if they were going to war against the Pathet Lao. Our small farm of only a few families, soon became the refuge for an uncountable number of families. They came from Long Cheng, Phak Khae, Pha Hoi and other places. Suddenly, tents and huts were set up and houses were built everywhere in the valley at the foot of the high rocky cliff, and up to the top of the hills. Our Vang cousins' brown-stalk cornfields disappeared within weeks. Then brown dirt emerged to take their place. Instead of worrying that their people had no place to live, some of the leaders started to talk about isolating themselves from the communist government. Each day there were more and more people coming to this tiny farm. It was not a refugee camp, but rather it was a refugee field. The families moved in with cats, dogs, pigs, horses, and cows, but no water buffaloes or elephants.

As soon as many people flowed into this tiny area, it seemed they also brought more diseases with them. Within weeks our chickens became sick and then died very quickly. We could not even kill many of them for food before they were all gone. Each morning more young and old chickens died inside the shelters or fell asleep everywhere. We were not able to treat or separate them at all because we did not know which ones were infected and which were healthy. We just kept burying the dead ones and waited to see how many were left after the disease was over. I had a nice grey rooster for fighting, but it became sick and died within two days. I was very upset for seeing him die. All the young chicks were gone, leaving only a few hens. I thought maybe they were strong enough to endure the illness, or they could just have been lucky. Instead of feeling better with more people in our place, I was feeling depressed to see all the birds were gone. The place changed to a different environment within months. The problem never ended. After disease struck our chickens, very soon came the war of the Chao Fa which we had never expected to happen.

At this time Nhia Tong *(Nyiaj Thoob)*, who claimed he was a former soldier serving some time under Vang Pao's command in Region II, had already moved his family with many cows to join the rest of us on our tiny farm. He moved there because he feared being persecuted. Also, the Kong Pachai Battalion and Pathet Lao were already well-established at many sites in Phak Khae, a place that once was the busiest market in the region. Nhia Tong thought the best way was to go to war against the Pathet Lao. He started to recruit people to form a brand-new army. It was his desire and compelling decision to gather soldiers when the drum started to beat, and it was appealing to the villagers to support him. Then the march was on to fight another war. Villagers started to pull out the weapons they had at hand and some started searching wherever they could to obtain more to get ready for the war. He believed that with his strategy, they could deter the enemy or at least delay them from advancing troops to oppress the Hmong people until Vang Pao returned to help them again. For Nhia Tong and most of the villagers as well, the belief of Vang Pao's return was imminent. They were very confident that if they started the fighting, then soon Vang Pao would certainly return to help them. Nhia Tong's character and attitude were impressive to the people in our farm village and made them feel like they had strong backbones again. However, there was one little fact of life they did not realize that in one generation there was only one wise and thoughtful leader. It did not mean that every single leader would lead them to victory or to have peace. To fight and win a war, there were a few things Nhia Tong should have determined at the time. The soldiers needed full uniforms and supplies, not like some of his guerrilla forces who were walking in their bare feet. He needed a massive army to fight and be willing to die, and a good strategy before he could win. Unless the other side screwed up their strategy so badly that they could not defend themselves, Nhia Tong could not win with his magic force. In reality, no matter how hard he fought, he would never win this war. However, none of these facts were pre-existing in Nhia Tong's brain. It seemed they thought they were going to fight the war with their magic power instead of using guns and bullets. It was a primitive strategy to use rifles to fight against the modern North Vietnamese army which had tanks and artillery shells bigger than their thighs. He underestimated the strength of the massive enemies while half of his people overestimated his capability and credibility. The people were being fooled. They should have known that if more shells flew onto their homes, where would they be hiding? If they lost the war, where did they go afterwards? They never thought that one day, not their village, but the thick jungles would be their permanent homes.

A week before Nhia Tong prepared his guerrillas to attack the Kong Pachai, the *nai kong* (ນາຍກອງ) in our village, told Father that he had met with the general in Phak Khae a few days earlier. He said the general was quite confident since he first arrived that he could bring the two sides together, despite their differences. At their initial discussion, the general told the *nai kong* to prepare his people to surrender. He wanted to take charge, oversee the surrender to make sure there would not be any harm to the civilians, and most importantly, to prevent any future conflicts in the area. At the time Father was quite reassured by the *nai kong* because of the general's promise. On the other hand, even though he promised them so, they were still skeptical about their future lives in some way, not wanting to bow their heads to the Pathet Lao. The differences between the Pathet Lao and the Hmong were not like putting horses and donkeys together. They would get along well with each other. Rather, it was like putting water buffaloes with cows in the same pasture. The water buffaloes could soak in the mud while the cows could not, which meant the Kong Pachai could follow the communist system while the villagers could not. They took very deep precautions and anticipated there might be some bad things happening soon. After their discussion and unaware of future trouble, they disseminated to the villagers what the general had promised them about their future lives. Soon some of the knucklehead villagers spread the story to Nhia Tong's ears. Once he heard the news, he prepared his guerrilla force faster than previously planned for a pre-emptive strike on the Kong Pachai Battalion in two days. His assumption was that if more people turned to the Pathet Lao, it might be harder for his guerrillas to go to war against them.

Nhia Tong's second decision to go to war against the Kong Pachai Battalion was also because he believed the Pathet Lao might turn the Kong Pachai Battalion to fight against the Hmong anyway if Pha Hoi village continued to be isolated from Phak Khae. They were angry about how they were portrayed as crazy Chao Fa. They built the temple to worship gods just as the Buddhists and the Christian built temples. It was a part of their religious beliefs. Once they practiced their worship, they were labeled as enemies and marked to be executed. It was like applying salt and hot chili pepper to their eyes. The Hmong believed they had the right to practice their religious beliefs. It was the Pathet Lao intention to diminish the core of Hmong existence. They believed that in any country on this earth if one group of people wanted to bring down another, that group could either use ideological and political influence, or even try to disintegrate the group with military power. That's why Nhia Tong stood up to fight for what he and his people wanted.

On the other hand, another group which did not like war argued and cautioned the guerrilla force to not engage in fighting a war. They did not want the Hmong in Pha Hoi to separate from their cousins in Phak Khae. They strongly believed there must be some negotiation between the two sides. There was a talkative slender man with wrinkled face and rising cheekbones, who had lost one of his upper left premolar teeth, standing with the group. He blasted off very loud with an angry crystal voice that they should look back to the past. The Hmong joined with the Lao right-wing and were supported by the Americans to fight the Vietnam War for 15 years, but at the end they got nothing. What they got during the war was the tasteless rice as allowance to feed their wives and children while fathers were fighting in the frontier. He asked them to reconsider to not fight another war again. Some people looked at him and were silent for a moment. He was right. However, it seemed talking did not work as well as going to war because the majority chose war instead.

By weighing all these bad and good things together, Nhia Tong's body was sweating with a temperature rising above 100 degrees. He decided to march his small force to pre-emptively hit the Kong Pachai Battalion in Phak Khae. Even though most of the people were confident about waging war against the Kong Pachai, others were still skeptical about Nhia Tong's failure to measure his strengths and the outcome of the war. It was a miscalculated strategy. They said, "If you cannot kill all the wasps at one time, then you should not touch their hives. Once you touch them, they will fly to follow you to the end." Those who gave advice to Nhia Tong were not educated, but sounded like they were naturally smart to foresee what was going to happen in the future, too. They kept repeating how they felt. What they saw were brothers going to war against brothers. However, to appease the brand-new leader's ambition, he went to war against the massive enemy anyway.

One afternoon, in the area below our home on the farm which was large enough for a soccer field, Nhia Tong mustered a total of 96 men, old and young, speaking a mixture of Hmong and Lao words. Half of them were barefoot, carrying a mixture of the American-made carbines and M-16 rifles. The group yelled together with their leader for half an hour, then stretched the line longer, and marched to attack the well-trained battalion.

He knew so well that to fight a war, besides the advanced equipment his soldiers would need, they must have months or even years of training. But, he verbally trained his little magic troop for only 30 minutes before they went to shoot human beings. Nearly 80 percent of his men had never been in the army and fought a war before. The skills they had were only to use their rifles shooting birds and squirrels. No one ever realized that shooting squirrels on the trees was different from shooting human beings on the ground. There was no doubt that in the fighting someone would be freaked out *(yoob)* while pointing his gun at the enemy. One hope was, as long as they did not pee in their pants, then it was good enough.

That evening the guerrillas moved forward for a surprise attack on the Kong Pachai. It seemed the enemy never anticipated that the Chao Fa in Pha Hoi would launch any attack on them. They probably assumed that the guerrilla force never had the guts to sneak up in the dark to throw grenades into the corners of their houses. This first time the guerrilla force attacked, the Kong Pachai Battalion did not even have soldiers on watch. It was the time the flame of the little cigarette lighter from Pha Hoi ignited the large oil tank in Phak Khae. Then the grief, heart break, bitterness of pain, anger, and bloodshed on both sides had begun.

Over the night some parents at home could not sleep, fearing that their barefoot sons might not return home the next morning. Whether they were drinking hot or cold water throughout the cool night, it did not appease their thirst. Instead of falling asleep, the fireplaces burned all night long until the roosters crowed, so they knew it was a new day. It was the longest night for the parents. One woman said her feet were tingling and trembling all night long, and she even had chest pains. They could not wait until they saw their beloved sons again. As the sky was clearing, they did nothing, but looked down at the narrow path below the village to see if their sons would show up at any moment. Fortunately, the evening before, their sons were protected by god. This would be the best way they would say. In the late morning they all came home without injuries to their bodies. However, some parents said their sons had lost their souls already. They needed to sacrifice chickens and pigs to do soul calling to prevent future ailments

After the first battle Nhia Tong's magic force launched against Kong Pachai, people believed that their enemies would not spare the people in Pha Hoi. They said the guerrilla leader had applied salt and hot chili peppers into the enemies' eyes. Certainly, they would now be chased to the end as they warned their leader before.

One day in November 1975, people started to worry that they would be attacked by the Pathet Lao soon. They kept asking their Mother Qeej if she knew when the Pathet Lao would come. She told them she did not have the answer yet. Then one day before the Kong Pachai attacked the village, Mother Qeej told the villagers the enemies were coming the next day. She said they would be coming from the northeast side of the village which was such a steep territory with thick bushes. This was an area where people did not believe the Pathet Lao would advance their troops through. The expectation of the people from her foretelling was high, but some people ignored her about the attack.

Early the next morning before the Pathet Lao attacked, Mother Qeej wanted all the young men who were going to fight to gather together in one place, so she could do a spiritual cleansing ceremony for them to get rid of the evil in case they had to go to war. Even though the day was going to be clear once the sun rose, she used the metaphor by saying that the day was very cloudy, and her mind was gloomy *(ntxhov siab tsis kaj)*, which meant some bad thing was going to happen to them this day for certain. By sunrise at about seven or eight o'clock while they were gathering for the ceremony, Tong Yang and his wife walked past villagers in the central village, going to the field to harvest rice. He was wearing dark civilian clothes, carrying a carbine rifle on his shoulder, a grenade clamped onto his waist belt, and a woven bamboo basket on his back. After a while the couple disappeared into the forest, heading to their rice field. Mother Qeej had not finished her spiritual cleansing ceremony at home yet, but gunfire and grenade explosions already sounded off from where the couple was going. The angry Kong Pachai launched their first surprise attack on civilians in the daytime. Maybe during the night, they had advanced their troops to surround the area, but the villagers did not know it. When Tong Yang and his wife got to a dry canal in the forest, a distance still very close to the village, two Pathet Lao soldiers hiding in the bushes above the path shot him with a barrage of bullets. He fell into the ditch below the path while his wife, who was not hurt, ran back home. The two Pathet Lao soldiers jumped out to wrestle with Tong Yang. Then he pulled the pin of his grenade still clamped onto his belt, based on the later assumptions of the investigation. It blew up and shattered all three of them into a mash like beef stew. The pieces of their torn clothes and flesh flew and splashed on rocks and bushes in the area. Their arms and legs were torn and mixed with each other everywhere; you could not tell which one belonged to whom. After the first grenade explosion, gunfire started to pop up from every corner of the village like popcorn popping in the pot. Then the group of people who gathered with Mother Qeej broke away and rushed to their houses to get guns to resist the Pathet Lao. From that moment, they hid in every corner of their houses, waiting to shoot Pathet Lao soldiers as they crawl up from the steep hillside below the village.

As gunfire and mortars or B-40 grenade propelled rockets exploded, houses burst into flame. Women and children were screaming, crying, and running to the bushes to climb up the rocky cliff on the north side above the village for safety. The men continued to fight non-stop, exchanging gunfire with the enemy until 10 o'clock before they retreated and rolled down the steep slope facing toward Phak Khae in the east where they had come from. Now it was the villagers turn to chase the Pathet Lao down the hill without fear until they all disappeared in the bushes. It was a surprise gift the Pathet Lao gave to the villagers. Therefore, in this first battle, three Hmong men from the Yang clan, Tong Yang, Chou Yang, and Fong Yang, were killed because they were not prepared or maybe it was just that in any battle there must be some casualties. On the other side, they had no information about the number of casualties of the Pathet Lao soldiers, besides the two men who were shattered by Tong Yang's grenade.

Tong Yang was our cousin's brother-in-law. While his father was on our farm, he was crying upon hearing the news of the death of his son Tong Yang. Some elder men told him not to cry because god only took his son to live with god. Soon he would return to earth again. But, he told them there was no one who ever returned after death. A human life after death would disappear just like pouring water to soak a heap of sand. The blood soaked the soil and the flesh decomposed thereafter. It was the end of a human life. He was disappointed, but there was nothing else he could do to bring his son back. The messenger told him that it was a bad time, so the villagers just buried the three men right after the enemy had retreated.

Even after the big loss of the Kong Pachai, it did not lessen the aggression of the battalion. The war swept like a tornado touching down among our homes. Our village, on top of a long narrow mountain stretching from the valley up to high cliff, received thousands of shells each week. These poor worshipers started to fight this relentless war in the tiny rocky cliffs, one battle after another. A week after the first battle, the Pathet Lao launched another offensive attack and burned most of the homes in Pha Hoi.

There was one battle when the Chao Fa knew in the late afternoon for sure the enemies were coming from their main position in the east. They scattered throughout the village to get ready for another battle. At 2 o'clock the next morning, the Pathet Lao opened fire with flames flaring up and bullets flying in the sky, flashing like sparkling stars. Unlike their enemies who shot multiple barrages at one time, the Chao Fa fired only one shot at a time when they knew for sure they could kill one life. Mortars and bazookas pounded the area, along with the extra shells that flew from Phak Khae to the high cliff in the morning darkness. On the farm we could see comet star bullets flashing in the sky during the battle. The remaining houses in the upper village were burning and their flames shed light to help both sides see to exchange gunfire. The guerrilla force could almost no longer resist, so they pulled back to the foot of the cliff to regroup at a better position. Then the Pathet Lao did not know exactly where to attack because the guerrillas did not stay in permanent positions throughout the fighting. It was confusing to the Pathet Lao. The battle continued until dawn when the enemy returned home. Even though the enemy retreated, their shells never stopped flying onto the guerrillas until 8 o'clock in that morning. They thought maybe by the time the battle was over, the exploding shells would sweep everything as flat as though it had been moved away during the night. As the sun rose in the clear sky, they went to assess the situation. All the houses that had not been destroyed in the first battle, had been destroyed by shells and fire during this battle. They found pools of bloodstains everywhere and small bowls, the ones the enemy carried with them for eating food, and water canteens were dropped everywhere on the ground. The guerrillas believed the enemy was confused and shot their own soldiers by mistake in the dark morning. Although the battle was fought all morning long, there was only one Hmong man killed in the predawn battle because he was hiding under a big tree when one shell exploded on top of it.

After the second attack, the Pathet Lao multiplied their troops to assault the guerrillas in the village non-stop. Then the guerrillas could only continue fighting to block their enemy from getting access to our village behind the high cliffs where hundreds of people had settled. It was good that after the first attack, civilians evacuated their homes completely. The village was not just quiet, but non-existent, leaving only ashes on the ground. That was the bad side. The good side was that no matter how many times the enemy tried to invade our territory during the war, they could not get through the terrain because of the limited access over the rocky mountains. Always before the Pathet Lao planned to attack the guerrilla camp on the hilltop, they fired their artillery from Phak Khae to scare the guerrillas first. This gave a signal to them that the enemy was coming close. Then they prepared themselves to be ready for the fight. While living on the opposite side of the rocky mountains, we could hear the explosions of the shells first; then the sound of the rifles followed. It shook our hearts and scared our souls from one day to the next.

While there were wars on one side of the cliff, the Chao Fa started to build their temple for worship and learning the Pahawh script on the other side. The temple was called *tsev kheej*, meaning round house. It had three levels of roofs which looked more like the shape of a Christmas tree. They also created their own national anthem and national flag. The anthem was to call upon god to come down to rescue the two ethnic groups, the Hmong and the Lao Theung. They were the suffering children of god. However, the Lao Theung later surrendered, bowed to their former enemy, and were recruited to come back to fight against the Hmong. The guerrillas called this group of traitors "those who turn their feet against the sky." *Cov neeg rov taw tuam ntuj.* It was such a smart strategy of the Pathet Lao. The Hmong flag was red in color with a first quarter moon shape and the sun. The moon represented the calendar as the earth orbits from one month to the next to give them guidance in life. The sun sheds light onto the children of god who live on earth. It was a light for them to see and earn their living. Later in the year in Phou Bia they also added a hat and a star to it. The hat symbolized an umbrella to cover above them. The one five-pointed star was to give protection when fighting battles. Everything was amazing and fascinating at the time, but I was too young to pay attention to those activities before we moved to Pha Daeng. What I remember the most was when they sang their national anthem during the evening sunset when the flag was taken down. It sounded very good and inspiring. I thought, "Now we really have something that belongs to us. It is the root of our lives." The Pahawh script, which had been prohibited for a while, was being taught once again. They believed this script was the only way that could help them communicate, but it was also the primary subject causing the Hmong people to be hunted down by Pathet Lao everywhere in the country. It was as if the people learned the Pahawh script, they would be targeted for execution. Very soon after they lost Pha Hoi, the new creation of the Hmong way of life disappeared again.

We set up a sturdy seesaw *(qhov cos)* in our brother's porch for pounding rice. As more people moved in, there were more people using it. Each day there were four, five, or six people waiting in line to use the rice pounding seesaw. Father often said that we would never win a war in this way. We had to plant rice in the field, wait until it was ready and harvest it first. Then we had to pound it and cook it to feed the soldiers. It was a long process. Before the country fell, Vang Pao just ordered the planes to drop the rice. We still went hungry sometimes and lost the war. It was an illusion and hallucination for the Chao Fa to go to war against the Pathet Lao.

Secondly, another weakness was that their weapons became scarce after so many battles. There was no supply of war materials and weapons, except searching everywhere in the area to get more of the leftover CIA war era ammunition. As the war went on and the desperate need for more weapons grew, a group of people went to dig for them in the village above our former narrow village. They were told that some people had buried some M-16 rifles with a few boxes of ammunition over there. If they ever found what they were looking for, could they win the war? Indeed, it was not worth risking their lives to climb up the mountain in enemy territory. The group went there all day, but they found nothing. On the way back home, the Pathet Lao shot one man dead. The others managed to get back home.

While the Pathet Lao were launching offensive attacks on the Chao Fa base on the mountain, men were sitting at our front door and backyard every day, discussing what to do about the war. Before the country fell, I never thought that one day our farm was going to be home to houses and tents everywhere with unfamiliar people. The area that once was empty, and where I once stood watching the airplanes flying from Viang Chan to Long Cheng every day, was now crowded with people. We no longer heard the noises of planes along the river as before. Instead, we heard the sound of artillery shells exploding and shaking the earth while startling and scaring us. It seemed we did not have enough water to put out the glowing flame from the oil tank as it kept burning larger each day. Each battle was like they just kept throwing more firewood under the burning oil tank. Even though the weather was cooling down during this time of the year, the new leader, Nhia Tong with about ten soldiers were running back and forth each day to the cliff and back home. His shirt was soaked in sweat and wet like he had just emerged from the river. His cheekbones rose higher and his personality changed from a normal peasant to an angry and anxious fighter in his dark, loose clothes. The decision he made to go to war a year earlier was nothing but a fiasco. The M-16 rifle on his shoulder seemed too heavy for him as non-stop battles raged and he missed meals. If they won the war, it might not mean very much for him and his people. If they lost the war, all his men, including himself, were going to be executed by their foes because of his vanity. We called this, "Living in the dark and fighting in hell with god's foe." Soon his people were not just fighting the endless war, but they also suffered from malnutrition. They could not grow enough crops to feed their families because the men were too busy in the front line fighting their foes.

In 1974, the caterpillars, the *scopelodes contrata* type, destroyed all the wild bananas in every valley in our area during the monsoon month. Their bodies were green, thorny, and poisonous too. If you accidentally touched them, it burned your skin just like poison ivy. The first week we saw some on the leaves. Within a week there were too many chewing around the edges of the leaves. They were so fat and heavy that the banana leaves were dropping down. In two weeks, the wild banana leaves in the valleys disappeared. What was left were only the stalks and stems. By this time the caterpillars disappeared too. When the guerrilla force was fighting the endless war, some elders believed the insects had already showed us the year before that one day the green army, the Pathet Lao, would wipe us out just like the insects that ate up the banana leaves.

One day a man came from Phak Khae to meet the people in our home. They suspected he was there to spy for the Pathet Lao. Suddenly, this large group in our yard surrounded him and questioned him intensively and wanted to arrest him, even though his son was with the guerrillas. He told them he came to join them, not to spy for the enemy. He challenged the group that if they thought he was a bad guy and wanted to kill him, he would be very happy to die. He was an innocent man. They should know it to be true that his son was with the guerrillas at the time; this indicated to them that he was not a spy. He would not turn his back on them while his son was with the group. At last the group let him go but warned him not to escape. If he ever left the place to go back to Phak Khae or any other place, they would just execute his son to pay for his crime. It sounded very bitter for both, father and son, to swallow.

Chao Lee, the man who claimed himself to be a communicator with god, lived with the guerrilla force in the base up on the rocky cliff. He had a very small device, which he never wanted to disclose to anyone to see it. He hid it inside his shirt pocket all the time. No one even saw what it was like. He said that it was given to him from the gods. During this time people called him sky father *(txiv ntuj)*, meaning the communicator with god in the sky. Sometimes he touched the device to produce a long high-pitched noise. He told them it was god talking to him. He knew when the enemy was coming to attack them and gave the soldiers some warning to prepare themselves. Whether he knew when the Pathet Lao were coming or not, they often fired shells from their base before each attack. Thus, the guerrillas were always prepared. After they fought many winless battles, except to maintain their base, his device was gone. He told people god took it back because they demanded impatiently to see it. He told the guerrillas that whoever god rewarded with the device, only that person could see it. When this happened, people lost confidence about winning the war. Some people feared without communication between god and Chao Lee, they might not know when their enemies were coming. Others were highly suspicious that it could be a small man-made tape recorder he obtained somewhere before the war. There were no such gods who issued a sound device as what Chao Lee claimed. This disappearance of the device led them to believe it must have run out of batteries, so he tossed it over the cliff. It was the end of the future hopes for some people in the guerrilla force. Some people in the group still could not believe why Uncle Blia Cha, who was in the military for many years, still could not identify the device Chao Lee possessed. Instead, he still believed everything Chao Lee said to him.

In the village Mother Qeej continued to play her amazing qeej. She said god told her to play to send away devils and purify the Hmong to extend their lives, so they could live longer. The villagers still believed that it was true that god must have granted her to play it because in those days no females had ever played that instrument. She told them that people would not die from disease or from fighting in battles. They did have a god who was watching, protecting, and providing them with prosperity.

One sunny morning when the guerrillas were unprepared, the enemy launched a surprise attack, and captured their base in the rocky mountain. Once the enemies occupied the area, they burned all the facilities and the temple. The guerrillas thought they had lost their base permanently from that moment on. However, a few hours later they managed to defeat their enemy and chased them back home again. Even if the enemy was able to occupy the base, soon they would all be dead. The guerrillas were going to block them in the back and some would push from the front. That would be the end. So, the guerrillas pounded the enemy with very minimal force and they just ran like a flock of sheep back home. One of their advantages was that it was their territory, so they knew exactly where to hide from their enemy. If the enemy got trapped, there was no way out for them. Either they had to jump off the cliff and die or return to the narrow path about eight feet wide and all get killed. Therefore, they probably figured it out that it was time to leave before they were all dead.

Whenever the guerrilla force had information that the Pathet Lao were coming, they prepared to organize a group to wait a distance behind and allow the enemy to enter the narrow path close to their base territory. The Pathet Lao marched in a line on the two-foot wide path about a quarter mile long from the village in the plain below. They outnumbered the guerrillas by ten to one in each battle. However, they waited until the enemies were in the place where they were waiting before they started the battle. Then every single bullet popping down from the cliff, knocked down the Pathet Lao, one by one. They could not make it through the narrow gate. When the enemy retreated and was on their trail back home, the group waiting behind ambushed again. Because of this unexpected attack, the enemy took very heavy casualties on the way home. This type of attack made the enemy confused about how they could encounter the guerrillas each time. They feared more of the attack from the rear than the front. Even though the guerrilla force was such a small group without proper training, militarily the Pathet Lao were no match in all these fighting aspects. The first few battles it seemed there were mostly Hmong soldiers from Kong Pachai Battalion in the fighting. As the war continued with many battles, the communist started to use more Lao soldiers along with the Kong Lorne, the civilian soldiers without proper millitary training.

In April of 1976, the enemy prepared to launch the biggest offensive ever, with troops and tanks to clean up the mess in Pha Hoi. The Hmong thought they might not be able to resist this time, but at least they would try everything before they abandon their base. That morning the Pathet Lao set their tanks, machine guns, and cannons in the flat area next to the school soccer field ready to send shells to pound the guerrillas on the cliff. In the meantime, the artillery in Phak Khae was also firing on them. For some reason after shells had been coming for a while to rip up the trees and shatter the rocky cliff, there was a big explosion in the soccer field area. A few minutes later, the artillery in Phak Khae was quiet too. Some people thought maybe it was an accident in which their cannon shells exploded. After the explosion, the Pathet Lao did not march their troops to attack the guerrilla base. It seemed after the explosion, the enemy just marched back home. Later in the day the guerrillas sent a group of people to assess the situation of what had happened down there. They found the place was bloody everywhere. It looked like many dead on the scene. Some people even believed it was the gods who helped the Chao Fa kill the enemy. Since then the Pathet Lao no longer launched troops to assault the Hmong on the cliff again. Our village of Pha Hoi became quiet with weeds growing everywhere.

In December of 1975, we moved back to Pha Daeng, the Red Cliff, our old place where we had lived in 1970. This place was separated from Pha Hoi by the very deep, steep valley of the Nam Ngeum. The village of scattered houses was smaller than before because after we left, people abandoned half of the village and moved to build houses together in the center. Within those five years, the area they abandoned became forest again.

The process of escaping a war at this time was more like moving during peacetime. The big thing was our rice. We had to put it in sacks and carry them to the river. From there we moved them across the water by raft to the other side. Since our field was closer to the river, it was easier for us than for some other people. Once we moved everything across the river, we transported it on horseback or carried it on our backs. It was a big hassle of carrying from the river and climbing up to the top of the mountain. Each round trip took about two to three hours. After a couple trips during the day with the hot sun, I just wanted to lay under the shade of the trees and not walk anymore.

After we moved back to Pha Daeng, every route had been cut off with no access to the market places anywhere in the country. The two things we needed the most now were salt and rice to feed our family later in the year. The Pathet Lao controlled all the resources while confining the Hmong to their villages up in the high mountain. Salt became scarce and had as much value as gold and silver. At the beginning of 1976, we started to eat everything without salt. Without the salt intake and lacking proper nutrition, some people became pale, weak and puffy in the face. We lived without salt from early 1976 to late 1978 when we surrendered to the Pathet Lao again in Meuang Orm.

In this village we were not free from the enemy either. Another Pathet Lao base was in Phou Kang (Middle Mountain Village) in the northeast. In the past, the local villagers along with the help of the people from Pha Daeng, fought a few battles against the Pathet Lao to force the enemy out of there, but they were not successful because the camp was well established. This was also due to the small force of the guerrillas. Even though they had fought a few unsuccessful battles in the past and without measuring their strength, the villagers were still talking about more fighting to get rid of the Pathet Lao in Phou Kang. Fighting the war became less and less an advantage for the guerrillas, but it was inevitable since they did not want to be ruled by the communist Pathet Lao. Believe it or not, these people liked only their own way of life; it was their favorite system. If the enemy wanted to attack us, it would only take them a half day marching, or we could also be reached easily by artillery from Long Cheng. However, one village between Pha Daeng and Phou Kang, the Guava Fruit Village *(Zos Txiv Cuab Thoj)* was neutral. Therefore, people in Pha Daeng thought they might receive some signals before being attacked. Father predicted that we would not be able to stay very long because the Pathet Lao wanted to clear up the region to make sure no more Chao Fa were left in any place. Our Uncle Tong Pao was very upset at the guerrilla force. He said the year before the Pathet Lao had not been hostile toward villagers. When they established their base there, they told people to stay where they were until they found a new place and they would transfer all the people to this new place. Suddenly, the guerrillas just attacked the Pathet Lao base, causing them much anger. Now we were all isolated from the Pathet Lao base completely. Above all, we were their worst enemy now.

One day an old man visited my father while we were still temporarily living in our Uncle Tong Pao's house. He was Tong Va Moua. His father died when he was little, and he grew up to be a farmer from his young days and throughout his entire life. Our grandpa also died when my father was about nine years old. He was very attached to Father. Father called him, (older brother) because he was older and their parents were related in some way. We called him Elder Uncle Tong Va Moua. He cried a lot while talking to the group of people inside the house because he missed his sons so much. They served in the army in Region II and had no choice but to escape to Thailand without him when Laos fell to the communists. He told my father and uncle that before the country fell, his sons told him that one day they would find a rice terrace and some water buffaloes for him. He could just use the buffaloes to plow the farm, so it would not be such hard work for him. Unfortunately, the plan his sons had for him went the other way. Suddenly, the country fell to the Pathet Lao. Unlike the Lao people who stayed where they were, the Hmong everywhere in the country were being pushed back to the mountains again. After his sons fled to Thailand, he cried many days and nights, but they did not hear him and they never returned.

Another matter beside his personal life, Elder Uncle Tong Va Moua continued to caution people about going to war against the Pathet Lao. He believed that the guerrilla force was too tiny and weak. If they could not kill all the Pathet Lao, then they should consider giving up. Once they wounded or killed one Pathet Lao soldier, they would follow the Chao Fa all the way to the end. Now, if they surrendered and the Pathet Lao had decided to execute all the men, there would still be the women and children left to live on earth. It was better than to keep fighting the war without winning. If any man thought he was brave enough to fight, people should lay him on the floor and chop him up with an ax. If the ax did not penetrate his flesh and his body was sparkling like a blacksmith pounding on red hot metal, then he could fight the Pathet Lao. With that kind of solidness of body, the man should not die from the fighting. If the man was being chopped and his body was bleeding like other human beings, then he should stop thinking about fighting. No matter how hard he fought, he would not win. The bullets would penetrate his body as easily as sticking a knife into a banana stalk because his body was not harder than that banana stalk. Elder Uncle Tong Va Moua also said that knew each man had only about 100 bullets for his gun. By using these leftover guns and bullets of the CIA era to fight a war, they were risking their lives to feed their enemies. In order to fight and win a war, they must have more ammunition than ten trucks could carry.

Meanwhile, my father also referred the Chao Fa back to the Crazy War, which was fought in 1919 to 1921. In the end the rebels were captured and sent to be killed in Xieng Khouang. They did not have prisons to keep the prisoners, so what they did was either kill or release them. All the captives were blindfolded, tied to posts in the hot sun, and later killed one by one by their foes. They had to pay 100 silver bars per captive to be released. Those who could not afford the 100 silver bars, were killed and went to hell. My father had a Yang uncle who joined Shong Ger to fight the war. Father's aunt went to ask her husband's relatives in the Yang clan to collect 100 silver bars to pay Kia Tong to save her husband from death. They refused to do so because it was too many bars to pay for one life. She then ran back to ask her brothers in the Thao clan for the 100 silver bars. The entire clan collected and came up with 100 bars to send to Kia Tong to release her husband from death. This was an example to indicate that if the Chao Fa lost the war to the Pathet Lao, they might be killed in the same way the people were killed after the Crazy War. These were two stories from the two cousins who did not like wars which reminded others to reconsider fighting. After this sad and long talking, Uncle Tong Va left the house and we never saw him again.

A few days later, another goofy old man named Chia Tou *(Txhiaj Tub)* with a couple of golden teeth and carrying a water bong, came to my uncle's house. He said people should not be weak and brainwashed. The Hmong should not be afraid of the enemy because they were the suffering children of god. They must fight to the end. They had fought many successful battles in the past in Phou Kang and Pha Hoi, where the enemy took heavy casualties. The Chao Fa did not have to shoot so many enemies to win the war. Whenever they went to battle, the soldiers had to wear their traditional Hmong clothes, so god was able to identify them from their enemies. The first shot they had to fire was from the Hmong black powder rifle (flintlocks) to call upon god for help. Once they shot a couple rounds at the enemy, god would jump in to shoot the enemy instead. That was one reason why they had won many battles with minimal losses. His fairytale sounded remarkable. There were about ten people in my uncle's house, listening to the man talk. Some people looked at him and said, "Who is this guy?" Those people who believed in him nodded their heads as his tale continued, but others shook their heads. They whispered to each other that this man did not know anything about how it felt when fighting in a battle.

Unlike Pha Hoi where it was difficult for Pathet Lao to invade, Pha Daeng was a place with open access everywhere for the enemy to get in. It seemed he had not washed himself in the river for months, but still tried to strategize how to win a war. One day he would live without food in his stomach. By then he might stop telling people his lousy joke. He stayed in the house for a while and after finishing his tale then took off, also gone forever.

After we moved to Pha Daeng, so did many other people. They came from Phak Khae, Pha Hoi, Phou San, southwest of Pha Hoi, and elsewhere. Unlike in Phak Khae, when Hmong Chao Fa fought against Hmong Kong Pachai as though brothers fought against brothers, Phou Kang was a different story. The Pathet Lao soldiers were mostly Lao and maybe some Vietnamese. The guerrilla force really wanted to get rid of these enemies, but they could not because the enemies kept receiving supplies by helicopters from Long Cheng. Therefore, they tried to use a new method to defeat their enemies by putting herbal poison *(puaj tawm)* in the stream where their enemy obtained drinking water, and of which they were not aware. Because this place had limited water, the small stream the Chao Fa poisoned was the only one the Pathet Lao soldiers could get water from. After putting poison in the water, they surrounded the area and did not allow the Pathet Lao to get out, except on the path to get water. A week later, they found out that the Pathet Lao soldiers had told the villagers they were very sick from diarrhea and fever; they did not know what the cause was. By the time they knew, the enemy had already packed and left their camp. The guerrillas considered it to be a successful strategy. However, this was only temporary. A month later the Pathet Lao launched another offensive battle against them in the village. The force this time was bigger and stronger. The Chao Fa could not defend their camp and lost it to the Pathet Lao completely. Then all the villagers in the four villages of Phou Kang, Phou Mee, Ha Ee, and Hoy Ha, about 50 houses in each village, felt not safe to live there anymore. They all moved to join us in the small place of Pha Daeng. Even though all the people abandoned their homes, this was not a concern for the enemy. They knew that the distance between Phou Kang and Pha Daeng was like moving your fingers from one knuckle of your hand to the next one. They let the villagers flee where they wanted to go. One day they could just come and bring them back when they were ready. The Chao Fa had a dead-end road ahead of them.

After the enemy retook the base, artillery shells started to fly from Long Cheng very often, landing on Hmong farms and ripping up crops in Pha Daeng. This was the way they tried to deprive the Hmong from having food to eat during the monsoon season and the coming year. If the villagers did not have food to feed their families, they would soon bow to the Pathet Lao. Then Mr. Bliaya Yang, another strong figure who lived in Pha Daeng, thought it was time to defend what the people had there. Unlike Nhia Tong Lor, who launched his magic force to attack the Kong Pachai, Bliaya Yang was to keep his force in place without bothering the enemy at this time. He prepared his guerrilla force to stand firm on the borderline to see whether the Pathet Lao would leave the villagers free or attack. He said if they lost their homes here, they would not have a place to go afterwards. He then combined the guerrillas of Phou Kang, Phou Mee, Ha Ee, Hoy Ha, and Pha Daeng together to join him.

After combining all these groups, it seemed the Hmong guerrillas grew bigger and stronger. Somehow, he failed to anticipate the future massive Pathet Lao army. They did not just defend the enemy from Phou Kang, but rather they had to fight against the entire enemy in the country like Nhia Thong Lor had fought in Pha Hoi. At the same time, they also lacked resources. Their weapons were too few and too old for their needs. Food was scarce since the population tripled in size. Nonetheless, he still believed if enemy ground troops did not invade our village until October, the Hmong army would become stronger again because their crops were ready to feed their people. But this was their only hope. Things did not go well as planned. Soon their future hope faded. They were able to block the enemy coming from Phou Kang for only a short period. The year had not yet ended and the crops were not ready for harvesting, but they had to abandon their homes and run for their lives by crossing the Nam Ngeum to Pha Hoi village for refuge. On the other side their bodies would be safe from being shot at by the massive forces of their foes.

There was another stronghold of Chao Fa in Pha Ngu (Snake Cliff), a place in the north. It was attacked by Pathet Lao a few times in the past, but it was a very difficult place to invade. The rocky terrain with limited access prevented the enemy from penetrating the village. Thus, the enemy never succeeded. In January 1976, we built our new house, so we could move out of uncle's house. While gathering materials to build this house, one of our Lee cousins came to help us carry the logs and bamboo. He was very attached to Father because his mother was Father's cousin. He called Father uncle, *"dab laug."* They often asked Father to do the shaman rituals for them. At the time he helped us gather the materials, he told Father that if Pha Ngu were lost to the Pathet Lao in the next few days or months, we did not have to build our house or even try to farm. It was more likely we would just have to leave the village. The reason for that was that the Pathet Lao were going to attack us anyway after they captured Pha Ngu, the most defendable Chao Fa base in the area. Then we would have to run fast to cross the Nam Ngeum back to Pha Hoi again, if we did not want to surrender or die. Otherwise, some people might be drowned in the river while the Pathet Lao were chasing them. His prediction was so true that later in the year some people took nothing, except their children with them when crossing the river to the other side. The enemy did not have to shoot anybody before they invaded our homes. All they did was just send shells from Long Cheng to scare the people before they came.

One day in March, our Vang cousin Blia Cha from our farm village in Pha Hoi, visited us. He said a week earlier his brother-in-law Neng Vue's younger brother, Xiong, was killed. Cousin Vang said they went in as a small group to attack the enemy base in Phak Khae. The Pathet Lao had expanded their perimeter of lookouts further from their usual boundary to where the guerrillas did not consider a danger zone. Thus, even before they got close to the enemy territory, the Pathet Lao had already shot him dead. His death was a shock to us and we missed him, too, because we used to live together on the farm before we moved out.

On a sunny day in March, Aunty Tong Pao Thao, her daughter Chong, and I went to the rice field. As we got close to the field, shells started to fly from west of Long Cheng, landing in the place ahead of us. Afraid of being hit, we rushed to hide under a big tree. Suddenly, one shell hit the tree above us. While we were plugging our ears with our fingers, the explosion was so strong that it shook our bodies and tossed us to the ground. What we saw everywhere were the falling leaves and small twigs from the tree. We looked up into what had been the thick leaves of the tree, but they were cleared away. We stood up and shook the leaves off our backs. We were scared, pale, and trembling after the explosion. We continued to hide under the tree for our protection for the next half hour while many rounds hit other places. Maybe the Pathet Lao knew very well that villagers would be going to their farms on the days of nice weather because shelling was quiet on rainy days.

The shells landed on our fields, but never reached the village. One possible reason was the enemy did not intend to drop the shells on us. Father thought it was not safe for us to stay in the house. Then he built a hut under a cliff in between our home and the farm in the east, but the cliff was facing west. He considered this would be safer for us children to stay during the day if the shells ever hit the village. From the middle of March to the day we left Pha Daeng, this hut under the cliff was our permanent home.

A few days before our homes were invaded, I went to see the farm with Father. While we were on the little hill, a distance away from our cornfield, we saw the field had many empty spots. We wondered what was wrong with the cornfield. When we got to the field, we discovered the empty spots were the craters of the exploded artillery shells that flew in from Long Cheng. It cleared off one spot here and one spot there. It was sad to see the young corn being destroyed. Father said the bad enemy tried to destroy our crops, so we would be hungry and surrender to them. On the ground close to one barren spot, I picked up a piece of metal about two inches wide and a half foot long. I told Father that I found a piece of shrapnel. He told me to throw it away right away because it was contaminated with poison. So, I tossed it a couple yards away.

July was the monsoon period with seven days and seven nights of rain. Artillery shells started flying from west of Long Cheng in the east more than ever before and landed on the Hmong fields and some even came close to the village. At this time, they did not just fire shells on the sunny days. For fear of being killed by shells, most Hmong families evacuated their homes and scattered to hide in the jungle or under cliffs. Some families moved down to the river to get ready to cross back to Pha Hoi and go to Phou Bia. The rain was nonstop, so the river became twice as wide and very strong. Its color turned brown. It was dangerous to transport families across on rafts. My family moved there with some Yang and Moua families to wait to cross the river when it became low again.

At the end of July, the river was low for some time, but we did not cross it yet. We thought it would be better to stay close on the river bank and going to get food at home would be much easier for us. If we moved to the other side, we had to cross the river each time we wanted to come back home. My third brother, Yeng, stayed at home. It was the time of losing grip for the guerrilla force and the villagers as well. The force moved back from Guava Fruit village, the neutral place, to the cliff above Pha Daeng village because they knew they could not resist at this time. The enemy kept pushing from Phou Kang in the northeast, coming ever closer. We knew for sure one day they would be at our homes. Then one morning before dawn, the Pathet Lao attacked Pha Daeng. They came from the northeast while the guerrillas were above the cliff in the east and on the far west.

When gunfire broke out, my brother and five others were at our home because they had abandoned their post the night before. The group in the high cliff was not attacked. Maybe the Pathet Lao did not even realize there was a guerrilla camp up there. When the Pathet Lao arrived, every house was empty. All the villagers had evacuated a few days earlier. My brother's group in the village ran to the small hill in the lower elevation in the south side of our home to observe how large the Pathet Lao force was. By this time, it was very clear and they could see everywhere. What they saw were many soldiers scouting in the flat plain area on the hill high above them. They fired their bazookas on the enemy a few times but did not even hit their targets. Then the enemy's mortars and B-40 shells were flying down from the hill, pounding them below where there were three houses. The area was treeless, so they could not find a place to hide. They were chased down the hill by the Pathet Lao like lions chasing gnus out of the grassy plain and into the thick forest where they finally were able to hide themselves. Once they ran into the thick bushes, the enemy lost track of them and stopped the chase. They did not offer any resistance either, even if they were in the better position. About thirty minutes later while they were still in the forest, shells flew nonstop from Long Cheng, pounding the village area. In the forest, my brother and the other five regrouped and ran down to the lower level to go on the south side then east and back to the cliff to observe the enemy again. By the time they got up to the Chao Fa camp to meet with the people there and looked back to the village, the enemy had already raised their flag to declare victory. For us who stayed in the deep valley, we heard the nonstop exploding shells one after another. We knew it was the end.

About one hour after the attack, my oldest brother with many villagers arrived at our hut. It was good they had stayed in another farmhouse away from our village during the night. The moment the

Pathet Lao attacked, they just ran down to follow us in the valley, hoping to cross to the other side. After a while more people arrived, then my father said we should keep moving on even though it did not appear that the Pathet Lao soldiers were following us. However, we were not sure of the whereabouts of my third brother at the time. Father said he told my brother the day before to stay in our home instead of joining the group in the camp. The reason for that was our home was in the lower level and not very visible to the enemy. Before they got to our home, they must go up on the hill above it. If he did as Father said, he should be fine. Down in the valley, we spent a half day using two small rafts to cross the wide brown river with its fast and dangerous current. In the late afternoon when we were in Pha Hoi already, my brother arrived with only his M-16 rifle on his shoulder. We thought maybe by then the enemy had a good life at our place, consuming the hundreds of cows, pigs, and chickens the villagers had abandoned. They would never go hungry since there was plenty to eat. Two days later the guerrilla army tried to retake the base they had lost, but they were unsuccessful due to the lack of supplies and their small force. Besides that, the Pathet Lao continued to receive supplies by helicopters from Long Cheng. It was all finished. The place had no life left in it and soon became another ghost town in the region.

6

THE ROAD TO PHOU BIA

---

*"Hmoob tsis paub tias xyov yuav ciaj los yuav **tuag** ua ntej Hmoob mus txog yawg hlob **Zoov Zuag**. Hmoob tsis xav nyob nrog nplog **liab** vim hmoob tsis muaj kev ywj **siab**"*

Once we were back in Pha Hoi, Father thought the best way was to move to the Phou Bia area, the tallest mountain in Laos. The hope was to go live close to Zong Zoua Her *(Zoov Zuag Hawj)*. His name meant "sharp beautiful forest mountain." He might have a better strategy to defend us. Obviously, neither Zong Zoua nor any strategy helped free us from the Pathet Lao. Wherever they ran away within Laos, the Pathet Lao would catch them one day.

We moved everything up to our previous cornfield, the place where I had lived and watched chickens a few years before. We set up our hut on the side of the field. The year we moved to Pha Daeng, another family had planted corn in the field. The corn was not ready to eat when we arrived there. By late afternoon of the third day, we started our journey to Phou Bia. As we passed through our former farm village, we saw there were countless houses throughout the mountainous place. The hilly place tucked in between numerous high cliffs on both sides, where used to be a thick mixture of wild bananas and elephant grass, now was only dirt and rocks. I looked from down below up to the hill where our house used to be, there were many more houses erected around it. The more I thought about my old place, the more my feelings hurt. We might never come back to this place again. As we walked past the village that afternoon, maybe half of the villagers also moved along with us. They believed they would no longer be protected after the fall of Pha Daeng on the other side of the Nam Ngeum. The village was so vulnerable, and they believed the enemy could just aim their cannons and 12.7mm straight at them from Pha Daeng, if they have any available.

It was the rainy season. The way to Phou Bia was very long and poorly marked at the beginning. From the Nam Ngeum to the main road, the small path was as wide as an animal trail, but it had been traveled by hundreds of people and animals ahead of us. It was also scary to travel on this route when crossing the main road from Ban Sorne to Phak Khae because the Pathet Lao soldiers might be anywhere waiting to shoot us. With our safety concern, we had to take a different route that did not go close to our Pha Hoi village, to avoid the danger of meeting the enemy. However, we were told that no more Pathet Lao soldiers came there after the last attack in April of that year.

After half a day, we passed Nam Yorne, another place which used to welcome hundreds of students from the surrounding area to attend its school each day. The old path was there still, but everything now was only weeds and bushes. There had been three buildings. One building was for first and second graders, another for third and fourth graders, and third one was for fifth and sixth graders. When we passed by the town, now the tin roofed school buildings had all disappeared. Maybe the Pathet Lao had torn them down during the year. Some people said the communists loved to take away the wooden buildings or anything else as long as they were good quality.

As soon as we crossed the main road going up the mountainside to the south, from a higher elevation I took a glance at the town in the valley for one more time, which could be the very last one. It was not raining in the afternoon, so the bright sun shone on the green valley. It was nice and beautiful, but the thatched houses around this valley had disappeared. There had been a road construction crew from Thailand and Viang Chan that lived in the lower area of the valley. In the past we came there and saw the yellow trucks and bulldozers moving around. Now the noise, the smoke, and activities were gone. Thinking about the past, I was about to cry at that moment. The huge green pineapple plantation that belonged to Nhia Her Lor was nothing but weeds. It could be that the Pathet Lao had dug all the roots up and transported everything to Xieng Khouang, or maybe they all had sunken down under the weeds. The only thing left in town, I thought, maybe were snakes and ghosts of dead people. After a while we were slowly moving to the other side of the mountain and leaving the nice valley behind. The one thing for me to keep was to record the scene in my memory.

By walking on the path crossing the side of the steep mountain slopes, one after another like the knuckles of your hand, we did not move very far that one afternoon. At sundown, we just moved to the side of the path to sleep without a tent in the forest during the night. There were many families resting behind and ahead of us. Once we stopped to rest, Mother and sister-in-law cooked dinner for us. However, there was one man who told all of us together that we should wait until dark before we could start the fires for cooking. In this way the smoke would not be seen by the enemy anywhere. He also told people to control their voices by not talking too loudly either. We did not know who the man was because after we crossed the main road there were too many strange people walking with us. Maybe he was one of the men who came from the Phou Kang area to Pha Daeng and then moved along with everybody. The man seemed very knowledgeable about everything. Like every other night since we left home, we again got hundreds of mosquito bites while sleeping in the open night air.

The next morning when we started our walk again, the path was a repeat of yesterday's pattern from dawn to dusk. The beginning path at Pha Hoi was like a goat trail which was wide enough for a person to walk on. But, after two days walking, the path was wide enough for a car. All the people who came from the lower Pha Daeng village from another route merged with us after crossing the main road. Thus, the weeds on the sides laid flat on the ground or were buried under the deep mud after hundreds of people and animals had walked through.

At the end of each day before dark, we had to stop to set up a little banana leaf hut, or sometimes we pulled out our two plastic sheets to set up a tent in the forest. This was mostly near a stream, so we had water for drinking and cooking. We burned a fire in the front of the shelter for cooking and for us to sit around to warm us up. After two days of walking at the pace of a three-year-old, in the late sunny afternoon we reached the Red Soil Village *(Av Liab)*. It was a small place of about 30 houses lying on a huge mountainside. By the time we arrived in the village, there were so many people who had stopped before us. The villagers did not welcome the newcomers either. It was also a place facing the enemy base in Hoy Kham, the intersections of both roads from Phak Khae and Meuang Cha. Therefore, even if it was close to dusk, we decided to move on. One of our uncles stopped and settled there with other people. They stayed there until early 1977 and then moved to join us in the Meuang Orm Valley.

In the late afternoon we continued to walk for about two more hours until we reached the Small Nam Mo. People name this the Small Nam Mo because there was another bigger Nam Mo flowing from Xieng Khouang to Vietnam. It was getting dark. The wild creatures started to sing in the forest before retiring for the night. Maybe they were calling and looking for their family members to go home because they had a home for the night. For us, we did not have a home to rest in for the night. We would be in an unusual cold place, which was not our way of life. We crossed the river to a cornfield on the other side which had already been harvested except the dry stalks left standing in the field. We set up our little tent on the ground close to the river. From our home in Pha Hoi to this region, there were always some wild bananas in every valley. Brothers cut small trees and bamboo to be poles staked into the ground for the structure, then the roof and walls were mostly covered with banana leaves. It was always for only one night, and we moved on the next day. When we got there, a family killed a pig to sell its meat. My second brother bought a piece to cook for dinner. That evening before we had our meal, there were more and more people arriving into the area, too. Many of our Yang cousins from Mother's side also arrived. We felt more secure because it was an area tucked in the deep river valley, remote from the enemy bases. So, it was okay to make loud noises during the night or early in the morning. During the night in the banana leaf hut, we heard nothing but the sound of the flowing river. It was such a charming and cozy sound. I wished our home was here forever.

The next morning after breakfast, our journey continued under a cloudy sky. We climbed up the mountain for two hours then we reached a different region that showers sprinkling or sometimes heavy rain. While under the rain, some families had enough plastic sheets or raincoats to cover themselves and kept going. Some families had to use banana leaves just to cover their heads and paused for a while until the rain stopped, if it did so. It was the most difficult and painful for the children to travel on foot along this goat trail. Our feet became sore and developed bad fungus after three days of walking. The children sometimes got wet, shivery, and very sick with fever from the soaking rain because they had no warm dry clothes. Besides the rain, they got too many mosquito bites and not enough nutrition. Each day we got only a small amount of rice. It was to keep us alive, so we could crawl up on the high mountains. Occasionally, we fell down in the mud because the path was too slippery and we were too weak. We had to pull on weeds or small trees on the side of the path to give us support. At the end of the day when we stopped, our clothes were wet and stained with dirt. So, we had to wash them in the stream and dry them very close to the fireplace to be ready for the next day.

On the fifth day, we reached a village called Ban Din Sai *(Zos Av Xuav)*, meaning, the Sandy Soil Village up in the mountain. It was a small place close to Nam Yeen (Cool Water Village) and Nam Mo village, the base of Xai Shoua Yang. When we arrived in the afternoon, one of our aunts was waiting for us. We had never met her before. My parents told us that she was our Aunt Jong Blong Yang *(Ntxoov Nplooj Yaj)* because she had married into the Yang family. She was in her mid-thirties and came there with a year-old baby. I remembered she mentioned the hunger of not having enough food to eat. When they arrived in this place, at first the villagers wanted to trade food for silver bars and old French silver coins. As more people came, food became scarce. Even though they had the money in hand, no one had enough food for sale. Food was worth more than silver and gold. They ended up eating wild things such as tree buds which they could gather each day. We had a little meal together outside a family's porch in the village.

During the discussion, she wanted us to go live with her family. Their home was hidden in the valley in the thick jungles about half a day walking from where she was waiting for us. My parents thought it would not be our permanent place to stay, but since we had traveled for many days, we should go there to rest for a while before moving on to the next place. After the lunch, we moved along with her to live with her family in the small separate village. That late evening, we moved into her house. There was not enough room for us to sleep. At night some of us climbed up to sleep in the empty rice stall. Our aunt was right. The village was not a good place because it was hard to find corn and rice. If we stayed there any longer, we would be too hungry. The new people were more numerous than the people who already lived there. There were tents setting everywhere in the flat area. We thought we might get diseases soon like in our farm village in Pha Hoi when people brought them to our chickens.

After we rested for a week, we moved on to the next place. Still our aunt's family was sad when we departed from their home. The next destination we aimed for that day was Nam Yeen, a place we had heard of, but never seen. Once we were back on the main road in the morning, we met many strange people who were all going to Nam Yeen. It was a long day of walking with heavy rain pouring on our heads along the way. This time the path was better because it was a region that there were more people farming along the way. We kept walking on the muddy path.

When the sun left the earth, we reached Nam Yeen. It was a small village tucked into a very narrow valley surrounded by thick jungle and less exposed to the sun. Some high cliffs were on the east and south sides. In the north and west were only high mountains with thick jungle. This place seemed very gloomy as the sun left the earth and thick fog came to take its place in the night. At the time my third brother-in-law, Leng Yang, also came to see us and help us carry things while we were on our way. He lived in Sarm Liam, the Triangular Mountain, remote in the east. We went to ask to stay with a Lee family which was related to him. This family had four children ranging from ages three to twelve years old. The mother was very pious and served us some fresh corn cakes in the evening. They were kind, but the house was too small for over twenty people. In the night we just dropped the plastic sheets on the floor and went to sleep. It was not a good place, but it was better than in the hut in the forest. The next day while we were there, we saw the sun very blurry through the clouds for only a couple hours before it left the village again. Other than that, it was showering, foggy, and cloudy all the time. The people there told us the climate was always like that from July to January each year. I thought life could be very sad without the sun every day.

After two nights and a day in between, we prepared enough food and left early on the second day. This day we were going on a path close to Meuang Cha where a Pathet Lao base was located. Nevertheless, we had to go on this path because it was the only route to Meuang Orm and Phou Bia, our destination. It was another day of walking on the path that cut across the slopes of many steep narrow mountains. Sometimes the path went from the top of a hill and all the way down to the bottom of the valley before it started up another hill again. It had been traveled by thousands of people before us during this rainy season. Thus, the path was very muddy all the way as the rain continued to pour down from above. In some areas, if the path was too deep in mud and we did not know how many bumps or holes were underneath, we had to pause. The men had to clear another path on the side for the family to walk through. This segment of path was the worst since we left Pha Daeng. With this muddy road and rainy conditions, we did not get very far in a day. As before, at sundown on that day, we reached a small cornfield which had two small houses. We stopped to rest there for the night. Even though they were not given by gods, we thanked them for the houses anyway. In the house Mother and sister-in-law gathered some vegetables in the cornfield and cooked them for dinner. It was warm in the house because we had many people together. It was also distant from the enemy, so we were not scared very much. It rained throughout the night. Along with us were two Green Hmong families who stopped in another house. They had two nice big healthy horses. That evening, their horses were constipated because the families had fed them too much shell corn and corn cobs the day we were in Nam Yeen. They should have fed the horses grass instead. During the night one horse died and the next morning the other died, too. The men were very sad because the horses had helped them carry many belongings. The families had to carry more things on their backs from then on.

Early the next morning we left the little house for a showery day on the muddy path again. During the day we walked mostly downhill to another huge valley. By late afternoon, we arrived in the valley of Plain of Rice Terraces *(Zos Tiaj Bleg)*. The sky was clear, but the sun had already gone down, except we still saw it shining on the tip of the high rocky cliffs ahead of us. There were many narrow high cliffs, like stacks of checkers surrounding us on the north, east, and south. In the west where we were coming from were only high mountains. In the flat valley the river was called the Nam Cha, coming from the north, cutting through the east side, and going down south to Meuang Cha village, with flooding everywhere in the rice terraces. It looked like half of the rice fields were submerged underwater.

Not knowing where to go in this strange place, we went to stay with a family in three farmhouses. This family was also moving to Meuang Orm. Since the river was too high to cross at the time, they had to rest there for a while. The husband was very sick, too. Father asked them why they stayed in that little house. The wife told Father that the people in the village were very stingy and did not allow any newcomers to stay at their houses. The villagers were angry at people who escaped from their homes. They said the newcomers were too cowardly to fight the enemy. Thus, they should not be allowed to stay in their homes or to sell food to them. It was unusual in our culture to be so rude in that way. Father said that someday the enemy would be there to chase them out of their village. By then they would know why we escaped from the enemy. Since the villagers were stingy, he wanted to have us cross the river the next day. The people in the house were laughing because they thought Father was crazy. One man in the house said Father might want his family to get killed by the water currents. Crossing the river would be like going to hell. Father said maybe the man was right because Father was too anxious to get away from this place. The point was, he wanted us to move away as quickly as possible from the Pathet Lao base in Meuang Cha, which was close to this area. He feared that the Pathet Lao might make their routine patrol to the village. It was as though we were living with the enemy again. All the families must cross the river, but it was too fast and twice as wide as normal. There were no boats or rafts to paddle across it as had been in Pha Daeng and Pha Hoi, and it would not have been such a good way to do so even if we had a raft at the time. We had to wait until it receded to normal.

Three days later the rain had stopped. The sky was clear. We were able to see the sun again and the flooding water had receded to the river bed. Father said it was about time to move on. We packed and moved to the river. It was a long, stressful day. The river had shrunk down almost to where it used to be, but it was still fast and difficult to cross. The bed of the narrow river was about six to eight feet deep and about ten yards wide. We had to transport not just people, but pigs, cows, and horses, along with us. These animals could swim across with the help of the people dragging them. For the people it was a different situation. The little old wooden bridge had been washed away, except some posts were erecting there. The only way to have the families cross this river was to rebuild another temporary bridge. So, the men had to cut down trees and hauled logs to make a simple bridge, using three logs for each link with a total of six links crossing to the other side. It was a little crazy just to build the bridge to send the families across the river. But whatever the reason, it must be done. With the fear of the enemy, we needed to get out of there fast. We also did not want to go back to stay in those farmhouses to wait for another day. It was the monsoon season, so there certainly would be more rain soon and the river would rise again. We knew for sure that the rain would not stop until October. That day could be the best time to cross.

At about 3 PM, the bridge was completed. The men quickly moved the families across in about a half hour. The people went over the bridge while the animals were dragged through the water. Once everything was on the other side, we continued our trip. We walked in the late afternoon until sundown and then we reached another small village. We were complete strangers to the people there. With nowhere to go and wet ground everywhere, we had to go ask the families to allow us to stay temporarily in their houses. Some families either went ahead of us or stayed behind in the woods. The Green Hmong families who had the two dead horses were not with us in the village that evening. They may have gone ahead already. One family allowed my sister-in-law's family and my family to stay in their house overnight. They said if we could not move on the next day, we could still stay there as long as we wanted. They knew that the weather was bad at the time. It was a bad time for us with the foggy or showery conditions every day since we left the Nam Mo. Inside the house in the evening, we were wet and cold and pushed ourselves toward the fire to get warm. The wife brought in more firewoods to throw into the fireplace to keep us warm. Life was very miserable. For dinner, we had nothing but rice with some boiled vegetables, which were provided by that family.

The next day the weather had not changed either. It was clear for a couple of hours but was still foggy on the peaks of every cliff and mountain. We decided to stay for another day or two while my parents went out to buy corn in another small village that was close to the one where we stayed. It was their lucky day since they met one of my mother's cousins. It happened to be the family who lived in Sala Village and left there a year before we did. The family took my parents to their farm to pick some fresh corn. By late afternoon, they came back with two big baskets of fresh corn on their backs. That evening we ground the kernels to make corn patties for our trip.

On the third day we continued our journey in the morning to Meuang Orm as the weather was better. It was a happy day for us, but sad for the family we had stayed with. The moment we were leaving their house, the couple greeted sadly with Father. They knew that fighting was everywhere now, so some day they might lose their home as we had. Father told them no one knew where peace was because the area where Hmong people lived was so tiny compared to the area of the entire country. We moved to Meuang Orm to find a better place, but maybe some day there might be another war over there, too. Then we might have to come back to their home again. No one could predict the future. We then left their home.

It was a repeat of the pattern of those previous days. The day was a long day of walking on a muddy path in fog and showers. We climbed steadily up the high cliff, which was called Pha Ka Tai. Its name sounds like cliff of the rabbit. On the way each person just walked at his or her own pace. But, if we children were very slow, our parents were always walking behind us. What I hated the most was the back basket on my back. I felt that it got heavier each moment while we were walking on the uphill path. When we reached the top, it was lunch time already. We rested to have lunch of corn patties. After a short rest, we went down the steep hillside on the other side. When we started down, it was sunny, but the path was still very muddy. By sundown, with sore feet and very tired bodies, we got to a small farmhouse on the mountainside below the road. It looked like some people had just left that morning because the ashes in the fireplace were still warm. We had to stop for the night. The sun left the earth. It was getting dark. It was not in a forested place, so there were no bird songs or ground creature sounds. Now, we had only my sister-in-law's family of four people with us. We did not know what happened to the other people. The small house was next to a small stream. The water was very clear and fresh. It had been a long day for us already, so we were ready to rest and snooze. We washed ourselves in the stream. Our feet were sore from walking up and down hills. Thus, before we fell asleep, we had to scald water to wash our feet, so they would feel better for the night and maybe for walking the next day. Father burned a lot of logs in the fireplace to warm us up. We children came to sit around the fire to get warm. Soon some were nodding their heads and fell asleep. Some leaned against the wall and fell asleep right there. At dinnertime, some children had food, but others did not because they were sleeping already. It was another day gone and we thought that we had been over too many mountains, but we were still alive. The hope was to have a better day when the sun rose again.

The next day we left the little house very early without breakfast. The traveling distance was faster on flat land than crossing many mountains and valleys as in the past few weeks. But still we had to cross many streams or small rivers throughout the day. It was a different landscape with a sunny day and a dry path. The area was called Pha Lo village and was close to Meuang Orm. By noon we passed that place to reach the main road from Meuang Cha, which no longer had vehicles traveling on it. From there we had to go up another high side of a mountain before going down to Meuang Orm. It was a long day without resting. At the end of the day we stepped into Meuang Orm territory, a huge valley surrounded by mountains on the south and east and rocky cliffs on the north. The Nam Orm, I later discovered, ran through the middle of this valley flowing eastward and then curling down south by cutting through a pass where two high mountains came together. It was getting dark, but we had not yet reached Mother's cousin's home. The twilight noises of different creatures surrounded us on all sides. Half of my family members had gone ahead of us. Father kept telling us to move faster, but my little sister and the niece of my sister-in-law were grouching about their sore feet.

Just before crossing a small river, my sister-in-law gave her slippers to her younger niece to carry. Suddenly, she dropped one slipper into the river. My brother tried to catch it, but it was too late. The slipper disappeared into the fast river in seconds. We walked in the dark another 15 minutes before we all arrived in Mother's cousin Pa Cher Yang's house. The village was called Ban Hai, meaning Farm Village. We were in a warm place to eat dinner. It felt more like home again.

The next morning, it was raining very heavily. The water flooded every channel. The family we stayed with provided us some rice for our meals. They said we should not worry about food while staying with them, and when the weather was better we could go buy our own rice in someplace else. It was very crowded with so many children in the house. Even though the children were familiar to us because they had also lived in Pha Daeng in 1970, now we were all strangers. By late afternoon, the rain had stopped, the clouds began to scatter, and we were able to see the sun through the moving clouds. Still the tip of every mountain and cliff was cloudy. This seemed to be our final stage of moving.

Upon arriving here, my sister-in-law's father decided to go to live with his brother and nephews in Phou Sarm Liam. It was a part of our culture that he would rather live with his relatives than live with us, his son-in-law. Her father, two nieces, and one cousin, who came along with us all the way from Pha Daeng, left Meuang Orm early on the second day.

On that second day, my brother-in-law and his younger brother wanted to go back home in Phou Sarm Liam, the Triangular Mountain Village, which was far to the east. They wanted us to go live with them.

It was another mountain, which was almost as high as Phou Bia with showers and cloudy days. However, we were still tired and had sore feet from the long trip. After two hours of discussion about our future place, my parents decided to go visit the place before they moved our entire family there. We packed and left Meuang Orm at noon to climb up the high mountains. They then took my little sister and me with them to see my sister in Phou Sarm Liam. It was a long climb before we got there. Once we went up about half of our trip, we entered a place with thick jungle. We no longer saw the sun as we had down below in Meuang Orm Valley. There were even more showers on our way, so we had to cover ourselves with plastic sheets to protect us from getting wet. The trees, thick fog, and clouds blocked our view from seeing much of anything. Some places on the path we only could see a few yards ahead of us. Even though it was daytime, it was dark as though the sun had already gone down. I felt like I was having a daydream about walking in the dark. Once we were on the huge mountaintop, the path went up and down hills like our trip from Pha Hoi to Meuang Orm. With the high expectation of him knowing everything ahead of us, on the way I kept asking his younger brother about how many villages we had to pass before we got to their house. He told me the first place on the mountain would be Tham Sae village and then we would have to go through many rice fields before we got to their house in the jungles on the mountain slope, which was looking back toward Meuang Orm.

Each day of our walking, we always ended up in the dark night before we could get to a village. We kept walking without resting, and by sundown, we reached the small village of Tham Sae, close to the top of Sarm Liam Mountain. However, to get to the peak of the mountain, there was still a long way to go. Then, instead of going toward the east as before, the path diverted, going southward like a bent elbow. We were also very close to my sister's house. The sounds of birds singing, looking for their partners, and other creatures were heard everywhere. We walked on the dark path under the trees with rainwater dripping from branches above onto our heads. The dripping sound of water was always very disturbing to my ears. After a while we left the flat land and went downhill again and left the jungle behind. Then we went into many green rice fields. We made another turn toward the west, going down the slope of green rice field. When it was almost completely dark, we got to my sister's small house, which was hidden in the side of the very steep mountainside and was facing west toward Meuang Orm, just as the younger brother-in-law had told me on the way. They built houses under the thick bamboo trees. Before we got to their house, their father was waiting behind the house to meet us. He asked my brother-in-law which one his father-in-law was. He pointed Father out to his father and said this was my father-in-law. They met and shook hands before entering the house. To me, the place did not look like a village. Instead, it was more like many cabins. It was a lonely place. The kitchen and dining areas were on the ground level, but the living and sleeping were on stilts high above the ground. That day was also gone, and the night was coming in to take its place. It was another night in a different place for us. That was our refugee life without a permanent home.

The next day the rain had stopped and the sky was clear. I looked down into the deep valley below, but I could not even see the Nam Orm because of the dense trees. On the right side or north side, of my sister's small house, was a beautiful waterfall flowing down from Tham Sae village which we have passed the day before. It was a really nice waterfall, bordered by thick jungles and a mixture of wild palm trees *(toov laj)*. During the day we had no place to go, except to confine ourselves in the house, looking outside through the cracks in the walls. There were many stilt houses in the row, but no children played anywhere.

We stayed there for three days and then returned to Meuang Orm. My sister was very sad because my parents told her we would rather stay in Meuang Orm. We felt this was not like a real home to us. Father thought everything could be very difficult for us to adjust. Thus, after breakfast, we walked back to Meuang Orm. On the way, I did not pay much attention to anything. There was the path and then we just kept going. There were only my parents, my little sister, and me returning.

It was showering sometimes during the day. The trip seemed shorter when going back.

That year in July a kind of little green wormlike insects, not exactly like caterpillars either, destroyed half of the rice fields in the area. At that time, the rice was still tender for the insects to chew. It ate up some fields more than others. As we walked through the rice field again in the daylight, I noticed it was the type of rice they grew in the fields. Two owners had two fields next to each other, but the insects ate all from the leaves down to the stalks in one field and not the other. Some people even said maybe that owner had done something against mother earth's regulations. Some said there would be bad things happening to them soon. So, this was an indication to them to leave the area.

Later that afternoon we were back in Uncle Pa Cher Yang's house in Meuang Orm, Father told us that he decided not to move to Sarm Liam. It was going to be very difficult to farm up there. Also, it was not a good place to raise cattle because there were no pastures. It would be better if we stayed in Meuang Orm since the environment was better suited to earn a living. There were more people, so it would be easier for us to find food. It was more like a real village to us. Father said we had to build our own house as soon as possible, so we could move out of our uncle's crowded house. The next day, Father and older brothers gathered materials in the woods for making a thatch roof and other logs for the structure of our own house. Since it was the raining season, it was difficult to do everything. Thus, Father planned to build a little house to stay in temporarily until the weather became dry. Within five days we had built our little house on the far western side of the village.

It was peaceful in this huge secluded valley with many villages in every corner. I called it the surrounded valley because mountains and cliffs were all around it. We heard no more gunfire because there were no more wars. It seemed this was a good place to live. However, food was scarce since the new crops were not ready for harvesting. Like everywhere else, people kept coming to Meuang Orm every day. The former villagers held back their rice, not wanting to sell to newcomers.

In fact, the rice they harvested the previous year was just enough to feed their families. So, they could not spare very much for sale. Then the newcomers like us ate more corn than rice because corn was cheaper and the villagers were more willing to sell it. Besides what our money could buy, each day my parents and brothers went out to the neighbors asking for work to get corn. At the end of the day, the villagers gave them each a bushel of corn in pay. It was a way to earn a living which Father said he had never done before. He said it was embarrassing to go around to the neighbors to ask for work to be paid. It seemed life had become harder than before.

It was unfortunate that half of our family became sick after living a month in this place. We had yellow fever, diarrhea, and other symptoms of unknown diseases. There were no medicines to treat the ailments, except some herbal medicines. Father performed some shaman rituals, but they were not very helpful. He said the reason we were sick was because we moved to a new place with a very different climate. However, the truth was too many people were coming from different places to live crowded in one place. Since our house was right next to the path going to Pha Lo and Meuang Cha where we had been before, we saw new people passing our house almost every day. When there were more and more people coming in, the villages became slum places.

One of my sisters-in-law died with a high fever while giving birth to a third trimester baby. Because of her pregnancy, it was not good to give her much herbal medicine for her ailment. After she was sick for two days, she delivered a baby boy in the late afternoon. The baby was already pale and dead. Right after the baby was born, she became weak and not able to eat anything. She never regained any strength thereafter. Father sent my third older brother to Sarm Liam to get her father to come down to see her. The next afternoon my sister-in-law died before her father arrived in the late evening on horseback. It was shocking, sad, and very unfortunate that her father arrived too late.

We were very poor with 11 people living in a house as small as a hut. When she died, we had to do the funeral for her, too. With our poor condition, the old neighbors who used to live there contributed some rice for us to feed the guests who came to help us with the funeral. Life was very sad. Everyone in the family was very depressed. It seemed everything was torn apart in our family. Mother blamed herself for not being able to do anything to help her daughter-in-law. She also blamed the politics, oppression of the Pathet Lao, and the war caused us to move to the new place and remain suffering. She believed that if we were in our old place in Pha Daeng, her daughter-in-law would not have died. During this time, not just our family lost one person, but other people died almost every day, especially young children. As the year passed beyond the rainy season to November, the weather became cooler. Then the people were less sick.

Sometime between August and November 1976, a respiratory disease struck the animal population in Meuang Orm, mainly the water buffaloes and cows. The buffaloes were the ones that suffered the most. The disease blocked their airways, causing them not to be able to breathe, and some animals were affected in the lungs, too. There were no medicines to treat the illness. The owners just waited and let the animals struggle with the disease to see how many would be left after the disease was gone. My mother's cousin, Ying Yang, had close to fifty water buffaloes, both white and black in colors. Whenever the animals died, the owner sold them very cheap to the Lao Theung people. They did not care much about the disease because they were hungry. One day Ying Yang killed one big white buffalo when it was getting sick. Then he invited Mother to go get some meat at the place where they killed the buffalo. She was there for almost two hours and returned with a heavy back basket of meat and a large piece of hide. We cooked the meat for soup and some was dried as smoked jerky. She cut the skin into small strips to dry and later she fried it to make crunchy sticks. We were so hungry that we just ate the meat, not realizing we might become infected with the disease. After two months the disease was over, but it had killed close to one-third of the animals. I was glad our cow and calf were fortunate not to get sick and die.

In December of 1976, we had the New Year celebration in Meuang Orm. It was a great New Year celebration with many people. The place was so peaceful just like Laos before the Pathet Lao took over. Meuang Orm comprised of six Hmong and two Lao Theung villages, all governed by one mayor. During the New Year they had both water buffalo and bullfights. Besides the bullfights, there were the remarkable amateur soccer and volleyball games, too. It was fun to watch the untrained players getting leg cramps while chasing the ball around the field.

On the third day of the New Year celebration, Hmong key leader Zong Zoua Her, who was a former CIA soldier, came from Phou Bia to visit the Hmong people in the valley. He lived in a place high up in the middle section of that rocky mountain. The host was mayor Nhia Chou Yang, who was still governing the valley. Before Zong Zoua arrived, there were old and young people lining up along the side of the dusty road in front of the mayor's house for about two blocks, waiting for him to come. Most of the people had never seen him before. What they heard was that Zong Zoua was a big and tall, the most powerful man in the region. By late noon, he arrived in a formation about a half block long, with his bodyguards marching in front and behind him. It was a time when the people felt their Hmong leader had arrived once again. He had about 15 or 20 people in civilian clothes with him. They carried M-16s, carbines, bazookas, and B-40 rockets. In front of the mayor's house, there was a young man dressed up with traditional clothing with dangling silver coins, playing a qeej (mouth organ), dancing to welcome the leader. On each side of the way were young girls lining up to welcome the group and bow their heads as Zong Zoua approached each one of them. The people behind that line of young girls were standing on tiptoe to make them a couple inches taller, so they could get a glimpse at Zong Zoua for the first time and maybe for the last one, too. As he walked close to the mayor's doorstep, people pushed closer behind him to see their leader in his dark grey uniform. There was a silent moment as he passed in front of the people before he went inside.

Above the mayor's house on the south side, was a steep natural slope elevated like a football stadium, filled with spectators, looking down on the courtyard, waiting for Zong Zoua's speech. As Zong Zoua and his team disappeared from the doorstep into the house, people were circling the large half block wide courtyard. After about twenty minutes, he came out onto the courtyard again.

To the people in Meuang Orm, the arrival of Zong Zoua was much like god descending from heaven to visit humans on earth. To Zong Zoua, this welcome was like people waiting to see their king. That was the good and strong expectation of the people in the valley. On the bad and weak side, he was experiencing hardship in the tiny region that had not been invaded by the communist yet. He did not know what to do to defend his own people. Nevertheless, people were still convinced that he would have a good strategy to fight and protect them from the invasion of the Pathet Lao in the future. One thing the people failed to realize was that the Pathet Lao would not leave the guerrilla force alone in Phou Bia, the most defendable area in the country, until they were completely wiped out of the picture.

The two tallest men in the crowd were Mayor Nhia Chou Yang and Zong Zoua Her. They both stood side by side without a microphone, facing up to the people. Zong Zoua delivered his sad 20-minute speech, which was what the crowd of people had been waiting for all morning long. In the middle of his speech, he had a lump in his throat and tears falling from his eyes, running down on his face without wiping them off, as he stood in front of the crowd. It showed how vulnerable a leader he was. He believed there was no one in the region his people could look up to, except him. He was in the best position to fight a war while the Pathet Lao had less advantage to invade the area. He wanted his people to be independent from the communist government, but it seemed his weakness was greater than his strength. For one thing, his territory was only a tiny area, as one knuckle compared to the whole hand. Secondly, he had no weapons, food, or medicine, and not enough army personnel. He did not get support from other countries. It seemed during the speech he showed the signal cues to people that it was the end of resisting the communist without telling them exactly what would happen next. Even though he delivered this sad and powerless speech, the people did not seem to grasp its core. They still considered him to be the central post of the house, which stood and held the framework together. Since there was no one else, they believed in him by seeing his uniform, his stature, and above all, his calm character that he was the only person they could rely on. Whatever the reasons, they believed their leader still existed. They felt twice as strong and more confident after seeing him in person. On the other hand, by seeing the cheering crowd, Zong Zoua Her believed that his people really wished for peace and to gain independence. But he did not have anything for the people except his plain words that he was their one-time leader in the crowd. The inspiration of the people and the emotional stress of the leader faded away the moment he ended his words. After the closing of his speech, Zong Zoua went inside the house again. That was the first and last time I saw him. After a while the crowd began to scatter everywhere. To this day I still hope that some people in the crowd would use their eyes as cameras to picture him for a long time like I did. Four years later after we surrendered to the Pathet Lao again in this valley, Mayor Nhia Chou Yang who stood side by side with Zong Zoua Her here, was arrested and sent to prison, but no one knew where. Zong Zoua, who was lucky and learned the lesson that, "Never surrendered to your enemy", was still hiding in Phou Bia and the Pathet Lao had not caught him yet.

The following evening, they held the party right in the dirt courtyard, where Zong Zoua had given his speech. This was the entertainment they showed to welcome Zong Zoua as their leader. The yard was packed with people, both old and young, including childen. They felt like they were at peace without realizing that one day shells would fly from Meuang Cha in the west, down on them. Many people sang folksongs and one young man with crystal voice sang the first very popular Hmong song of "Purple Opium Poppy" *(Paj Yeeb Ntshav)* without music. The person who sang the best folksong I remember was *Taseng* Waseng Vang. He was young, popular, and had good vocal ability. There were also some skits or short funny plays. It was great fun.

In January of 1977, we built our second bigger house behind our small house, but on the other side of the path. Father said we should build it farther away from the large pond below our small house or not too close to the sloping hillside. This way was better with nature to live in healthy conditions. At this time, my oldest brother and his wife had two children. They decided to move out to build their own house. Thus, they built their house next to ours.

With every route cut off and no communication with the outside world, we could not get any more detergent for washing clothes. We discovered another substance to replace it. Before washing our clothes, we put ashes in a piece of cloth and poured hot water over it to drain the liquid into a bowl, then let it cool off a bit and use it as our detergent. It worked very well. Some people even used it to wash their hair, but I heard some people said it was not good to use it too often. It could make hair fall out.

February of 1977 was the time to begin field work, but we did not have a piece of land for a rice field. Thus, Father decided to clear up the grassland very close to the village to grow rice. It was difficult because there were animals running everywhere. The big village was like an animal farm. We had to put a fence around the field to protect the crops from the animals. One good thing was there were many families who made their fields next to ours, too. So, we all worked together to put the fence around the fields.

Even though we were in a peaceful place, life was poor and our future was uncertain. Our cornfield was east of our house about three hours walking distance. After we cleared the fields, we planted corn in April and rice in June. It was a lot of work. Everyone in the house had to work, no matter how young we were at the time. The one thing we were hoping was there would be no more war, so we would not go hungry again at the end of the year. There were still more and more people moving into this area, so food was scarce. No one wanted to sell food because the villagers wanted to keep their rice to feed their own families. Therefore, from April to August, we did not have much left of the rice we bought when we arrived. It was not just our family, but about two-thirds of the people also did not have enough to eat. The good thing was that the country was very rich in wild things, which we could gather and cook to feed our family until our crops were ready. At first, we started to eat wild potatoes mixed with rice. From June to August before our corn was ready, we ate palm pulp mixed with rice. The palm trees were the salvation from starvation for the people. One of my brothers went to our cornfield with our cousins to chop down a huge palm tree. The trunk was about three feet in diameter and about a half block long. They cut and chopped away the outside bark to get the pulp (flesh) inside and sliced it into small pieces to dry so it would last longer. It was very rich in nutrition. Sometimes we just chopped and pounded the raw pulp, added water to it, and then squeezed the juice to filter through a cotton bag. Then we left it for a couple hours until the milky juice settled to the bottom of the bowl and drained off the water. The flesh would be like dough. We mixed it with rice and steamed it for a meal. During the four months of June to September we mostly ate this kind of palm pulp.

At the end of August our corn ears were ready to eat. We were not hungry again. From November 1977 to March of 1978, we had rice and enough food to serve on the table as we had done before. Additionally, we had more chickens and pigs. In September our cow gave birth to another female calf. We had a total of three cows now. In October of 1977, Father said we had to kill a cow for a ceremony to have a happy party for us because in the past years we had been through many difficult situations. We killed our one and half-year-old calf for the ceremony, about which I was very upset. Father said in the past we had so many cattle in Xieng Khouang, but we did not kill one for food. Instead, when we had to abandon our home, we let them run into the woods. They became meat for the Pathet Lao after we left. This time we might have also to leave our home some day if the enemy came after us. Thus, we killed the cow and invited a lot of our relatives to join the party.

While we were still in this peaceful Meuang Orm valley, rumors spread to the people in the area that a man named Vang Bee had returned from Thailand to visit Phou Bia. I have never seen this man, so don't know what he looked like. Once this news was heard, people were even more confident about the return of Vang Pao. Whether Vang Bee really visited Phou Bia or not, people were aroused big time. They thought despite the poor living conditions they had to endure now, they would be liberated soon, now that their leader had returned. However, it was only a dream. It had been one of their biggest wishes to see the return of Vang Pao since day one of his departure to Thailand two years earlier. Their imagination of having a leader or even a piece of land of their own soon led them into the jungle to suffer more. The people who returned to the Phou Bia area from Thailand as the "Team" put the civilians in the region more in jeopardy. First, they continued to prolong the resistance against the Pathet Lao, so the people suffered death in battles, by disease, and malnutrition. Second, their wishes never came true. There was no one who ever showed up to rescue them.

Unlike other places where Chao Fa guerrillas were well organized, in Meuang Orm there was no organization. We heard people say that the Chao Fa and Pathet Lao had fought a few battles in the past on the way going to Phou Bia, which caused a massive killing of Pathet Lao soldiers. At the time it seemed that Meuang Orm was such a secluded place where villagers lived normal lives as though in peacetime. Nevertheless, most men carried their American manufactured carbines and M-16s wherever they went while performing their daily work. One of the common things as in every other place was the worship temple. In this huge valley, Pa Cher Yang built his temple on a nice flat hill surrounded by many beautiful ponds close to the old airstrip. Below the temple close to the ponds was the small guesthouse. Worshipers gathered themselves together to pray inside the temple as a basic routine. Also, villagers came from many places in the surrounding areas to worship. They called upon gods to help them. They also went there to pray for god's cure whenever they were sick. In the temple they gave holy water for patients drink. Anytime they considered it to be a good or special day, Pa Cher Yang held a handful of burning incense, stood before the altar inside the temple, and asked for help or blessing from Yang Shong Lue, the Hmong Mother of Writing, who had already died. He, along with the people, wanted to be freed from the ruling Pathet Lao government, so they were praying and hoping the enemy would leave them alone in this place. Somehow, one day the enemy's Russian made artillery shells would fly from the high mountain in the east of Meuang Cha, land, and shatter their homes in the peaceful valley. The Pathet Lao tanks and soldiers would march to burn their newly built temple in Meuang Orm. The words Chao Fa were the trigger to the Pathet Lao's ancient hatred.

It was so true that very soon they did not have the peace they had wished for. Their fate was fading. In early 1978, Hmong people were chased out of their homes again by the massive Pathet Lao forces. Their worship temple was eventually burned to ashes when the Pathet Lao arrived in the valley. The sacred place was run over by Russian made tanks. Their souls were scared by the explosion of artillery shells. Instead of having peaceful lives in their homes, the thick jungles became their permanent refuges. The buds of trees and palm pulp became their main diet to keep them alive while enduring illness and deprivation in the jungles. For the first time ever, some of their babies were born into this beautiful world, but into the wrong time and wrong place. The babies were too hungry and weak to the point the sound of their crying was like a kitten's meow. Without knowing what went wrong with the babies, the parents still believed that the illness was caused by the loss of their souls. Without a real home, they did not do the three-day soul calling ceremony for their babies. Thus, their souls were sad and had left their bodies to go back to their ancestors in heaven. For nutritional purposes, they were weak and sick because their mothers did not have good nutrition and did not produce enough milk to nourish their babies. Some died while others lived with hunger.

7

RUNNING IN A CIRCLE

*"Xav hais tias tsis **khiav** los ho ntshai ib tsam raug nyab laj liab muab rho **siav**. Lawv thiaj khiav mus nkaum rau tej qab **roob** los nplog liab tseem tuaj muab lawv tua tuag tu **noob**. Thaum lawv swb rog caub **fab**, lawv raug coj los nyob ua tsheej npoj zoo li cov neeg ua tub **sab**."*

After the fall of the Chao Fa positions on the north side of Phou Kang, Pha Daeng, and Pha Hoi, the Pathet Lao shifted their focus to the southeast side, surrounding the Phou Bia area. Pha Ngu was the only base in the north that had not been washed away by the Pathet Lao's military because it was a very difficult base to invade. On the southside Phou Sarm Phiang, Phou Sae, Phou Het, and Meuang Orm were quiet at this time. Most of the battles were fought only at the end of 1975 to the beginning of 1976. The people in this area were not under the control of the Pathet Lao and lived normal lives. The sole isolated base in Nam Mo, which belonged to Sai Shoua Yang, was also free of assaults by the enemy. One possible reason was that the Pathet Lao re-energized their capabilities before they waged another war against the Chao Fa. No matter what reason it was, their plan was still to clear up the region to become free of guerrilla forces. Their main future target was to advance troops, tanks, and artillery from Meuang Cha, the main camp in the region, to set up in Meuang Orm and then send soldiers to search for hidden Chao Fa in every corner of the jungles. Their assumptions of the south area were that they had less area to cover and it would be easier than before. It was their central place that they could send shells out in any direction in 360 degrees. They would accomplish their mission quickly with minimum force. However, the war went longer than thought, and they never have completely cleaned up the mess because of the mountainous region. Once they were in Meuang Orm and went to search in the valleys, the guerrillas moved to the mountains. When they searched the mountains, the guerrillas moved back to the valleys. They tried to clear up Phou Bia from the beginning of 1978 to the end of 1979, but Zong Zoua with his force was still there about ten years later, or until his death. On the other hand, during this wave of war, the guerrillas did not offer much resistance, except against those who went straight up Phou Bia. Elsewhere, civilians mostly just ran and hid from place to place or moved down south to the Mekong River to escape to a safe haven in Thailand.

Early in 1978 was the time of losing our home again. In March Father and I were in our cornfield in the far northeast of Meuang Orm to harvest opium. One night a flare parachute popped up on the mountainside very close to us. We realized that the Pathet Lao were coming close to our territory. They came from Tha Thom, the deep valley where the Xieng Khouang River cuts through in the northeast. This flare could have been a signal to their other troops. Two days later Father thought we had to return to our home in Meuang Orm because people were talking about the Pathet Lao coming soon. The vast majority of people harvesting opium in the fields had also gone back home to Keomanang and Meuang Orm, or wherever they lived. In the afternoon when we returned to our home in the sunshine village, we heard rumors that people had spied more Pathet Lao troops in Meuang Cha. We knew something was going to happen soon, so we prepared food in case the Pathet Lao were coming.

Three days later, at dawn, we heard gunfire in the village between Pa Hia and Keomanang on the northeast side, a place at the foot of the high mountain. The place that was attacked was close to where we saw the flare a few days earlier. We grabbed as many things as we could and ran up the steep mountain on the south behind our village. On the way up people were climbing with crying children and heavy packs on their backs. Once we got to the top of the mountain, there were many more people than we had thought. At the same time, some people in the village decided not to escape. They thought it was better to surrender to the Pathet Lao since there was no other way to go beyond Ban Hai. They were exactly right because later in the year we had nowhere to go other than to come back to our homes. Blia Neng Yang was on the top of the mountain, too. For a while he urged the men to move their families to the other side of the mountain and return to fight the Pathet Lao in the attacked village. Some men, instead of nodding their heads, shook their heads. They said the dam had been broken and the flood water was running everywhere, so it could not be stopped again. It was impossible because they were lacking so many things. There were not enough men who could go back to fight the enemy. Besides that, they also did not have good weapons. What the people had at the time were only those they had collected from the leftovers of the Vang Pao era. Each person had only about 50 to 100 bullets for his gun. It was not possible for them to go to war against the massive Pathet Lao army with its hundreds of tanks, and many Russian-made artillery pieces. If the Pathet Lao only fired their artillery shells from Meuang Cha to Meuang Orm, it was more than the Hmong could endure. Now it was too late because the enemy was in every corner of our homes and in good positions. The guerrillas would never push them back to the woods again. After debating for a while, people milled around the area without finding a solution. The mortar shells and B-40s continued exploding non-stop in the village, some houses burst into flames. As the exchange of small gunfire continued, the bullets flew up in the air like comet stars.

My third older brother, Yeng, was still in the temple. We hoped he was safe, even though the enemy was going to be there soon. Now there was no imminent attack on our home yet. If the enemy attacked our village, my brother should be able to find his way out of Meuang Orm.

The place where we rested was facing the attacked village. As we looked down from the mountaintop into Meuang Orm Valley for a while, it was completely clear as the sun rose from the east. However, there was no sunray that hit down into the deep bottom of the valley yet because the sun was blocked by the high Keomanang Mountains. The fog still covered the Orm River flowing from the west of Meuang Orm to Keomanang village in the east. The people rested to catch their breath by the sides of the path which cut through the field of dried brown rice straw, one group here and one group there, waiting for the arrival of some of their family members who were left behind. We did the same thing by waiting for our brother to show up before we moved on.

We waited for a while, but brother did not show up. Father urged us to move on to the other side of the mountain in order not to be targeted by the enemy. Then we moved slowly with the people on the way. Once we were on the other side, we no longer heard any of the loud gunfire. From there we continued to walk approximately two hours downhill before we reached a deep narrow valley with a lot of sugarcane and banana trees. The place was called Tong Noy or small valley. We passed that place and went up the other mountain. Here was another rice field with dried brown rice straw. My parents moved us into a thick wooded area next to the field, but without other families. At this point my third older brother had not reached us yet.

We were worried, but still had hope he would be safe. We rested the whole day there, not going anywhere. In the late afternoon, he came with our two cows. He said during the day it was quiet again. However, it was over if we did not want to go back to live with the Pathet Lao. This meant we would never have a home again in Meuang Orm.

The next morning my third brother went back to our home again to butcher a pig for food. By two o'clock he returned and carried a little dead pig completely cleaned on his back. He said some people were still fighting against the Pathet Lao in Keomanang because he still heard gunfire was continuing. As we had seen when we were there before, some people in Ban Hai did not even bother to evacuate at all. It was quieter, but not completely cold yet. We should just stay there for a couple of days to see what happened before we moved on to a different place.

On the third day, Father decided to return home to see if there were any Pathet Lao soldiers at our home. He was gone all night long. At about 8 o'clock in the morning, he arrived at our temporary camp while I was watching our cows grazing. He told me to take the cows back to the tent right away because we had to move on. We might have to kill our cows soon and eat them. I was shocked. My heart was pumping fast for fear that something must had gone badly wrong. I thought if we killed the two cows then we had nothing left. Father said we no longer could return home again because the enemy already moved their tanks into Meuang Orm. I grabbed the rope and lead them back to the tent as he directed. Once I got there, Father called everyone to come together and explained the situation. He told us the story about what had happened that early morning. While he was in the house, tanks were roaring on the road from Meuang Cha in the west. The sound of gunfire was coming toward our home. He rushed up the high mountain we had climbed a few days earlier to return to our camp. He knew that the Pathet Lao Army was advancing their troops from Meuang Cha to Meuang Orm within the last 48 hours. He did not have much time to do anything, except grab a few of the household tools such as axes, sickles, and knives into his back basket and rush to come back. It was time for us to move on, maybe further down south.

At noon after lunch, we packed and moved to another village in the southeast. In this group we had only our family along with my oldest brother's family moving along the road. We passed a few streams before we got to the intersection of two joining paths. There was another path coming from the northeast that merged with the path we were on. The scenery of this area was hilly just like the knuckles on your hands. We had to go up and down, up and down. We then met our Thao cousins and many more people, who we never knew before, coming from a village on the mountaintop very close to Sarm Liam. One of the cousins had an injured foot and walked with a single cane. I thought walking on the path up and down hills like that must be very difficult for him. I saw him just for a moment while my brother chatted with him. Then we walked past each other to go to the next point. It was the last time I saw him in Laos until we met again in 1984 in Minnesota. After we left them behind, we kept walking, but knew nothing about where we would end up in the night to come. It seemed there were many people who had gone ahead of us because weeds and grass on the sides of the path had died from the people stepped on them in the last couple of days. At sundown, we reached another rice field on the side of the mountain. It had only one small house, but many families had set up tents in this place already. Some people had been there two or three days before us. One family killed a pig a few hours before we arrived. One of my brothers bought two kilograms of the meat to cook for our dinner.

Escaping families by Danny Yang Xaiphia

That night we did not have a place to sleep. So, our entire family went to sleep by a pile of hay. It was good that during this time of the year there was no rain at all. The night was cool. It was interesting to watch the moon and stars, but life was very sad without a home. The next day we did not have any breakfast before we moved on. During the past three days while we were in the thick jungle, many families had moved ahead of us. On the way to the next village that morning, we kept meeting more families resting along the way. The weaker families just wanted to hide out, hoping to go back to their homes one day when the Pathet Lao left. This was just their hope. The stronger families had the goals of going southward and cross over to Thailand. They knew life was going to be bad at home because they did not like the Pathet Lao. We walked until noon, then reached a village with most of the villagers gone. It was called Tong Pa Koy, meaning plain of the banana forest. We moved into a house that belonged to an old Green Hmong lady, who welcomed us. She said the people had evacuated the place about a week earlier. Since then she went to stay in the farm to take care of the chickens. Her daughter and son-in-law with their five children also had left her. She did not want to go with them because she was too old. She would rather stay on the chicken farm and feed them. Some people looked at her and thought she must be crazy to live in that place where there was nobody else. Without the new people like us moving into the village for a short time, she would be there by herself like a ghost wandering alone.

On the second day in Tong Pa Koy, Father decided that we had to kill our cows for food. The decision to kill the cows was to get rid of them so we could go to Thailand. So, we killed the cow in the morning, leaving the 7-month-old calf behind. In the afternoon Mother's cousin from the Yang clan asked if he could use the calf for a ceremony. His child was sick and he needed a cow to do the soul calling. A cow had a higher spirit power, which would make the child healthy again. We gave the calf to him, but we still kept all the meat. At first, I wondered why we lost our home, the pigs, the chickens, the horse, and finally the cows, too. It was very sad for me to see the cows gone in one day, but, on the other hand, I thought it was time to forget about everything in the past. If we surrendered to the Pathet Lao to save our animals, it was like we were pushing ourselves into hell by living with the enemy. Father had the experience of how the communist system was. He was sick and tired of their seminars. Without the animals, our journey would be easier and faster if we went to Thailand.

In the afternoon on the second day, a man with a young wife arrived in the house. His name was Blong. My brother knew him because they had met a while ago in Meuang Orm. He had returned from Thailand to accompany his relatives to Thailand. However, he could not find the people he wanted to take with him. On his way back, he was offered a new wife by an old couple. He was the lucky guy, I thought. They gave their daughter to him and hoped she would have a better life in Thailand or in another civilized country. The parents hoped one day their daughter and son-in-law would be able to help them if the parents were still alive. If they died, the daughter was given free to the new son-in-law.

My brother asked him if he could bring us to Thailand since he knew the way back. He said he needed a silver bar for each person. Also, on the way to the Mekong River, there would be some people who died, either from gunshots or starvation. It sounded like he just wanted to take the silver from people but was not responsible for what he was doing. My brother thought we should just forget about him and follow other escaping people as they went. One silver bar per person was too much and that small guy would not be able to carry that many bars with him anyway. There were only three chances for us. First, if we got caught by the enemy, we just had to surrender to them. Second, if we were shot at, we probably would just die on the way. Thirdly, if we were lucky, then we might just get to Thailand. That evening after we decided not to go with them, the couple left the house. We never met them again.

In this village there were more people coming to stay or to pass through each day. There were also some cousins from Mother's side and one Thao uncle with his family of 11 children, who came to stay with us. On the fourth day the daughter and son-in-law of the old lady, who let us stay in her house, returned home with their five children. They had been hiding in the valley. They came back to get more rice and wanted to continue their journey to Thailand. They both asked their old mother to go with them at this time, but she kept saying she was too old. It was not worth the effort for her to go. Whether she went with them or stayed, she would have an equal chance of suffering. So, she would rather stay and feed the chickens on the farm. They told her that she was old and could not do any more farming to feed herself. Thus, she must certainly go with them. Besides that, some day there would be no more people in the village. She insisted that there always would be some people around. She said she could not do any farming, but planted a lot of yuca and yams, so she would just eat those for food. The three of them debated for a while without an agreement. The young couple was very sad. The next day the young family left the village again. I felt so sad.

On the sixth day in Tong Pa Koy, we were hungry for fish. All the young men and women decided to go poison the fish in the Orm River which was very close to where we stayed. We started to dig up many roots from a kind of small vine *(hmab txhais)* for two hours, bundled them up, and carried them to the river to poison the fish. Some guys said they had used these roots in the past in some small streams. After they washed the juice of the roots into the river, the fish got dizzy or sick and floated up to the surface. Then they were easily caught for cooking. They were not sure about a big river like this Orm River. We carried as much as each person could down to the river. Once we got there, we pounded the roots with bats, heavy sticks, or even rocks until they were all smashed. Then we washed them all together at one time into the river. After 30 minutes, we ran down the river to catch the stunned fish on the surface of the water. We ran as far as a mile down the river for one hour, two hours, but caught nothing. We saw the fish were still dancing under the rocks in the water. In the meantime, some people started to feel an itching on their bodies. The poison started to bite the people. No one had been told that the juice would irritate the skin and cause itching and blisters like chickenpox if they came in contact with it. After two hours, we got no fish, but we had skin blisters. Overnight and the next morning, it was even worse. Most of us had puffy faces, especially children who had played more with those roots. We blamed each other for what we had done. It took seven to ten days for the blisters to dry before the skin peeled off.

On the eighth day in Tong Pa Koy, some people returned from Meuang Ao, a place far down in the south. They said that my oldest sister-in-law's younger brother, and one of our Yang cousins had been killed when they were on their way to the Mekong River. My sister-in-law covered her face with her palms and cried as the people explained the situation. The two young men were killed by landmines. They were not the only two men who got killed that we heard of. There were many more people who died in the same manner on the way, but no one ever took account of them. The people who returned from the trip said it was too difficult for families with young children. It could take months to get to the Mekong River. People would not be able to carry enough food to last for this long journey. Some part of the journey would have to be cut through thick jungle where there was no old path to follow. Some part of the way would be too dangerous to cross because the Pathet Lao made their routine patrols very often. The landmines could go off at any time, or the enemy would be concealed someplace to shoot whenever people approach them. Once we heard this tragic news, Father hesitated to continue our trip. At the same time, Father also feared surrendering to the Pathet Lao because they might use young men for soldiers. Both these bad and good things combined his mind, two days later Father decided to let three of my unmarried brothers go to Meuang Ao and go on to Thailand. Then our family was reduced to eight people--my parents, two sisters, my oldest brother, his wife, their daughter, and me.

When the Pathet Lao chased us out of Meuang Orm, they also chased the people in Phou La, Pha Phai, and Nam Thien out of their homes. Later in the year, we learned that people suffered a big loss within this short period. Those in the southern region, from Meuang Orm and all the way down to Meuang Ao, ran southward to Paksan, going to Thailand. While they were in the south not even close to the Mekong River, about one half of them had died. This group suffered the biggest losses. No one had the exact number of dead people but estimated many hundreds of them died. The distance was too far, and they could not carry enough food to feed their families. Mostly, children died from starvation and overdoses of opium tranquilization for the fear of being captured by the Pathet Lao. The parents gave opium to their young children and infants, so they would fall asleep when they were close to enemy territory. Some were saved not being captured, but many of their children died from the drug. Besides the children, the elders died from starvation because they could not eat wild things to strengthening their health. Thirdly, people died in gun battles, from illnesses, and landmines. Along the way they were also ambushed by villagers for silver. Those who were lucky made their way to Thailand. Others turned themselves in to the Pathet Lao to save their lives when they were too weak to crawl up mountains or slide down hills. Those in the northern region such as Phou La, Pha Phai, and Nam Thien climbed up Phou Bia all the way to the top. This group suffered more from starvation. With no food anywhere to keep them alive, they ate some big lumps that grew one or several on vines that were on the ground or climbed trees (noj pob caus ntoo). Some of the lumps were as big as soccer balls. When chopped up and eaten raw, they were tender, flavorless and crunchy like potatoes. Later they surrendered to the Pathet Lao and their stories were told. Some of the people like us, who decided to hide in the jungles around Meuang Orm, did not suffer much loss.

A few days after my three brothers left, one Yang cousin and I went walking around the village. On the way we saw most of the houses were empty and even scary. As we walked to the far side in the west, we finally saw a small house on the right side of the road with the door still left open. There was also smoke coming out from the roof. Even though our hearts were beating fast in fear of ghosts, we thought it would be good just to check to see who was there. When we looked inside, it was our Lee cousin by himself. His name was Thao Lee. It was strange that every house was cold and without people in that area while he was the only person who lived in the house. His wife died in Pha Daeng a few years ago while he was still in the army. He said he was sick and coughing up a lot of phlegm. He was on his way to Thailand, but once he arrived here, he started to get sick and could not make it any further on his journey. He knew me very well because we used to visit them in Nam Phai when we lived in Sala in Xieng Khouang and later in lower Pha Daeng, too. I was too young to engage in conversation with him, but said I was feeling bad that he was sick. All I said was I hoped he would get better soon. I asked him where his three brothers and their mother were. He told me they used to live in Pha Phai, but he was not sure where they were now. They might have gone to Phou Bia, Nong Ong, or even surrendered to the Pathet Lao and moved back to Xieng Khouang already. He said he picked up a nice crossbow a few days before on the other side of the village, but he was too weak to carry it with him. Someone left it in the house when he was there. If he still had it with him now, he would just give it to me for hunting birds. After we chatted for a while, my cousin and I said goodbye to him and returned to the place where we stayed. When I got back home, I never mentioned this to my parents that I met our Lee cousin either. It was the last time I ever saw him. Later I felt guilty for not talking to him enough at the time.

A few days later, we received a message from my sister Mai and brother-in-law Leng Yang, who used to live in Water Falls Village in Sarm Liam. They were somewhere in the jungles beyond Meuang Ao in the south. They said we should not buy any more rice. If we needed some, we could just go get theirs in Sarm Liam. They might never come back again. If we did not follow them, we might never ever see each other again in the future. No matter what happened they were going to Thailand anyway. It was a heartbreaking message for us.

That same afternoon we heard rumors that the Pathet Lao were coming to where we stayed. Then we thought the best way was to move and hide down along the Orm River. The dense banana forest would offer better protection if we hid there. The fear of the Pathet Lao led the elders to psychologically believe that the forest and deep valley would give them protection. It made no sense at all. We packed everything to move there before the enemies could catch us. When we got there, we saw more and more people moving to reside along the river with us. A lot of Xiong families from Keomanang stayed to the north of us. By then we did not have a real home anymore. All we did was to build a little temporary banana leaf hut.

Since we stayed right next to the river, my Thao cousins and I had a lot of time to play in the water every day. Life was peaceful in this place, but we had no future and soon we would not have anything to eat. The river had a lot of fish, but we did not have the equipment to catch them for food. All we did was walk up and down the river to search for crabs under the rocks. The water was very clear on the sunny days, so we could see as deep as five to ten feet down to the bottom. All of a sudden, we had some Lao Theung children join us. These Lao Theung children were better swimmers than we were because they used to live close to the river. Fishing and being able to swim were their daily life. Once we saw those boys who were smaller than we were but were very good swimmers, then we started to learn how to swim. It was very difficult at the beginning since there was no one to teach us. In real life, Father never knew how to swim, and he often cautioned us to be careful when going into the water. The Hmong children played in the shallow area while the Lao Theung children were diving and swimming in the deeper part. One month in the river, I finally figured it out and stayed afloat like the Lao Theung children. My cousins still could not swim because they were too afraid to be in the deeper area.

One sunny afternoon, we walked down the river further south; we saw a group of young men swimming ahead of us. They jumped from the big rocks into the water and yelled very loud because they were having fun. Once we approached them, a guy yelled at everyone that he saw a school of fish dancing under the big rock close to where they were swimming. One guy, who had his left hand cut off at the wrist, grabbed a rifle, which they called an eight-round rifle *(phom yim tes)*, the M-1, and jumped on top of the big rock. He stood there and aimed the gun down under the rock for a few seconds, then shot three times into the water. We watched for a couple of seconds after the gunfire, then we saw some fish floating up to the surface with their bellies facing up to the sky. The guys jumped into the water to catch them. Some men were laughing. Some said, "Let's start a fire, so we can cook the fish for lunch." One guy said the fish should not be put on the hot rocks because they would all be cooked by the time they got the fire ready. After we watched them catch all the dead fish and put them on a flat rock, we continued to go further south, even passed the place we tried to poison the fish a few days earlier. We spent a few hours walking and digging crabs under the rocks. When we returned to the place, the men were gone.

One day Father took me with him to visit our uncle and aunt, a Xiong family who stayed along the river to the north. They were from the Xiong village in Keomanang. This couple was as old as my parents. Without having children of their own, they adopted some from relatives. They were very kind to us because the aunt did not have any brothers. Even though she was only Father's cousin, she called him, "Brother." There were many families stayed along with them.

After visiting them, we crossed the river to the steep mountainside to visit my sister's home, the Water Falls Village, below Tham Sae, which they had abandoned a month earlier. The mountainside surrounding their homes was all cleared up for rice fields. It had one dead tree here and another there throughout the field. At this point it was so steep that it blocked our view, so we could not see the top of the mountain yet. As we walked up to the other side higher up, we could see straight from there to the falls of the Tham Sae River. The thick bamboo trees over my sister's home we had visited two years earlier had vanished.

This was an area of about three miles from the river up to the huge mountain with nothing else but dry brown rice stubble after the rice had been harvested. The thick wild palm trees below the bluff on both sides of the falls I saw two years ago, now had been cleared up. Some palm trees were cut down by people while others had been destroyed by fire. Further up on the mountainside to the north, going toward Keomanang, was also a treeless area with brown rice stubble. Once we walked up close to the village, we were on a higher level. At this point we got a better view of the huge mountains. One was coming from the Tham Sae and Sarm Liam and the other was south of Meuang Orm from the west. The two mountains met where the Nam Orm cut through.

It was such a hot afternoon. We were sweating and thirsty from climbing up that huge mountain. As we got closer to the village, Father said we had to rest for a while before moving on. I climbed up to sit on a big dead tree trunk lying on the ground, facing down toward the river with my feet hanging over the side of the trunk. Father was standing, whistling, and waiting for the breeze to come from any direction to cool us off. We believed that if you whistle, you are calling for a breeze. It was such a pleasant moment in the field to see the dry rice stubble mixed with the green weeds. In truth there was no more life in the place. Even without war interference, soon villagers would abandon it any way of land depletion. After we caught our breaths, he said, "Let's go", and he jumped off the log to the ground. I followed him. We walked for about ten minutes and arrived in the village of about 30 houses. We toured around the village and went to find out who were the people now living there. We found that the former villagers were all gone. All those current people happened to be Mother's relatives who had just moved in a few days before. Her two brothers' families with many nephews and grandchildren were there. During the conversation, they told us that the two houses tucked into the forest very far on the top were still occupied by the original villagers. They decided not to go anywhere. Father told me to play around with our Yang cousins while he checked to see if there were any empty houses left. Most of the houses in the lower section had been occupied because the area was flat and better suited for children to play. He left me with them while walking further up. After he was gone for 30 minutes, he returned to one of Mother's brother's families. He said he found a few vacant houses on the top of the village. By now we had been gone long enough already. The sun went down lower with a shadow cast on the mountainside above the Nam Orm. He called me while I was playing with my unfamiliar cousins in the backyard, that it was time to go back to our temporary banana leaf hut in the deep valley. Father told them that if we decided to come to live with them, we would take one of those houses up on the top. Then we returned to the valley again.

One month passed without Pathet Lao action, but we could not go back home in Meuang Orm either. Also, we had not heard any news from my three brothers who were on their way to Thailand. In April of 1978, Father took me and three other cousins with him to live in my sister's village, the place we had visited a month earlier. We left Mother, two sisters, my oldest brother, his wife, and their daughter in the little hut in the jungle. The plan was to get a place first, then we would move everyone up together. In the afternoon, we went up to one big house in the very top of the village. We stayed in the house for two days and went back to pick up the rest of my family in the valley. Once we all moved up there, we had our entire family plus one of our Yang cousin's family, who was Mother's nephew. We had nothing to do now. There was no more farm work either. The days were nice and sunny. The temperature went up higher. It was hot from noon until late afternoon, but it was cool at night. During the day we went down to the Tham Sae River to cool ourselves off. It was not as big as the Nam Orm, but it was big enough for people to cool themselves off.

We did not know what was going to happen next because this place was facing Meuang Orm too. If the Pathet Lao wanted to fire their artillery shells on us, they would easily land there. So, we still steamed and dried more rice to get ready in case we had to run away again.

One day my Yang cousin and I walked up to Tham Sae village above us on the mountaintop. The place was cold with no people or animals as there had been a year ago when we had walked past it. Maybe the only creatures in the houses were animal fleas. It became a quiet and scary place. It was as though people had abandoned the place for months or even years already. All over the area the weeds had started to grow. The walls of the houses began to fall apart. The roofs started to collapse. We were young and not brave enough to go around, so we decided to return home after observing the place for a little while. We did not understand why our parents took us to this lonely place. We would not have any future. Everywhere we moved to was a sad place.

Life was boring with nothing to do. There was a wooded area close to our temporary home that had many squirrels. We searched and found some crossbows and arrows in the houses near us to shoot them. However, this species was very smart and fast. The whole time we stayed there, we shot only three of them.

At the end of April 1978, a Yang cousin who left his wife, a child, three brothers, and his mother in Sarm Liam and went to Meuang Ao, returned home again. When we heard he was back, we rushed to see him. He said escaping was complicated. The way to the Mekong River was much more difficult than people ever imagined. On the way to Thailand many people would starve to death or be killed in gun battles or by landmines. That's why he decided to come back to live with his family. Father asked him if he knew what happened to his three sons. He said they separated from each other sometime before he returned. There were a lot of people on the way who had no idea where they should go. They just used the sun as a guide and kept going southward, hoping one day they would reach the Mekong River. Even though they wanted to go, it was like a dead-end path for them because no one could ever possibly travel on foot for a month or two without knowing what was ahead. When we heard this troubling news again, my parents started to worry about my three brothers. They feared my brothers might just move along with people without realizing the danger on the way ahead of them. But then it was too late to get them back. All we could do was to wait and to see if there was any good news from them.

We lived in this Water Falls Village for another month. Soon bad things happened to us again as we had predicted. One day in early May of 1978, some people saw Pathet Lao soldiers on the mountain going toward Keomanang. We knew they were coming after us, so it was time for us to prepare to run. The next morning was a very sunny day. At about 8 o'clock, mortar shells exploded in the jungles where the Pathet Lao had been seen the night before. After a few explosions, it was quiet again. It could be that the Pathet Lao just fired some to signal us that they were coming. At the time, people in the village were yelling and running everywhere. Some had something in their hands and on their backs. Others had nothing except their children with them. For us, we packed what we needed the night before because we believed what people told us about seeing the Pathet Lao and they would be coming. We ran up to the wooded area next to the village where we used to shoot squirrels. There was nothing to hide in except bushes and trees. We had not had breakfast yet. We brought along with us a pot of rice and some water in a plastic container. In the wooded area, Father gave us some plain cooked rice with water. In the short time while we were eating, more and more people arrived in the area. In the meantime, as we looked up the hill, we saw that some people had already gone up to the mountaintop going to Tham Sae village. Our Yang cousin, who was living with us, said we should not run too fast. First, we should rest here and wait to see what was going to happen during that day. If everywhere was quiet, then we might go to Sarm Liam Mountain. The plan was to go there, then down south to the Mekong River, if that was possible. Father said it was not very different from those past couple months that we just moved from one place to the other. He wanted to follow the group because he did not want to surrender to the Pathet Lao either. Even though we were talking about abandoning this village, the two original families, who had always lived there did not make a move. It looked like they decided to stay there, and if the Pathet Lao came, they would just surrender to them. We said they would just raise their white flag.

For a while after the villagers evacuated their homes, the place was completely quiet. Those who were moving up the hill disappeared. Father told us to move from there to another location above the two original families and close to the path going to Tham Sae village. This area had more trees for protection. We got out from the bushes to run back down to the treeless area in the village where the path was, then rushed off to the place where we wanted to hide. Once we got there, we found two of our Thao and Yang cousin families there already. There were no more gunfire or mortar explosions.

We hid in this place all day long while it was quiet in the village. We were not allowed to talk out loud or even let children cry. At about 2 PM, Father went back to the house to gather some more belongings and cook more rice for us. About two hours later he came back and said we must leave the area because the village was empty except for the two original families. We must be fast to catch up with our Yang cousins who had gone ahead to Phou Sarm Liam early in the day. He served us the meal with rice and water again. It did not taste good, but was just to keep us alive. After our meal, we put our packs on our backs and said good bye to Water Fall village. It was so sad.

That afternoon even we wanted to leave the village by going to the jungle, we were still not sure where we would wind up along the way in the evening. After climbing up the hill and passing Tham Sae, we met dozens of people who were ahead of us and going into the jungle. They were the Xiong and Lee families who used to live along the Nam Orm and somewhere in the rice fields close to the hills where we had heard the mortar shells explode that morning. The people were walking with packs on their backs. Some held one child in one hand with another one on their back. While some families stuck close together in a group, others were left behind taking a rest and not following their family members. Some people were skinny and weak while others fat and strong; some were healthy, and some were sick. Without knowing what was ahead, we kept walking until dark and reached a grassland area which once was a farmland, maybe a couple years earlier. The grass, weeds, and reeds were growing tall already. The wild creatures were singing everywhere as we had heard them in the past. Everyone was tired and hungry. It was time to stop to rest for the night. We moved about 20 yards from the side of the path. Father set up a temporary tent for five of us to sleep in for the night. My brother set up another one for him, his wife, and their daughter. Our Thao cousins stayed down the hill close to the stream. That evening we left behind our Yang cousin's family, who had lived with us in the same house. We did not know whether they still followed us or had decided to go back to the village. The people we met on the road that evening were mostly unfamiliar faces while we were losing our close relatives. It seemed people were careless about each other and moving on their own way in life. In this area we did not know how many families were stopping for the night. All we heard was the noise of babies crying here and there along the way, as though they no longer were afraid of their enemies anymore. Throughout the night the sky was clear and beautiful. The temperature was cooling down, too. We slept without a home through the night while watching plenty of stars above us.

Early the next morning of our second day, we heard the birds singing, but not a single rooster crowed. Everywhere was wet with heavy dew on the grass. People made noises without any fear while starting their fires to cook breakfast to feed their families before they would move on for the day. At the time the sky was clear as the sun started to rise, and the smoke rose everywhere for about two blocks along the path. Some children cried. More mothers yelled instructions to their children. My brother still had two chickens with him at the time. He killed them for breakfast before we went on. But the cooking and eating must be done quickly. As soon as our light breakfast was done, it was time to go again. We walked for about 30 minutes then we got to the divided path. One path went downhill to the valley toward the north, and the other was going straight to the side of Phou Sam Liam in the east. Our parents were a distance behind us while my little sister and I were with our Thao cousin's family. Some panicked crazy people behind us came running fast and screaming that they saw Pathet Lao soldiers were following them. My little sister and I did not know which way to go, so we just followed our cousins to take the path going downhill. We kept running down the steep path along with other people for a while and finally reached an old rice field, which still had thick brown stubble after the rice had been harvested. There were many people who had stopped in this place already. Now we realized that we were there without our parents. Our cousin's father, Uncle Joua Vang, told us not to worry. We should just stay with them for the time being. He told us that our parents would follow us there later. With the hot sun above us, Uncle Joua Vang moved us into some emptied huts people had abandoned next to the rice field. We moved a total of 16 people into one hut on stilts. We were too many people living together to feed at one meal with our limited food. As we were resting in this place for the day, there were still more people coming and passing by us, going down into the deep valley below. My sister and I hoped that our parents would be with the crowd of those people. We waited and waited until dark, but our parents never showed up. Life was so sad because one day your family all lived together and the next day everyone was gone. Our aunt and uncle assured us again that if our parents never showed up in the evening, we would go back to find them along the other path the next morning. It was as though we had become orphans and lived with an adopted family.

The next morning, which was our third day, we did not go to find our parents either. Instead, we waited until late afternoon when Father came to our hut. He said they went the other way when people screamed about the Pathet Lao soldiers behind them. Later they found out that no such thing had happened. He said overnight mother was sick. So, he stayed with us for a while and decided to return to where the rest of the family was. On his way back, I thought I should go with him to see their place. We left my little sister with our cousins for the evening because we knew for sure we would come back there the next morning. We walked all the way up to the top of the mountain, which we had run down the day before, and then went toward the east on the other path. Mother and brother were staying in a rice field that had just been cleared up and burned and ready for planting rice this season. In the field were many families living in banana leaf huts while others had plastic sheets to set up as their tents. We slept there for the night. That evening I kept thinking that maybe it was difficult for my sister to stay alone with our cousins throughout the night.

On the morning of our fourth day, we packed and came to the place where my sister was with the Thao cousins. This place later I found out was called Nam La. It was a region facing down toward Tha Thom, the enemy territory. Once we arrived in the place to be re-united with my sister, we rested for a day.

On the fifth day, after breakfast we moved on again. We had no home, no future, and knew nothing about what was going to happen to us even in the next minutes. Our plan was to hide in this region or to go up north to Pha Phai, a place close to the Xieng Khouang River, or further on to Nong Ong, to surrender to the Pathet Lao. Below the rice field the jungle was very thick with rattan vines and palm trees shooting up their tops above the giant trees. We were instructed by the elders just to go down there. We walked past the rice field and into the jungle on the path thousands of people had trod before us. The path had been there in the thick forest for years already. The trees were so big that maybe three people hugging them with extended arms would not be able to touch each one's fingers. It was dark. It was cold and scary.

This day our walk was on the path that was going down in the valley for a while and climbing up the high mountains again. Then it was going down into a smaller valley and across small ridges all morning. When the hot sun was straight above our heads, we reached a field where all the brush had been burned, maybe a few days earlier, because a few dead decomposing stumps and stalks were still on fire with smoke rising constantly. It smelled good. A young boy, who was much older than I, came along with us. He lived with us in Pha Hoi village before the country fell. My cousins, he, and I were sitting on a big tree trunk to catch our breath while waiting for our families who were behind us. He unclamped a green grenade from his waist belt and disassembled the neck from the body part. I was scared to death by seeing what he just did. I moved to sit further on another log. He mocked me by saying that if I were the enemy he would crack the egg in front of me already. I threw his muck back in his face by saying that maybe the egg would crack in his face someday if he kept playing with it. By then it would be too bad to do a funeral for him, except digging a hole ready and shovel whatever was left on the earth's surface into the hole. At that moment my cousin did not pay much attention to how we verbally fought. But I looked at his face, instead of turning red, it turned pale like a dead face. It seemed my jinx really hurt him a lot. In our culture if we say something like that to someone, they believed the bad thing that had been said would happen to them. That was why he was scared and turning pale. We stopped our fight. My family arrived first at the scene. We moved ahead of him. We never saw each other again until this day.

When the wild creatures started to sing, we were in the dark thick jungle. There were no watches, so these wild creatures were our timekeepers to tell us when it was the end of day and the beginning of night. My cousin's family and my family moved to the side of the path to set up our tents and rest for the night. Some families had already stopped before we did. Others were still moving past us to go ahead. Soon it was very dark in the thick jungle, so we did not even see the stars or the moon in the sky. Life was poor. We did not even have a flashlight to use. The light source was from the fire. For dinner we had steamed rice with water again. After the meal, everyone was tired. Father just dropped a plastic sheet on the ground under the tent, so we snoozed. My oldest brother was very sad about what could happen to us next if we did not know where we were going. He leaned against the big tree next to the fire. After a while our cousin's mother came to check how we were doing in the dark evening. Everyone talked quietly because we were scared the Pathet Lao might be somewhere close or even have followed us. It was good that some people were behind us, so in case the enemies were following us, we would be alarmed. It was a nightmare. The night was quiet, with many mosquito bites, and we feared that snakes or centipedes might crawl over us.

The next morning on the sixth day, we counted that one bad night was over. Hopefully, things would be going well for us the coming days. At dawn Father urged us to get up to move on without breakfast. We just quickly put our stuff on our backs and then hit the path. After ten minutes of walking, we were climbing up the hill again. At this point, the path either was zigzag or went straight up. The people, adults as well as children, grasped small trees or anything on the side of the path to give them support and strength in order not to fall backwards again. They rested on the way as we walked past because the high elevation caused people to get tired very fast. There were always some people who we met along the way, both familiar and unknown faces. I was so exhausted at one point and sitting on the side to catch my breath. One Yang family who used to live with us in Pha Hoi, walked past me. It was a big surprise to see them escaping on the same path with us. By noon we reached the top of the high mountain. Then we went down a few blocks distance where there was a channel with a small stream. Everyone in my family and my cousin's family was very hungry. Father said we could not go any further without eating something first. We moved to rest on the side of the path again while many people passed by. Father went to the stream to get some water in a pot. Once he brought the water back, Mother poured some of the dry cooked rice from the cotton sack into the pot of water. She let it soak for a while to soften and then shoveled a couple scoops into the small bowl for each one of us. It was not a real meal, but at least it was something to appease our hunger. Maybe that was how our jungle life started. While we were there eating our rice, an old man followed us to beg for rice. He was from the Xiong clan and used to live in our aunt's village in Keomanang. We knew very well who he was. We did not give him any rice because each family just carried enough for its members. He then walked past us and disappeared. My brother reminded everyone that he was from the village where people were very prejudiced. The people in that man's village were very stingy. He knew in the past they treated newcomers badly. Brother said that even if we had more rice than we could all eat, we still should not give him one grain.

Once we were done with our little meal, Father urged us to continue our journey. We walked and walked without stopping until late afternoon when we reached a place on the rocky mountain where people used to grow opium poppies. The dried plants were still on the ground. The smell of the weeds and dried stalks brought back my memory in the past year of my own farm. I thought life was lonely on my farm, but quiet and peaceful. At this time the shadows were already cast over the field because of the high cliff above. It was easy to look down into Tha Thom Valley with the Xieng Khouang River cutting through it from the northeast going down southward. The sun was still shining down in the valley. The rice terrace was shiny green and beautiful. It seemed a good life was down there in the valley while hell was where we were at the time. We missed our homes so much and wanted to have a peaceful life as the Lao people in Tha Thom had. We knew that we were coming close to our cornfields again. The people who arrived there before us had set up their tents everywhere in the field. Father thought we were in a place that was so obvious for the enemy in Tha Thom to see. It would be better in the woods than in the open plain area. So, we must move to the jungle on the side of the opium field to stay for the night.

After several months of moving, it was senseless to go back closer to face the enemies from whom we had escaped. I thought, why in the world were these people so crazy to move constantly from one place to another without knowing their future. We should have surrendered to the Pathet Lao in Pha Daeng, Meuang Orm, or even in the Water Falls Village in Phou Sarm Liam instead of kept on running in a circle. Infact they were not crazy, but the reason was they did not like anything about the communist Pathet Lao. They believed life was bad if it meant living with the communists.

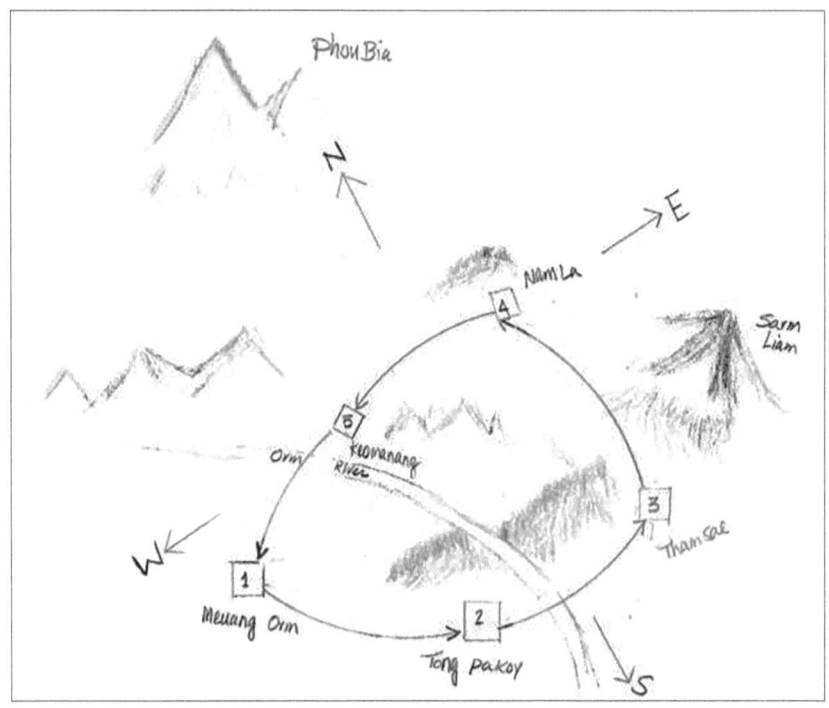

Running in circle

The next morning, on our seventh day, after breakfast, we walked for a few hours straight back to our cornfield. The plan was to rest there for a few days before moving to Pha Phai, our destination. Then, if possible, we would move to Nong Ong to surrender to the Pathet Lao. Now we had only our Thao cousin family staying with us in this place for the night. The next day, our eighth day, our Xiong uncle came from the jungle to see us there. They stayed in a place below where we had been the day before. He invited Father and brother to go with them to their home in Keomanang to kill their pigs for food. However, he was not sure how they could get the pigs because they had run into the woods and become wild. Nevertheless, he really wanted them to go with him anyway. Thus, Father and brother went with him for a half day. In the late afternoon, they came back with one half of a small pig. Our Xiong uncle and other people had still not arrived at our place. Once they arrived, my brother put some banana leaves on a huge flat rock behind the farmhouse. He dropped the meat on top of the leaves and chopped it into small pieces, so it could be cooked for dinner. We thought that we would have a good meal with the fresh pork. When he was done chopping the meat, but we had not cooked it yet, our uncle arrived in our place, very exhausted. He said we had to run because they saw the Pathet Lao soldiers were following them when they left the village. Without any delay, brother wrapped up the meat again. It was time to run to the woods. Before we got our things ready, our Thao cousins had their belongings packed. They were heading on the path to Pha Phai in the north. Father told them we would follow them once we were ready. However, after our cousins left, our Xiong uncle said we must follow him to stay with them in the jungle. Our aunt needed us to be with them, or else she would be very depressed. Then Father moved us along with our uncle to the jungle instead of following our cousins to Pha Phai as he promised. We put everything back on our shoulders and followed our Xiong uncle into the jungle. It seemed Father could not keep his word to our cousins. This was the last time we lived together, and we never saw them afterwards.

After we ran for our lives up and down hills for a while, we arrived in a place of thick forest on the mountainside facing Tha Thom. The place was comprised mostly of wild palms *(kuj yem)*, bamboo *(xyoob)*, and rattan *(kav theej)*. It had a very clear stream flowing in a small channel, which provided us with good fresh water. In the afternoon and throughout the night we rested under the trees without a hut. Even though it was not certain how many days we would be there, we had to build a shelter. The next day we gathered palm leaves to make roof thatch and chopped bamboo to make the walls and beds. This was the place we spent the next two months of our lives, living like Tarzan. Our food was wild things that we could gather, such as leaves, tree buds, and bamboo shoots. It was not a livable place. Instead, it was a life survival situation.

The end of May 1978, my second and fourth brothers and a Yang cousin returned from Meuang Ao. They thought it was too dangerous to go to Thailand, so they decided to come back to stay with us. The Yang cousin's father was Mother's brother. He and my second older brother were very good friends since they were little boys. My third brother did not come back with them. He separated from them in Meuang Ao by going to Thailand with our Uncle Blia Cha, who had been in the CIA army. They said when the three of them got back to Phou Sarm Liam, the place was empty and cold. They did not know where we were at the time, but decided to follow the path that so many people had been traveling on lately. After the Pathet Lao chased us out of Water Falls village and every mountain, they did not follow us to Nam La valley territory yet. People were still settled along the path in the area. On the way they kept asking all the people they met and finally they found us in our quiet jungle home.

We had less and less rice to eat in this place. Sometimes the adults would try to go back to Keomanang Village at night to get rice. They went there just like robbers went to steal from someone else because the Pathet Lao were everywhere. When they were lucky, they brought something back. If the enemy was there, people just returned with nothing. Since there was not much to eat, we cut down the young palms and rattan almost every day to cook for food. Soon the small lower palms in the area had all been destroyed.

One morning our Yang cousin and my two brothers went to chop down a palm *(toov laj)* for food, then the Yang cousin slipped and a dry palm needle jabbed into his foot. One broken piece was still inside. We did everything we could, but could not get it out. At the time his mother and two sisters were in Pha Phai, near Xieng Khouang. We forwarded a message to them with some people who were going there. Within five days, his mother and two sisters came back over the dangerous route to arrive in the jungle where we lived. His mother was concerned about him so much because he might not be able to walk. Fortunately, by the time they arrived the foreign object had been pushed out after the infected wound became worse. The wound was healing now, and he was able to walk without wearing a shoe. They stayed for one night in our place and took him with them to Pha Phai the next day. Later in the year when we surrendered to the Pathet Lao in Meuang Orm, they also surrendered in Nong Ong. Then they were forced to move back to Phonsavan, Xieng Khouang. We have been separated since then.

Palm trees

There was a kind of vine with edible sour fruit, we called *txiv kub nyuj*, meaning cow horn fruit, which also produced very sticky sap. If cut and the sap was drained and allowed to dry, it became rubber. I thought I was going to make a lot of rubber strings like rubber bands or straps for slingshots. I went to cut the vines climped up against the big trees and drained the sap into a few small bamboo tubes as big as pencils. When I got them all filled, I brought them back to heat in the fireplace to make them dry quicker. While I was heating the tubes in the fire, our Yang cousin and one brother were sitting very close watching me and laughing about it. They thought it was such childish stuff while I thought it was a part of a child's exploratory stage in life. Suddenly, one tube was too hot and exploded, sending the sticky sap flying everywhere. It seemed half of the sap flew onto my brother and cousin's pants and stained them badly. The sesame seed sized spots on their pants were bad now, but luckily, they were small enough to not penetrate and hurt any part of their legs. It was good the juice did not shoot high to get to their faces, either. They said it was amazing. My fourth brother, who was sitting further away on the bamboo bench, released his anger on me by asking why I was nuts to do such goofy stuff and not be careful. Maybe he was worried that the Yang cousin's white pants would not be pretty anymore with these brown spotty stains on the legs. I told them I felt bad about the accident, but I did not anticipate it would blow up like that, and neither did they. He was very mad.

While living in the jungle, people were talking about how the Pathet Lao were spraying poison everywhere to kill the Hmong. No one knew what it looked like or even what color it was. We were cautioned to boil the water before we drank it. This might neutralize the poison. Some people never paid any attention to this at all.

In the middle of June 1978, we heard that the Pathet Lao planned to search every mountain and valley to get all the Chao Fa back to Meuang Orm. The Pathet Lao recruited Boun Chan, a Lao Theung man, to join their army. They gave him the rank of general. He became the Pathet Lao's number one hunting dog to chase after the Hmong everywhere. Also, while the Hmong were hiding in the jungle, most of the Lao Theung had surrendered and established their new village alongside the Nam Orm. The new Lao Theung general, Boun Chan, recruited many of his own ethnic people to serve under his command and chase after the Chao Fa, or to provide security to his own people. Under his leadership, Boun Chan planned to call the people hidden in the woods to come back home. He changed the strategy to no longer killing people who surrendered to the Pathet Lao. He knew that if they kept killing people, the Chao Fa would be very angry or become wild. If so, they would never be able to clean up this region to be free of the Chao Fa. Then the chase began. Even though Boun Chan's strategy was to save the Chao Fa who came out to surrender to them, his Lao

Theung soldiers killed hundreds of them when they were out of sight of his supervision. One reason was that the Lao Theung soldiers found that Chao Fa had a lot of Chinese old silver bars, French colony era silver coins, and the heaviest silver necklaces. These items made the Chao Fa targets for murder before they had a chance to surrender to the Pathet Lao. When we came back to Meuang Orm, one day I saw Boun Chan walking in the village with dozens of Lao Theung soldiers. Most of them carried the American made M-16 rifles and some wore green army uniforms, while others just were in civilian clothes. The Chao Fa believed the Pathet Lao only used Boun Chan as bait to lure them back to the village. Later in the year, people lied that he had been executed to pay for the crimes of thousands of civilians who were killed by the Pathet Lao in the jungles.

During this time shells began flying from Meuang Orm into our territory, exploding, and ripped thick jungle where people were hiding. This was the time they started to clean up the woods to clear out the Chao Fa. One afternoon we heard non-stop gunfire to the east of us. Its purpose was to scare children and make them cry so the soldiers could hear where the people were. We knew the Pathet Lao soldiers were coming close to us. We abandoned our hut and ran down the steep valley with other people and crossed over the path people traveled every day, to hide in the difficult steep terrain. The hope was that the enemy would not follow us down there. On the way, we stumbled upon some skeletons of dead people. Their bones and clothes were disintegrated everywhere. Maybe their souls still wandered around there, too. After a short distance, we stopped down in the steep area along the stream. There were more than ten families gathered together in one place. Suddenly, the rain came pouring down very heavy on us and we had no roof to cover our heads. The Pathet Lao soldiers were pushing closer and closer to us.

The next day people thought we had no other choice than to surrender to the Pathet Lao. The families could not sustain themselves for a long time with these poor living conditions. This place was even worse than our previous one. Some areas were as steep as a wall. Then the young husbands and single men decided to separate themselves from their families. They wanted to hide in the woods while they sent their elders and families to stay close to the route where the enemy would come. The plan was to have the families surrender to the Pathet Lao and go back home. The young men, however, feared being executed if they turned themselves in to the enemy. They told their families if within a week no Pathet Lao found them, the elders should just turn themselves in to the Pathet Lao in Meuang Orm. Some of the young men moved to Phou Bia, but some lingered in the area to observe what was going to happen to their families. If the Pathet Lao treated their families well, they might come out and surrender. Otherwise, they would rather be wild in the woods the rest of their lives or hope someday someone would liberate them. My two brothers separated from us, too.

In the late afternoon, we moved back close to the path, which we had often walked to Keomanang, assuming it was also the way the Pathet Lao soldiers would travel through. If they did so and saw us, we would just go with them back to our homes. However, it was a very dangerous situation for us because we did not know whether the enemy would harm or save us when they met us. Together, there were five Xiong families, our Xiong uncle's cousins, with us at the time. We came to stay in a place that had a high cliff above, but was very flat and dry underneath. This place that once was the home of other wild creatures now became ours. All the families moved to this place for one night. The next day it was quiet until late afternoon; then we heard gunfire again one round after another from where we had been a day earlier. After a while we heard a person calling in Hmong language that everyone must come out and surrender. He said people should not be afraid because they would not kill anyone. They fought the war for the country because they needed more people, not just more land. Soon the call came closer and closer to where we were. Finally, the call came very close to us, a place which had been cleared for farming but had not been burned yet. Our Xiong uncle tied a piece of white cloth to a long branch and walked out to the path where it was obvious the Pathet Lao could see him. He waved the white cloth as a flag to show the soldiers that we surrendered. He also responded to their calls that we would not run away anymore. We were there waiting for them to come to take us home.

After a moment, five soldiers appeared down in the cleared field. Two climbed up on the branches of dead trees to observe while the other three moved toward us with their AK-47 rifles at their chests, pointing directly at us. They seemed very tense. It was a frightening moment for us, not knowing what would happen next. I stood a few feet behind Father and other elders, looking down at the ground and once in a while I took a glimpse at them. All the women and children were still under the cliff, ten yards away from where we were. We, indeed, feared that once they got close to us, they might just shoot us one by one. Then we would just all die together. Even though they had not arrived at our camp yet, I already felt as though some bullets penetrated my body. I did not know how others felt, but my heart was racing when I saw the soldiers in green uniforms carrying their AK-47 rifles pointed toward us. The people were extremely scared. All the men and women held tightly together with their children in a group. I thought only two things could happen. First, if the soldiers killed us then we all died together quickly. Second, if they set us free, then we all lived. They kept coming toward us without fear because they were trained to kill and die. In a few minutes, they were in front of us. They were in their 20s. The first soldier in the group was Hmong. He spoke Hmong to Father and our Xiong uncle the moment he arrived in front of them. The second man was a Lao soldier who was able to speak broken Hmong language. Father and Xiong uncle walked a few steps closer to them on the path to greet them. The soldiers did not shoot anyone or search us for anything. They asked for guns, but the response was that we did not have a gun. After they were told by the elders that we did not have any guns, the soldiers cooled down and were more relaxed. Their rifles were no longer pointing at anybody while they stood with our elders.

The Hmong soldier repeated to Father and uncle that we should not run away. The Pathet Lao fought the war not just to get the land. They fought because they wanted the people. We knew for sure that now they might not kill us. The fear stopped, the temperatures came down, and everyone was relieved. The feeling of bullets penetrating my body was over. I thought the people who we had escaped from for years now would spare our lives.

Within minutes, more soldiers came from below with Hmong families behind them. The people, who had already been captured with packs on their backs and children, were following the soldiers like a large flock of sheep. Everyone at this time was powerless and had to do exactly what the soldiers said. Those few soldiers who first arrived in front of us told us to pack and get ready to go. We rushed to get everything on our backs. Before we left the area, one soldier asked my oldest brother if there were any Chao Fa ahead of us. He said he was not sure, but maybe there would not be any Chao Fa soldiers hiding in a bad place like that. It seemed the soldiers believed what he said. One Lao soldier shot his B-40 rocket grenade ahead of us before we moved on. It hit tree branches and exploded very close to where we were going. It shattered trees and leaves fell down after the explosion was over. Another one in front aimed his AK-47 rifle ahead and fired a whole clip at one time. Some children tried to plug their ears with their fingers and held tightly to their mothers while the barrage was fired. His magazine was empty after he fired. He pressed to eject the magazine and put it back in his holster. Then he pulled out another magazine to insert into his rifle before he moved on. They walked ahead of us while others were far in the rear of the line to stop the people from running away. Our working continued again, but it was a different quiet subdued way of moving. The authority figures were with us along the way. We climbed up the path, cutting through the rocky cliff. The path was like a goat trail. The soldiers kept firing their B-40 rockets and AK-47s as we came up to the farming territory. As the bullets cut the tree branches, the leaves and small twigs rained down while we were moving up the steep path. On the way we also feared that if Chao Fa guerrillas were approaching us, they might be angry at seeing us with the Pathet Lao, and they would fight against each other.

When we arrived at the farm, higher up above the cliff, it was much flatter. In this area we became less panicked because we could see everything surrounding us. They took us on another path; not the one that passed our cornfield. This path was going further on the south side to Ban Nong Sa, close to the way going to Phou Sarm Liam. Walking was very slow since there were so many children. The line on the path back to Keomanang was about a mile long. What we saw with our own eyes at the time, it seemed the soldiers were very patient and polite. Maybe it was their way to not intimidated people. In the line of walking, the soldiers may not have noticed or realized that there were more women with children than men. Most of the husbands were still hiding in the woods.

At sundown, we got to the side of Ban Nong Sa where they instructed us to stay in some of the empty frayed houses for the night. It was still far away from the central village. To go from there to our home of Meuang Orm was about 2 hours walking. All the first group of people with us were put in five houses. The soldiers stayed in another house. Some houses had only one wall left standing. The floor was very dirty, but we just cleaned as much as we could to stay for the night. One good sign at the time was some of the soldiers really enjoyed talking with the elders that night.

After we settled down, Father went to the next house to talk to the soldiers. It seemed they had been isolated too long from their families or were in the jungle for so long. When they greeted Father, they addressed him as Por, meaning, father in the Lao language. I was with him at the time, watching them converse. The mess cook, who was called Ai Liang, handed a bar of dried corn cake, about two inches wide and four inches long, to Father while he was cleaning the pot before steaming rice for dinner. Father thanked the soldier for the bar. He peeled off the thin clear wrapper and broke one half for me. I took a bite. It was crunchy and powder-like. They were talking about a few things of life in Lao language such as working on the farm. He said that once we settled down in a place we would be able to go back to work on our farm. I comprehended about half of the words. Soon Father thought he did not want to take too much of the Ai Liang's time because the soldier had to cook. So, we returned to our junky place. As I noticed when talking with us face to face, he was just like ordinary people except for his uniform. So far, the soldiers had not shown any signs of hatred or hostility towards anyone. Father said Pathet Lao soldiers always appeared to be nice from the outside while hiding the bad things very deep inside. We said the tiger has stripes on the outside while human beings have stripes on the inside *(Tsov txaij nraum daim tawv, neeg txaij hauv nruab plawv)*. One thing we and the soldiers had in common was that we all smelled the same. We had been in the jungle for so long and had not washed for months.

That evening more soldiers and civilians arrived in the cold, dirty village. Our Yang cousins, who we had left behind in the opium field a few months earlier, also came. The Pathet Lao went through every path, up high in the mountains and low in the valleys to make sure they got everyone out. However, they did not get everyone because some people moved to another place when they were being chased in the jungle. They were very good at hiding if they wanted to. During the night the soldiers were on watch and making rounds to every house to make sure no one sneaked out into the woods. In reality, the people had been penalized and were powerless, so no matter what, they would not leave again for fear of being killed. Our Xiong uncle and Father did not sleep throughout the night. They kept burning firewood to light the house. As the soldiers were roving around in those houses, they did not say anything either. The night was not very long. It felt like only a few hours before dawn came. Suddenly, the birds sang again. It indicated that the fearful night was over and the new day was coming to take its place. In a short while the sky was clear. Our only hope was that the day might be brighter ahead.

Then the Hmong soldier came around to remind us that after breakfast, they would take us back to Meuang Orm. Unaware of the restrictions, our Xiong uncle asked him if they could go back to their home. He said it was not the plan because Keomanang was out of the control of the Pathet Lao. It was close to the territory where more Chao Fa hid in the forest. However, it might be possible for them to go back there in the future after they cleared up the rest of the area to make sure there were no more Chao Fa. Besides that, they wanted to take us to Meuang Orm to register and organize us first.

The Lao soldier, who came along with him, asked each family to see if they had enough rice to feed their families. But people told him they had enough for the day. He said if any one did not have rice to feed their children, please do not be shy to ask. They had more than enough to give to the families. "Once we got to Meuang Orm, there should be plenty of food," he said. It was only their expression to save face. In reality, the communists did not have plenty of food.

After finishing our light breakfast of rice and water, the sun was already hot. It was a beautiful, sunny morning like those days Father and I used to experience walking from Meuang Orm to our cornfield, and when we were in the field, he would go up on the big rock to whistle or sing Hmong marriage songs. Without any expression on my face, I missed my home, fields, horse, and cows very much on a particularly nice morning like this. Everyone seemed to be happy and eager to be back home in Meuang Orm Village. But, I was sure Father was not happy to live with the Pathet Lao because of his past bad experience in Nong Het and Sala. The soldiers came to check each family if they were ready. The men also urged the women and children to be quick because they did not want to upset the soldiers who might have to remind us a second time. Everyone who was ready should just put everything on their backs and march on the path under the soldiers' instructions. By late last evening, more people came to join us, and now we saw some unfamiliar faces in the group. The line on the path was much longer than it had been the day before when we left the jungle. The soldiers were also twice as many because they came from many groups and joined together. We were walking on the road like a herd of animals again. In the clear light of day while walking, we saw our real physical appearance. We were dirty and stinky, wearing torn clothes. Health was the real issue. The people were thin, weak, pale, or even sick, but did not feel that way at the time.

On the way to Meuang Orm, we walked freely. Some soldiers were in the front, some were in between, and some were at the end. They wanted to guard us, so no one escaped into the woods again. We walked past Keomanang, past the former Lao Theung village next to the Orm River, and finally, past our village of Ban Hai, too. Where the path we used to come from Ban Hai in the south side and merged perpendicularly with the big road going in both directions, Keomanang in the east and Meuang Cha in the west, was a new Pathet Lao army camp just below the road. Above the road was an artillery piece. Later we were told that the gun was Russian made and had sent thousands of shells to us in the woods. This area was a very nice dry grassland with a few fishponds along the stream cutting through the road. Those big fishponds used to be owned by the former villagers of Ban Hai. It was a really nice place. That's why the Pathet Lao built their camp there. After passing the camp and crossing another small stream behind it, flowing from Ban Hai which merged with the Nam Orm below, there was a new but very well established Lao Theung village. This village had been built early in the year right after they returned from the jungle. It was heavily populated, but only with ethnic Lao Theung people.

The soldiers took us to another empty Nong Sa village to the west of Meuang Orm, going toward Meuang Cha. As we walked close to the airstrip of Meuang Orm, I looked toward the round temple to see how it was. At this point it should have been very obvious to see it on the little hill. It had disappeared. Most likely the temple had been burned or torn down by the Pathet Lao, since it was the subject matter of their hatred against the Chao Fa. It was like salt and hot chilli pepper to their eyes. They wanted to destroy everything they possibly could to devalue the principles of Hmong beliefs. This sacred place, once the Hmong worship area, had nothing left but maybe ashes on the ground with weeds above. It was very sad. For a while, we arrived in Nong Sa. It had many houses but was not as dense as Ban Hai. The soldiers let each family chose the house they wanted to live in. So, we moved up to the house on the top of the village near the forest with our Yang cousins. Most of the Xiong families took those houses in the lower area near the main road going to Meuang Cha in the west.

LIVING WITH THE FOES

*"Hmoob khiav khiav los yeej khiav tsis **dim**, vim Hmoob yog cov neeg tag tswv **yim**. Khiav xyoo xya caum rau tawm xyoo xya caum **cuaj** ces raug nplog liab muab tseem coj los kaw **nkuaj**. Cov txiv tsev ntshee cuag ua **npaws** vim ntshai tsam raug nplog liab **ncaws**. Cov niam tub nyuaj siab tsis xav noj **mov** vim nplog liab hais tias lawv yuav muab cov txiv tsev faus nyoos rau hauv **qhov**. Thaum lawv zoo li plis nkag mus **cuag tsov**, lawv mam nco txog leej txiv tshaj plaws uas yog yawg hlob **Vaj Pov**"*

We would not have been chased around the country for many years and suffered from malnutrition and bad diseases if people did not start the Chao Fa activities at the beginning of 1976. When the Pathet Lao took over the country, the villagers should just be stable by not moving too much. Once some of the high-ranking officials were sent to prison, others should slowly look for a way to get out of the country and leave the ordinary peasants stay where they were. This way it would not trigger tension between the villagers and the Pathet Lao. This guerrilla war did not pay off the loss of thousand people who died during the war from fighting and starvation. Contrarily, many people believed that this resistance deterred the aggression of the Pathet Lao offensive war against the Chao Fa. It also altered their war strategies. With this Chao Fa resistance, Boun Chan, the new general, planned not to kill, but tried to call people in the jungles to come out to surrender peacefully. The more you kill people, the more good people would run away to resist.

Meuang Saisumboun in Lao language means the city or region of complete victory. When we arrived in Meuang Orm, I heard people said it was called Meuang Saisumboun. I wondered why they called it thus. It was named so because in 1979 the Pathet Lao thought they had won the war over the Chao Fa completely. However, Chao Fa continued to fight and live in the jungles until the early 2000s when those last group who had not died from starvation, diseases, gun battles, and could not maintain their life cycle, or other reasons, came out to surrender.

It was the beginning of July if using the lunar calendar. On the third day after arriving in this place, we had to attend the samana sessions, which were conducted by the Pathet Lao soldiers. It was an educational session for people to learn about their policies, laws, government system, and way of life, all which people had heard more than enough already. The *samana* was held in a green grassy area as large as a soccer field in front of former Mayor Nhia Chou Yang's house in Ban Hai. This area was a place for our New Year celebration two years ago, but now was occupied by the Pathet Lao.When we got to the field that sunny morning, it was full of people, males and females, old and young, and some children together. The adults were sitting on the grass like whole bunch of apprehended criminals. They knew very well that they must stay focus and pay close attention when the Pathet Lao soldiers conducted samana session. Otherwise, trouble would come to them soon. It was our first day, so we did not know if these were all the new people who attended or if they called just a portion of the people to attend for the day. The soldiers surrounding the area were carrying their AK-47 rifles. It seemed everyone had to go through some sort of disciplinary sessions before they could become good citizens. Whether it was at home or in the field, Father often whispered to us that this was how the communist system worked. No matter what happened and whether you liked it or not, they had to teach every human being since birth about their system. To use a metaphor, they wanted to cut down the old trees and plant the new seeds. This way the seeds would grow to be better trees in the distant future as the old trees had already been penetrated by insects. This translated that they wanted to teach the younger children who had not learned anything about capitalism, so they would grow up and blend into the communist system better. Unlike the younger ones, the old people had learned more about capitalism and they would not obey the new system.

In front of the audience, a small table had been set up, but without a microphone and speakers. Once the people convened there, a Hmong gentleman in army uniform came forward to the table. My oldest brother told me, "the man was Pao Moua". People always called him Pao Tzong Ma *(Pov Ntxoov Mas)*, by using his father's name with his name because his father was the famous Hmong mayor in Xieng Khouang. His introduction was to welcome everyone back to the village. He encouraged people not to run away and said there would soon be an end to the Chao Fa era. They wanted to clean out every corner from the mountains down to the valleys to make sure that it was cleared of Chao Fa. The people should not follow the *Sak tu,* meaning enemy. The Pathet Lao had chased them all the way out and they would never return. Those American backbones *(backers)* were the losers. Then he moved on to agriculture. He said it was a little too late to grow rice on the dry farmland. However, within the next few days the government was going to send plows and water buffaloes to us; then we could grow rice in the rice terraces. It was not too late to do so. Every family had to work together on the same farm. In truth, they did not want people to own anything for themselves, and one person cannot be richer than the other. That's why they put every family to work on one farm. They did not care that people did not have enough food to eat and just let people suck in air to live without food. After he finished his brief speech, he turned to become the interpreter for the Lao man who would talk in deeper detail to press for guns. This Lao man told the people to disclose how many guns each family had and to hand them over to the Pathet Lao. The longest time was spent on gun issues. When Mr. Pao called on people to raise their hands to see if anyone possessed guns, some did raise their hands. He then wrote down the name of the person, the gun type, and where and when they could get it. We spent four hours from 8 to 12 noon before the session adjourned. Then they told people to go home and come back for another session the next day.

On the second day our whole family with all the villagers went back to the field. It looked like more new families showed up. They proceeded with the same story as the day before. At first Mr. Pao Moua wanted to make it clear to everyone to understand the process. When he got to the gun issue, he asked people to raise their hands. Some people still raised their hands to show they had guns. At the end of the second day's session, the Pathet Lao indicated that it was hot and difficult for women and children to be in the field. So, they just wanted the men to attend the third day's session. They let the people go home.

On the third day, we convened in the field with the same procedure. There were still more people who raised their hands about possessing guns when the Pathet Lao pressed harder. It was getting to be a hot situation when the Pathet Lao lost their tempers. Their body temperatures rose up, when more of those same people who had already attended the session for two days still admitted they had guns. The Pathet Lao told the people through the interpreter that they would continue on the fourth day because people did not tell them the truth. It seemed there was a lack of cooperation. For three days when they pressed harder, more people disclosed more guns. On the fourth day, the soldiers were going to dig deep holes in the ground to bury the men alive right up to their necks. Then let them die there unless they disclosed all the guns they had. They were suspicious that people just gave up some, but hid the rest of their guns in the jungles. If they wanted to go back to join the Chao Fa, they would have their own guns to use again. At this point Pao Moua did a little bit of mediation by stepping forward to tell the men in Hmong language that if they wanted to give up their guns, they had to tell all that day. No matter what the Pathet Lao asked, there should be no more guns on the next day. It must be the last day to give up those guns they still had. By doing so, it would appease the Pathet Lao's thirst for guns. If each day people disclosed some, but not all, then the soldiers would lose their patience. If the men did not do what he said, it could result in someone going to re-education camp, to jail, or being slashed in the throat or chopped up into pieces. This time, the men learned their lessons. On the fourth day, everyone zipped up their mouths. When the Pathet Lao pressed for guns again, people said nothing. It was an easier session than before. By noon it was the end of the samana. We came back home, but were living with the enemy.

While we were in Ban Nong Sa, my second older brother was still hiding in the jungle with a carbine rifle. He loved the gun so much and did not want to come back to live with the Pathet Lao. He hated them and feared of being conscripted to be a soldier. Father decided to go get him back to live with us since there were no other choices. He believed that my brother would not be able to hide in the woods for the rest of his life. The only way was to get him out of the jungle and someday we would have to find a way out of this place. He went straight to tell Pao Moua that one of his sons was still in the forest and wanted him to come out to surrender. Pao Moua asked for his gun, but he said his son did not have one. Then Pao Moua told Father to go get him out of the woods and assured Father there would not be any harm to my brother once he came out. However, they had to report to Pao Moua when he came home. In about a week, my second older brother sent us a message that he was hiding in the rocky mountain above our cornfield. He was doing fine, but had no food. Tree buds and palm pulp were his main diet. Then one morning, Father carried a basket on his back, pretending he went to gather food in the field. He went directly to our cornfield where my brother was hiding. When Father got there, he whistled to call my brother to come out. Once they met they decided to hide the gun by burying it in the dirt in a dry place under the cliff because Father had told Pao Moua my brother did not have a gun. They came home that afternoon. Two days later Father took him to report to Pao Moua. They let him be free. The gun he loved would soon be destroyed by ants and termites.

In the meantime, we saw a soldier ride our horse on the road in Ban Hai village, about four miles away. Father went to ask Pao Moua to claim his horse back. He asked if my father knew for sure it was his own horse, then he would give him a note to take to the soldier to get his horse back. They had the policy not to keep people's property. Father told him that he was absolutely sure it was his horse. Then Pao Moua gave him the note and he took it to the soldier where he stayed. After reading the short note, the Lao soldier nodded his head. He then handed the horse in the stall to Father. These soldiers who lived in the village were not real soldiers. They wore green army uniforms, but worked mostly with civilians like civilian personnel. They were called in Lao language as *phanaknga*, which was similar to civil servant.

After getting the horse, we walked back to see our house next to the main Ban Hai, a village that was established in 1976 when we first arrived. As we arrived and toured the area, we saw the houses we used to live in had all been destroyed, either by humans or animals. One of the reasons was that in this area people did not use very strong materials for building the houses because they considered their homes as only temporary. When the Pathet Lao came, the area had been evacuated completely. When the people were all gone, the animals invaded the houses. That's why when we came back six months later, it was all cleared of houses. It was sad to see our house had disappeared. There has nothing left, except dirt for me to remember. It was better to go home to the new place and forget about the empty one.

Once back to our new place in Nong Sa, my job for the next two months was to watch the horse grazing. I joined my Yang cousins to watch our horse with theirs every day in the pasture that was close to the village. It was fun to be with them until one day we went to pick some large grapefruit and used them as soccer balls to kick on the field with our bare feet. We divided into three people on each team to play the game. After playing the game for a while, one of the Yang cousins who was Mother's brother's son, started to play bad. He kept kicking the grapefruit away, not letting us play like a real game. It was bothering me, and I could not hold my anger any more. I picked up a bamboo stick from the ground and hit him very hard on his leg. Some of the boys were freaked out while others raised their eyebrows. How could I do that to him? He cried aloud right away and ran home, leaving us in the field. The rest of us did not bother to follow him either. Later in the afternoon when I came home, I went to see our other cousins near their house. I saw him sitting with his father at their front door. He did not want to look at me at all. I really did not feel guilty for hitting him either. Since then I decided to hang around with other Yang cousins, but not him anymore. After a few months, they moved to Nong Ong in Xieng Khouang province.

After we came back to live in Meuang Orm, we still went back to pick vegetables in our cornfield, east beyond Keomanang. One day we went to the farm and stopped by at the divergent path coming from Ban Hai, close to the big army camp, waiting for our cousins to come before we proceeded to the field. It was the place where the army camp was next to the small stream with a few large fish ponds along it. Above the road was the big Russian-made artillery which they used to fire onto people in the jungles. When we were there on the path on the other side of the stream looking back to the army camp, we saw the soldiers killing a dog for food. It was a dark brown dog. As we watched, a soldier used a stick as big as a baseball bat to hit the dog once in the head and it was unconscious. The group poured hot water on it a couple times, then the dog woke up and cried again. The soldier hit it with the stick one more time and it was unconscious again. They poured more hot water on the dog a second time. After the second time, the hair on one side of the dog was scraped away with a knife. From what we saw, it had completely hairless white skin. It woke up and cried out a third time. The soldier hit it with the stick again. It was unconscious, and they still poured more hot water on it. It seemed the dog was dead by then because it did not sense any more pain. They continued to pour hot water on it and scrape off the hair. It was the end of that dog's life. When they were hungry for meat, it seemed they did the cruelest acts on earth.

During this time the Pathet Lao had not established any schools for children yet. Two months later in September, there were still no schools built anywhere, and most likely they would not build any in the village. It also had been two months, but there were no plows and water buffaloes delivered to the civilians to farm as Pao Moua had told them during the samana sessions. Obviously, the Pathet Lao could not perform as fast as they had promised. Everything was not stable in the village yet while they were still busy chasing Chao Fa in the jungle. Beside the current unsettled situation, the government did not have the equipment to provide to the people as they had said. In real life, instead of using water buffaloes and plows to do the work in the field, they used a gang of people as slaves to dig or plow the soil and plant rice. Thirdly, they could not organize everything together as fast as they had expected. The people were coming in and moving out all the time. There was no one who wanted to work on the farm together as a group since this was not their traditional way of life. Father thought we would starve to death in the coming year because we had planted no crops. In the meantime, we just gathered rice wherever we could, one bushel from here and one bushel there to feed our family. He believed we must move out of Meuang Orm as soon as we could before anything happened. If we stayed any longer, the government might change its plan and send people some place where they did not want to go. Also, during early September, we had received a letter from my third brother from KM52, a place very close to the capital, Viang Chan. He had survived. He could not cross to Thailand when he was on this trip with other people to the Mekong River, so he surrendered to the Pathet Lao in Paksan, a place down south of Viang Chan. After he surrendered with his group, they were transferred to KM52 which had a very big population of

Hmong. Once Father heard this news, he figured it would be better to ask permission from the Pathet Lao to move to KM52 where his son was. His main concern was that one day we might not have food to eat. Also, there could be conflict between Chao Fa and Pathet Lao in our area again in the future, and we would be in the middle of it.

In Meuang Orm there was another Pathet Lao Army camp next to the old airstrip. A couple of soldiers who spoke broken Hmong language used to come from this camp to visit us. One soldier claimed he was Hmong, but he was sent to live with the Lao people at a young age. That's why he did not speak Hmong very well. When visiting us at our home, they loved to volunteer to help people do work, either house chores or other things. They helped our family often, especially the women. My sister-in-law asked them to bring some of their rice for her to make noodles because their rice was harder, so it was better for making noodles. A couple days later they brought about two kilograms to my sister-in-law. One day the Lao guy came and he had sewn two pieces of Hmong embroidery on the butt and two on the knees of his uniform pants. My brother asked him why he sewed them onto his clothes. He said he liked them. They looked colorful. He might be busted for violating their army dress code. It was also a sign of not knowing our culture because the embroideries belonged to women's clothing only. Some girls joked that he was half man and half woman when they saw him wearing the pants. While they were in our house, Father asked them if there would be any school for children to attend soon. Their responses were sort of unsure, but one guy told Father to send me off to attend school in Viang Chan or Xieng Khouang. He told Father to send me soon while I was still young, so I would learn faster. Father said he would think about the situation first, if he could do so. The soldier's recommendation was unbelievable and impossible because it was going to be very difficult for a little boy like me to stay away from home.

My brother had a glow-in-the dark face watch, made in Japan. At night it turned sparkling bright and green. It was beautiful. The soldiers liked it very much, too. They kept asking brother to trade for two kilograms of salt or a pair of army boots. Asking for one time was not enough. They asked him again the second time when they came, and the third time. Each time brother was very fearful of them, but refused the trade. To the soldiers, the watch was worth more than gold. It was the only thing they ever wanted. To my brother, it was a souvenir. It seemed trouble was coming to him unless he traded the watch, or we must find a way to get out. Since then he took it off and hid it in his pocket. Whenever the soldiers came, brother grabbed a back basket and a sickle and walked out of the house, pretending he went to gather grass in the field to feed our horse. It was the only way to avoid contact with them. They kept coming to visit us so often during this time. They had been separated from their families for too long, so they were very happy to hang around with civilians. However, Father did not want to see the soldiers come to our house anymore. In September 1978, he went to see Pao Moua to request permission to move to KM52 where my brother was. Pao Moua denied the permission to Father because he knew if we moved to KM52, we could just flee to Thailand easily. He told Father he only granted permission to go northeast to Xieng Khouang, but not southwest to Viang Chan territory. A few days later some families were granted permission to move to Pha Ngun, a place above the dam on the Nam Ngeum. This place was relatively close to Long San, a region that had been under communist ruling before 1975. For some reason half of the people who requested the permission decided not to move out anyway. Father, along with some of our Yang cousins, asked them to give us their permission slips instead, so we could leave with the other half of the original people. They were willing to give us their travel papers. He thought the sooner we moved from there, the better it would be because Meuang Orm was not like it had been before. It was quiet without the sound of gunshots as it had been in the jungle, but it was only a temporary place for people to stay until they cleared the Chao Fa out from the woods. The place was not as secure as it was before the war either. It was always in Father's prediction that the Pathet Lao might move people out of there to other places in the country sometime in the future. If they did, we did not know where we would be sent.

After he got the permission to move, Father, along with half of the group waited until the end of October 1978. During this time of the year, the rain had stopped and the road conditions were drier. Thus, our long trip would be better on the way. When the time came, we packed and headed out on our journey. We had the impression that the trip would be a good one. However, our Uncle Xiong and aunt did not want us to leave. They said the current situation was stable. Soon they were going back to live in their home in Keomanang again. We should be doing the same thing. But by then our home had disappeared, leaving only its dirt floor. If we stayed, we would have to build another home. Their beliefs were that Meuang Orm was a good place to earn a living. Once you established a rice terrace, life was easy. The cornfield was not far from home either. It was the Hmong way of life. Their hearts would be torn apart if we left them. Father expressed that he wanted to stay, but he foresaw that the place was not going to get better. Without telling them the truth, his idea was to go to Pha Ngun, the place above the Ngeum Reservoir, and finally, move to KM52 in Viang Chan to be re-united with his third son. It was the time we had to leave Meuang Saisumboun forever.

Before our departure, our aunt and uncle came to stay with us and talk during the night. The next morning, we had an early breakfast together before leaving. It was a very sunny day. The sunrays cut through the Meuang Orm Valley and clear blue sky. A heavy dew was sparkling on the grass as the sun rose. It was a scene to remember for the last time, as we would be gone. I thought there would be no more trips to our cornfield in the east or a time to hang around with our Yang cousins in the pasture watching the animals. Once we were ready, we put everything on our backs and the horseback, then abandoned the house. The neighbors were watching us leave our home. Some wished us luck on the road. Others were surprised seeing us leave because they had no clue what was going on. Our aunt was crying a lot. She said she might never see us again. She might see us in heaven or in another life only. This was true. When they moved back to their home in Keomanang later in the year, her family was robbed and all were killed by some devils. That morning she followed us all the way up to the mountaintop looking down to Pha Lo between Meuang Orm and Meuang Cha. She was very sad before she returned home because she did not have any brothers left in that place.

On our trip from Meuang Orm to Pha Ngun, there were Lee, Yang, and Thao families ahead and behind us. The day we walked from Meuang Orm to Meuang Cha was a long day because we were without shoes, sandals, or flip flops on the rough road covered with small rocks. Each day we had to get to a certain destination where there was a village in order to be safe. We must cross many mountains and valleys before reaching our destination. We went by the side of Pha Lo, the village we had crossed through one time in 1976. Since it was slow moving, at sundown we had not made it very far. We got to the side of the mountain next to Meuang Cha, not even to the top yet when it was already getting dark, but it was still a long distance to where we had expected to be at the end of the day. Then we moved to an old army camp above the road to stay overnight. It looked like they had abandoned the camp a few months earlier because weeds had grown about a foot tall already. We dropped our packages on the ground and moved to the trench to stay quietly throughout the night. We did not start a fire due to the fear of being attacked by either the Chao Fa or Pathet Lao. Father cautioned us not to go anywhere in case there were some landmines in the trench. We were terrified. It felt like hell throughout the night staying in this place. Without a fire, the night was too long and cold. To say anything, we must only whisper because there once had been some fighting between Chao Fa guerrillas and Pathet Lao in this area. Whatever the situation would be like, we must stay quietly throughout the night, hoping we would still be alive the next day when the sun rose.

The next morning before the sky cleared and the sun rose, it was time for us to get out of there. Father urged us to get everything back on our backs and get away from this ghost place. We moved down to the rough bumpy path again. Over the night our feet were better. Now they were going to be sore one more time before we could have another rest. It took us about 30 minutes to walk up the hill. On the mountaintop we could see buildings ahead of us not far away. However, the road going down to the valley was a zigzag, so it was going to be a long way before we got there. Father told my two brothers to lead the horse ahead of us since we were in a safer place. When they got to the village, they had to cook breakfast and be ready for us. It might take us longer than expected to get there since our feet were sore again, not able to walk fast. My little sister was crying and wondering how much longer we had to walk. My parents assured her by pointing their fingers to the village that soon we could be in one of those tin roof buildings in the valley. It looked beautiful in the early morning sunshine.

By the time the hot sun hit the valley and we had pounded our feet on the rocks for two hours, we finally got to two public buildings next to the rice terraces. About couple blocks further to the west, was the Nam Cha cutting through the foot of the high rocky cliff and going southwest. The place was very beautiful indeed. I wished we could have come there in the first place a long time ago. It had been a famous school town with hundreds of students from many places attending before the country fell. None of us knew which buildings the former schools were because we had never been here before. The small houses were destroyed. Those still standing were the ones built with stronger materials such as concrete or stones. At this time, it seemed there were still no civilians. Next to the buildings we stayed in, I noticed a big, long building. It was the place where the Pathet Lao sold fabrics. Further down in the south on the other side across the river, on a higher flat hill, were a few buildings with a dirt parking area. One or two buildings were built with stone walls. The army lived in those buildings. Some green army armored vehicles were parked in this area. Up to the north where the river was coming from, were high, rocky cliffs. They stood up just like a wall of stacked checkers.

When we got to one of the buildings, we met the group of young people who left Meuang Orm ahead of us the day before. These young people also came to buy fabric for making clothes. They stayed for another day because they wanted to pick guava fruit in the terrace village to the north behind those rocky cliffs. During this time the guava trees were full of very ripe fruit. They were a group of five who went to pick fruit. One young girl was our aunt's adopted daughter. My two brothers wanted to go with them, but Father would not allow them. He feared that if anything happened to them, it would be difficult for us on our long journey. The place they went to was in an area often contested by both the Pathet Lao and Chao Fa. Sometimes civilians passing through were killed by the Pathet Lao. They were gone for almost a half day. By late afternoon, they came back without any problems. Each one of them carried a full back basket of fruit. Our aunt's adopted daughter carried more than she should because she wanted to give us the extras. They were supposed to return to Meuang Orm the same day. However, when they got back to our building, it was late. Thus, they decided to stay another night with us. The next morning those young people said goodbye to us and walked back to Meuang Orm.

We also planned to stay for another day to recuperate from the sore feet before moving on. Late that afternoon, there were three army trucks going to Na Tu Na Luang, our last destination before the road branched to Pha Ngun. The trucks were empty. My brother went to ask one of the drivers if we could just ride with them. One young skinny Lao driver, who was the most popular one in the group, allowed us to get into his truck. However, they did not want to transport our horse, two sows, and five pigs. We really needed our horse for future use. Then we decided that Father and one brother would walk with the horse, which carried something on its back. The rest of us would ride on ahead with the truck. Once we all climbed into his truck, the other two empty trucks left the scene for Na Tu Na Luang. While we were waiting in the truck, the commander called the driver to go back to their headquarters. He drove us fast back there to see his commander. When we got there, the commander said he had changed his mind. He wanted the young driver to stay. This was too bad for us. He did not take us back to the building where we had stayed. Instead, we had to get out of the truck, unloaded our stuff, and walk for about fifteen minutes back to our building. Once we got back to the building, Father said we would continue our walk the next day, which would be our fourth day on the journey from Meuang Orm. We spent one more night on the concrete floor before leaving that building forever.

Early the morning of the fourth day, we had a breakfast and left Meuang Cha. The day was sunny with the cool breeze. We walked all day without any rest on the same road covered with dirt and small rocks as it was from Meuang Orm to Meuang Cha. Soon our feet were sore again. It was painful, physically and mentally, to see so many mountains ahead to be crossed before we could get to our final place. It rained in the late afternoon, but that was ahead of us. We did not get wet while walking on the wet road. We tried to walk as fast as we could to get as close as possible to our destination. By sundown we got to the Mo River, a river that we had crossed one time in the north in 1976. The place had three buildings set below the road in a flat area tucked into the deep valley next to the river. They looked like barracks for the construction workers who had built the road before the communists took over. One of the buildings was occupied by a group of Vietnamese soldiers. So, we moved into one of the two empty buildings.

The next day on our fifth day, the Vietnamese soldiers came to see us. The group leader said he did not want us to move on. He wanted to send us back to Thong Hak, a place on the mountaintop we had just passed by the day before. Father then showed him the letter of authorization from Pao Moua in Meuang Orm. He was Vietnamese, and maybe was able to read up to third or fourth grade level in Lao language. After he finished reading the short letter, he nodded his head. He said he would let us move on because Father had permission to do so. Father told him that we wanted to stay there for another night and leave early the next morning. They were okay with it. During the day it rained for a while. The sound of water dripping from the trees onto the tin roof was very noisy. We killed a little pig to cook for food and salted some to smoke and dry. We gave about two kilograms of meat to the soldiers to make them happy. In that same afternoon, a group of soldiers came back from the woods with many green bananas. They were from the banana trees planted by the people who used to live in this area before 1975, maybe by the construction workers. Because the soil was very fertile, the banana trees never died even though they were sunken under the forest for many years. It seemed they had a good life in this place.

On the sixth day, we set off early by putting our feet on the hard-rocky road again. We walked across the Nam Mo Bridge, then went up the mountain for a while to reach the junction of the road from Phak Khae and Meuang Cha. It seemed there no longer were any vehicles traveling on the road going to Phak Khae. This place was Hoy Kham village. It means valley of gold and it used to be a busy market place for the entire region before the country fell. Where crowds of sellers and customers had been, now weeds grew tall. Now we knew we were close to Na Tu Na Luang, but it was so painful for our feet that they did not want to move anymore. It was our wish to get there soon, so we could take a rest. The day was sunny as we walked on the road. At this point we felt safer. Regardless of the circumstances, we had to push ourselves until the end of the day to get to Na Tu Na Luang. The road never had been straight. It was crossing through many channels of streams, bending like an elbow. By late afternoon, we arrived in Na Tu Na Luang, a Lao Theung village. It was a beautiful place in the flat valley with a very clear river running by its side. Alongside the river, green rice paddies were on each side and further down southwest. The main road from Meuang Cha and Phak Khae going to Ban Sorne crossed on the northside above the village. The climate was another different factor. It was warmer in this region because it was further down in a lower altitude. The men wore more short pants or towels *(pha phae)* while women dressed in Lao short skirts as their traditional costume.

Even though it was a late afternoon, a lot of people soaked themselves in the river to cool off. Life seemed more peaceful and enjoyable. It was a real human life.

When we arrived, we met a Yang Family who once lived with us in Pha Hoi, along with three other Yang families. They had just arrived two days before us. These families came from Meuang Ao after they surrendered to the Pathet Lao. The father of this Yang family was a CIA Forward Air Guide, or in the Spy Team. Before and now he did not want to mention any of his past identity. Instead, he pretended to be an ordinary peasant. These families also planned to go to Phou Sarm Phiang together. It must have been good luck to meet all these people who would be living with us in this unfamiliar place. One of the three families had lived in Phou Sarm Phiang before. After the communists took over Laos, they joined the Chao Fa and fought against the Pathet Lao for a while until they lost Phou Sarm Phiang to the enemy. This one family fled east to Meuang Ao. There they united with other Yang cousins after they surrendered. The family which used to live in Phou Sarm Phiang wanted to take other families with them to go back to live in their old place again. That's why they were all there together.

On the second day in Na Tu Na Luang, we killed another pig for food. After we killed the pig, a soldier who was stationed there, came to ask to buy the pig organs. These soldiers, called Kong Lorne, mostly provided protection to the villagers. When we completed cleaning up the pig and pulled the organs out, my little sister wanted to eat the heart. After a while, the soldier came back to get the pig organs. My brother told him that we could give him everything but not the heart because my little sister really wanted it badly. The soldier was mad and did not want to buy the organs unless we gave him the heart, too. We thought why in the world was he so crabby. It was good that we had not eaten the heart yet. My brother realized that communist soldiers could be mean if we did not give them what they wanted. So, we should not upset him. My brother gave him the heart along with other organs.

That same afternoon the young driver, who had dropped us off at his headquarters in Meuang Cha, arrived with a patch of white gauze on his temple. At noon they arrived at the Nam Mo Bridge and he dropped a grenade into the river to kill fish. The water was too shallow and when the grenade exploded under the bridge, a piece of shrapnel flew up to hit his forehead. We said that one problem was they had too many grenades while there was no war to use them, and two, it must be god punishing him because he kicked us out of his truck in Meuang Cha. It was good he was still alive.

My brother had a crossbow and a few arrows with him. Four soldiers came to challenge and test my brother if he could shoot and hit a target. They made a circled paper of about three inches diameter and set it at a distance about five yards away, then watched my brother shoot it. He shot only one shot and the arrow hit right at the target. They were laughing. They asked him if the crossbow kill birds and animals. He said not only could it kill birds and animals, he could shoot at their bellies and they could die from it. They were shocked and left the scene with perplexed faces. I thought, "Oh no, he will get into trouble for saying bad things to those foes."

After three days resting there, we moved on to Phou Sarm Phiang as planned. We left the village to cross the river on the side of Na Tu Na Luang, through the rice paddies, and then went up the mountain. After we were on the mountaintop next to the side of this village, we had to go down again into another long valley. Here we walked on the zig zag path along another stream by the side of the mountain and then crossed the stream again. We kept repeating this pattern many times. By late afternoon, we reached another mountainside Lao Theung village, which was close to the Nam Mo. We kept walking without resting until sundown; finally, we got to the banks of the river. This part was wider than where we had crossed two times before in the northeast. We had to stay there overnight because it was getting dark and the children were too tired. Father started a fire on the sand without a tent. There was a large sandy area close to the water. Some of the Yang cousins and I loved to run over to play around in the sand in the moonlight until we were very tired. It was good night for us again to watch the moon and stars in the sky.

The next morning brother picked some wild vegetables along the river to cook for breakfast. After the meal, we climbed up Phou Sarm Phiang. It took us a half day to reach the top. This was a long narrow mountain, stretching from the east to west. We called it "the straight skinny mountain" *(roob yiag)* because once we were on the top, we could look down on both sides very far below. When we arrived, we moved to the side of the village to build our temporary hut. It was a big surprise to meet my oldest sister-in-law's cousins who had moved there a month before us, and who we knew from Sala village since 1965. We never thought they would ever be in a place like that. We stayed in this temporary home from November 1978 to the beginning of January 1979. Then we moved to Pha Ngun, which was our final destination for the year.

While we temporarily stayed in this place, we were provided five kilograms of rice per person. Besides the rice, the Pathet Lao government also distributed four yards of black fabric per person, but only one time. The cloth was the poorest quality because after we sewed it into clothes and wore and washed them, they shrunk too much and were not good to wear a second time. They were very wrinkled, too. The rice was distributed twice a month to the people who had moved from the Meuang Saisumboun area. We went back to pick up the tasteless rice in Na Tu Na Luang at the beginning of the month and in the middle of the month. We continued to receive this rice assistance from November 1978 until June 1979.

While living in Phou Sarm Phiang, two of my brothers and other Yang and Lee cousins went down to Viang Chan to buy clothes for us. It was their first time of traveling to the capital city of Laos. My parents gave them the old French silver coins to exchange for paper money to buy the clothes. After they were gone for five days, they returned home with some new clothes. My brother did not mention how much it cost to buy a shirt and pants. When they arrived, my second brother explained to me the illusion on the asphalt road from the dam of the Nam Ngeum all the way to the Morning Market in Viang Chan and how beautiful it was. The scenery straight ahead of the bus was a long row of palm trees on both sides of the road with the dark road surface looking like a snake. He told me about the statue of three elephant heads, on the side of the road before coming to the Morning Market. This symbol on the former national flag represented Lan Xang, meaning a million elephants. His story also took me on a tour of the temple in Viang Chan. He explained to me about the beauty of the coconut trees around the Victory Monument (*Patuxai*) in the capital city. The golden Wat Thak Luang was very beautiful during the day and flashing with lights at night while they were walking around. It sounded gorgeous, but my thought was of many earlier stories. "Why had Hmong people been robbed and why the name calling of 'Meo' before?" I asked him how safe it was in the capital. He said the whole time they were there it was fine. No one did any bad thing to them as they used to do before 1975. It must be that the new government cracked down on the gangs after the Pathet Lao took over Laos. Also, there were more Hmong living in Viang Chan at the time. That was the end of his story. He handed me a pair of new black pants and a light pink shirt. They were the Lao and western style and a little bit too long for me, but he said I would outgrow the clothes soon. I thought, "No", he just tried to make me feel good about it.

In December 1978, my two brothers and a Yang cousin returned to Meuang Orm for the Hmong New Year celebration. When they told Father, they were going back to Meuang Orm, he was not very happy, but he allowed them to go. The morning before they left, Father burned a bunch of incense, held it facing the north, and asked for mother earth and gods to protect the three young sons while they were on their trip. Three days later some people came from Meuang Orm. They told Father that his three young sons had been attacked while they were on the road between Meuang Cha and Meuang Orm. They were riding with the Pathet Lao soldiers in their army truck. The Chao Fa fired a bazooka onto the truck along with many rounds of rifle shots. They jumped off the truck and ran to the forest. Unfortunately, their Yang cousin was injured by a bullet in his leg. Later in the day they were re-united and managed to get to Meuang Orm. It was just all trouble and trouble only. Father was not very happy and concerned very much because this was only a story being told. No one knew for sure if the three young men were safe. While hearing this bad news, the Yang cousin's older brother was having mixed feelings of concern and anger. He said he did not allow his younger brother to go, but he was so stubborn and went anyway. It was about a week later, they came back home in Phou Sarm Phiang. The Yang cousin's wound had healed. They said they were attacked in the area where we stopped for a night. We must have been very lucky that night.

In January 1979, we moved to settle in Pha Ngun to farm there. In this village were some Green Hmong families who had lived there for a few years already. We, the newcomers from Meuang Saisumboun, all moved together to a new area next to the old village. We were on a high mountain where we could see the great Reservoir of the Nam Ngeum far down below to the southwest. Pha Ngun and Phou Sarm Phiang were two parallel mountains divided by a deep valley with a clear cool river in between. The weather was cool during the night and throughout the morning, so people needed a light jacket. During the day the temperature rose to 70 or 80 degrees Fahrenheit with a cool breeze from each side of the mountain because both sides were thick with jungles. The environment and the nature were cozy with many birds singing, but the life style was very primitive. We had to build a new home before we could begin farming. It took us a month to gather logs, bamboo, and palm leaves to build our house. This time we built a large house with four bedrooms to stay temporarily. After the house was built, the next month we began to clear the forest for farming. Our future life was not certain in this new place since some new families who came with us fled to another place much closer to the Ngeum Reservoir, due to the scarcity of food. There was no more war, but food was a problem that would arise soon. It was a very isolated place from which it was harder to go to other places to get rice. The people who had lived there for a few years were fewer than the new people, and they did not even grow enough rice to feed their families for the year because the good flat farmland was very limited.

We still received rice assistance from the Pathet Lao government at this time. Each month we had to go back to Na Tu Na Luang to pick up our meager portion of rice assistance. We must leave home at dawn to walk down two deep valleys and climbed up two huge mountains before we got there. Most of the time, we arrived before sundown to get the rice ready for the next day. The next morning, we left before dawn or before the sky had cleared. On the return, with the heavy rice bags on our backs, we usually did not make it back home the same day. Often, we stayed in Phou Sarm Phiang to rest for the night. On the second day we left early again, to arrive at home by late morning. Instead of distributing twice a month as before, now the government gave us only once a month and the amount was reduced to three kilograms per person. It was not the good quality rice we used to get either. This rice was hard and smelled as bad as mold. By the end of each month we often ran out of rice before we got the next distribution. It was hard to tell when they were going to stop the assistance, so we lived day by day and worked on the farm as each day came. We hoped that by year end we would have our own rice and not rely on this assistance anymore.

Even though I was not so lonely on the mountain by hanging out with some of my old 1975 classmates from Pha Hoi, life seemed brighter and better down in the town below the dam of the Nam Ngeum. Each day we went to our cornfield in the southwest where we could see half of the reservoir. We always wondered what was down there beyond the dam. Our minds were always unsettled with wondering how we could cross over to the other side of that huge liquid pond below. We were like the birds locked inside cages with no way out. To go down from our home to the intersection of the Meuang Cha and Ngeum rivers, it would take about a half day. However, the return trip climbing up on the steep slope could take the whole day to get home. The villagers often went to the intersection of Nam Cha and Nam Ngeum to buy fish from the fishermen, but they could not go any closer to the water or to Viang Chan because the fishermen controlled the check point at the port. People had to have permission from the village chief to cross the reservoir to the dam. In those days to obtain a travel pass to go some place else was not easy. It was quiet and peaceful on the mountain, but it was a poor and isolated life with no communication to other places. The only things we saw were fields, trees, and houses. Therefore, the tribal villagers did not want to live up there anymore.

The old system got back to us again. In February the Pathet Lao ordered villagers to work in one farm which belonged to everyone. The farmland they wanted villagers to work on was not in our village. Instead, it was in Mong Pheng, about two days walking to the north. The village chief gathered one person from each family to walk and clear the field for planting corn and rice. The group went there for a week and returned home.

They spent four days for travel time and three days to chop down brush. After they returned home, there were many things going on in the village. Some people moved out. Some new people came into the village. The village chief spent more time on organizing and disciplining his villagers than on the farm that belonged to everyone. They did not have a time to go back to burn the dried brush to plant corn and rice. We moved out during the year and did not know what the Pathet Lao did to the village chief for not planting crops in the field.

During this time the Pathet Lao still tried to recruit young people to join them to work as volunteers in the region. They needed workers to go to each village to collect rice as taxes for the government. Some people just left home to work and never returned home, or only after a long time. If you were a good worker, the Pathet Lao kept you longer. If you were a bad worker, they might slash you in the throat and dump you in the ditch. This type of work was not my father's desire or for the rest of the people who had just come from the jungles. Soon when it came to our family's turn, one or two of my brothers had to go to work for them. Thus, in April my second and fourth brothers left with some of the Yang and Lee cousins going to Thailand. It was the only choice for them to get away from the Pathet Lao. Since the route going down to the dam on the Nam Ngeum was difficult to get through, they went back to Meuang Ao, one of the villages in Meuang Saisumboun territory. Then they walked through the jungles going down to the Mekong River on a long and very dangerous route. Some of the unlucky people did not make it to the river. After our brothers left, life was even sadder than before.

We were poor and hungry. One day in early April, Father, oldest brother, a couple of Yang cousins, and I went down to the reservoir to buy fish and carry them back to sell to the villagers in the Meuang Cha area. When we arrived, Father bought many baskets of raw fish for us to clean, salt, and smoke dry above the fire during the night, or we salted them raw and put them in the big bamboo tubes of about five-inch diameters and two feet long. There were plenty of bamboos in the forest, so we could just cut down one or two of them and cut the piece to hold the fish. We stayed there over night and then returned home on the second day. From home, we set out on our trip early the next morning to Meuang Cha. In that one day the two Yang cousins, my oldest brother, and I walked all the way back to Tong Hak, a village we had passed once before. In early 1979, the Pathet Lao moved people back to settle in this old area again. I carried only two tubes in my back basket which were still too heavy for me, and my oldest brothers carried four of them. They were very heavy for us and exhausted us by going up and down the mountains and valleys all day long. That evening we sold all the fish to the villagers in Tong Hak because they were very hungry for meat. We met a nice man who had just returned from the field. He was the *nai ban* of that village. He told us that it should be our first and last trip to this village. He knew that the villagers there were hungry and needed food, but the communist system was not easy. The Pathet Lao really hated people who did business to earn a living. Thus, we should not misunderstand his advice because it was not his intention to say so. He loved his own people and did not want anyone to get into trouble at all. We thanked him for his sincere advice and came back to stay the night with another young couple with one child. The next morning, we rushed back home again before we got caught by the communist Pathet Lao.

After my two brothers were gone, we burned the field which we had cleared to plant crops. In the middle of April it rained a few times, which soaked the soil deep enough to make us believe if we planted the corn, it would sprout. We planted corn and would plant rice in June. However, it was a very bad year for us. There was a drought after the rainfall in April. The corn we planted grew about an inch tall and then shrank back into the soil. The dirt became as hard as rock. Instead of growing corn, it grew only weeds, one green spot here and one there throughout the field. By June every family had no corn plants in the field, and even the weeds turned brown. There was no family could plant rice either. A few Lee families who farmed next to us left without letting anybody know where they were going. We were talking about moving out again because soon there would not be anything to eat if our little ration of rice assistance was cut off. It was to be believed that if the drought continued, soon only palm pulp would be our main diet like a year ago when we were in the jungle in Meuang Saisumboun.

Then my third brother, who was sent from Paksan by the Pathet Lao to live in KM52, Viang Chan, came to visit us in our high mountain village. He got married to Mai Vue and had a family while living with other relatives. KM52 was also a better place to earn a living than in the mountains where we lived. The market place, the communications, and ways of making connections to other places were better. The purpose of his visit was to take us with him on his return. However, the communists established a gate at the junctions of the Nam Ngeum and Nam Cha and did not allow the tribal villagers from the high mountains to pass through. It was the only route to get to Viang Chan. They feared that if people were allowed to leave, they would never return to their poor homes up in the mountains again, and the Pathet Lao did not want to lose people. When my brother came to our home, the communist did not check his documents for going up to the mountain. But when he returned, they checked for how many people were on his pass. It was good he put my name in his travel pass when he came to visit us. He knew he could not take all my family, so he took me with him on the way back home while my parents stayed up in the mountain village.

Upon arriving in the checkpoint where the two rivers met, the communist officials were hostile towards us. They said they did not like people from the lowland to visit the tribal people in the mountains so often. To them the travelers from the lowland were like a contagious disease, causing villagers not to want to live up there. If this pattern kept on going, soon people would all abandon their homes by escaping to other places. My brother argued that his family was establishing a good living in the mountains and had no intention of moving out. The one reason he came there to visit his family was because we had been separated for a while. A family should not be divided based on their political and ideological restrictions. The officials sounded very angry and told my brother to get his butt out of their sight quickly. After the argument, we walked for a few yards away and met a fisherman who was transporting a half load of fish in his two by eight-foot long boat. The man was taking his catch to sell to the Lao business people at the dam. My brother asked him to take us and paid him 300 kips for the ride to the dam. We left by noon. It was a long and fearful trip on the water because we did not have any lifejackets or rubber tubes for safety. On many occasions the strong wind caused the waves to swell. Our small boat was swinging from side to side and bobbed up and down a lot. By 3:30 PM we arrived at the dam, the man pushed his little boat against the shore to anchor it and to let us off. Without any ice to cool them and a long day in the hot sun, it seemed half of the fish were rotten already. My brother asked what happened to those fish which were rotten. The man said the Lao people still needed them any way to make fermented fish. There was nothing to be wasted. On the shore, flies were swarming so quickly to suck the juice from the fish. The fisherman got out and went in the other direction to see the business people while leaving his boat of fish in the water. I thought by the time he returned, the flies probably laid thousands of eggs in the fish already. We grabbed our suitcases and stepped out to put our feet on the sand. Our fears were over.

We climbed up the steep bank to the top where the bridge crossed the Nam Ngeum. Up on top of the dam, which was also a road, we walked across to the other side where there was a big flea market with many songthaews (ສອງແຖວ), pickups with two rows of seats in the back, waiting for passengers to go to KM52 where my brother lived, and on to Viang Chan. We jumped in one of them as it was ready to leave. On the way to KM52, there were many palm trees along the side of the road as my second brother had told me a year ago on his first trip. They were planted by residents, but they were not as beautiful and thick as those wild palms in the mountain where I came from. Alongside the road, there were also the beautiful rice paddies and pastures with herds of buffaloes, grazing in the sunny afternoon. It seemed this place was more civilized. With the fast moving of the *songthaew* and wind blowing against my face, after a while I felt my face was sort of numbed. Even thought my parents were still at home in the high mountain, I hoped one day they would be on the *songthaew* like we were at that moment, coming to KM52. By 5:30 PM we arrived at my brother's home. He was glad he had been able to fool the officials at the gate to get me through. Thus, came another ending to one of my trips, my second experience of riding in a motorized vehicle.

Into July it was still no rain in the mountain village where my parents were. The corn in KM52 was almost ready to pick and eat. It was too late for them to grow rice. Most of the new people snuck out to other places where they could find food to feed their families. Father went to the village chief, *Taseng* Nor Yee Thao in Phou Sarm Phiang, to request permission to come down to see us one time in KM52. When he returned home, my family just packed and left the place. However, once they got to the checkpoint in the reservoir, they were sent back home again. My brother in KM52 thought he must do something to get them to live with us. A few days later my brother hired two fishermen who lived near the reservoir to get my family in the mountain and bring them by boat across the huge pond of water at night. They were fishermen who lived on the water most of the time. Therefore, they could transport people across to the dam at any time without any notice from the Pathet Lao, and even if the Pathet Lao saw them, they just ignored them. Within 24 hours they brought my family at night all the way to KM52. We were all together again.

About three months later, we finally received a letter from Thailand coming through the Lao post office that my two brothers who escaped to Thailand had arrived in Ban Vinai Refugee Camp safely. They said they had spent a month hiding and traveling to the Mekong River before crossing. We were so happy once we got the good news from them.

9

THE YEARS IN KM52

*"Lub neej nyob nram **tia**j thiaj muaj kev mus khwv **nyiaj**. Lub zos lav 52 yog thawj lub zos hmoob los nrog blog nyob. Thaum Hmoob tej tub tau mus kawm **txuj** ces Hmoob yuav nrog luag tsim **nuj**."*

It was the first time we ever lived in the lowlands. In KM52 the climate was different from the mountains, where we had always lived. The land was flat. There were no rocky cliffs. The environment was better. It was more like a civilized town. However, the integration was the same as our previous mountain life. The Hmong still lived in one village while the Lao Theung lived in another, and they never built houses mixed with the Lao Lum village. The weather was very hot from March to August. During this time the temperature was as high as 39 or 40 Celsius. In the rainy season water flooded everywhere. Dried canals filled with water that rose up. Wooden bridges washed away. Along the main road the main electricity wires were running from the dam going down to Viang Chan and cross to Thailand. No one ever connected it to use in this town yet because people could not afford it. So, we did not have electric fans to keep us cool. When it was too hot you just used a hand fan waving back and forth in front of you. It was the only way to keep you cool. Even though it was hot and we were not used to it the first year, we were all healthy. We were not exposed as much to the mosquito bites as in the mountains.

The people in the area were a different factor. It seemed they were modernized and more educated than we who had lived in the mountains without exposure to foreigners. We saw different kinds of people, white and brown who we believed were Russians and Indians, traveling in the marketplace. However, one sad thing was that new people were coming to this place from everywhere and soon disappeared. Mostly they stopped by to search for ways to flee to Thailand because they did not like to live with the communist Pathet Lao. Since the newcomers kept doing this all the time, the old villagers disliked all of us. We were portrayed as dirty people by the villagers who had lived there for a while. Youth culture was another reason. In the old days before 1975 and now, boys wore pants with larger openings at the bottom. So, we were accused of being capitalist for wearing big bellbottom pants. Whether it was social or political, there were always some disagreements between the new and old people in the village.

Here, mostly people earned money by selling produce from their farms. The people could do business by selling goods to the merchants in the capital city, Viang Chan. It was a better place to earn a living. From July to August we could sell fresh young corn and green cucumbers. From September to October we sold watermelons. And from November to February we sold bananas, papayas, yams, pineapples, eggplants, and other things that we gathered from our farms. Early in the morning before dawn people from every village were on the road going to the flea market next to the main road. It was still dark, but very few people would use flashlights while others just walked by using their imagination. There were no horses to carry things as in our mountain life. The people either carried things on their backs or pushed two-wheeled carts. We did not make very much money. The watermelons and cucumbers were more than the buyers could buy. There was a lot of bargaining in the markets, and buyers tended to offer the lowest price at which the sellers did not want to sell. I remember one morning a man had a full bushel of big papayas. The Lao lady from Viang Chan kept bargaining to lower the price. The man did not want to sell to her. She asked him what he would do if he did not want to sell the papayas to her. He said that he would just take them home, cook, and eat them. She said how could he finish eating all those. He was angry and said with a loud tone that his family was going to eat one each day because they were ripening. The lady just walked slowly to search for other things in the area.

Sometime in late 1979, my sister Mai and family came from Phou Khao Khoi (Buffalo Horn Mountain) to visit us in KM52. We separated in Sarm Liam a year earlier and now we saw each other again. They surrendered to the Pathet Lao in Paksan while they were on their way to Thailand the year before. After they surrendered, they were transferred to live in Phou Khao Khoi which was close to the Long San River, a channel flowing from the east into the Ngeum Reservoir. Their father and more than half of their family members were in Ban Vinai Refugee Camp at the time. Their purpose in visiting us was the hope of moving to live in KM52 because in Phou Khao Khoi was difficult to earn a living. Besides that, the people where they lived were those who used to be communists a long time before Laos fell to the Pathet Lao. Ideologically, it was hard for my sister's family to blend in or adjust to those old villagers. The livelihood at their home was not as good as it was in KM52. After visiting us, they returned home one more time. A few months later they came back again and went to Thailand to be reunited with the other half of their family in the refugee camp.

The childhood and youth stages went by so quickly. Now I have already matured enough to learn the family role, the culture, and the religion within the clan in order to make the passage to manhood. In the sixties and seventies, the time I was on the farms, hiding in the bushes, or on the roll of the war was more than the time I spent with my friends. I did not have much of a good time in my childhood because we were constantly moving from one place to another. In the early eighties, my youth stage was better. I started to be exposed to a civilized society and learned how the world was. However, the place we lived, the school I attended, and the friendship still were only temporary. We met each other this year and moved away from them the next year.

The life of being a cow herder as I used to be before, no longer existed. We had no cows, horses, pigs, chickens, or even a dog as a pet. We no longer lived in the jungle home or in a war zone. Life in this place was quiet and peaceful. And hopefully there would be no more wars interferring with our lives again. Now it was the time to start education while integrating with the lowland people. The one thing I would not be afraid of them was to learn their language. It was a myth that when people went to the capitol city and they did not speak Lao, the taxi drivers would lure them into their cars and take them to the woods to rob and kill them afterwards. This haunted me all the time.

I planned to attend school again in September1979. However, first it was time to determine what grade I should start with because I had no schooling since 1975. It was going to be very difficult if I started at a higher-grade level. They offered some adult classes in the village which were equivalent to second and third grade levels. The Pathet Lao tried to provide basic education to adults so everyone could read. My brother thought it would not be such a bad idea to enroll me in those classes for two months before regular school started. It might enable me to read better. After that I could just go to regular school in September to do the assessment to see what grade I would fit into. Therefore, I attended the short hour adult classes for two months, from the beginning of July to the end of August. In September prior to enrolling in class, my cousin, who came together with my brother from Paksan and attended seventh grade at the time, encouraged me to go directly to fourth grade. He said there was not much difference between third and fourth grades. I was a little shaky about it and decided to enroll in third grade, based on my confidence. My adult school classes were very helpful when I entered regular school.

The school system had changed to a different way. The titles of a teacher and principal in elementary school had been changed. The teachers were called older brother teacher and sister teacher, while the principal was called father teacher. One afternoon when the principal visited us, the students addressed him as father teacher when they asked him questions. I was startled because it was completely different from what I knew in 1975. It was a new school culture that I had to learn and assimilate.

We did not have textbooks in class. The teacher had the textbooks for every subject and he had to copy everything on the blackboard. Then the students copied from there. My second day in class the teacher called me to stand up to read out loud the full blackboard of the reading chapter he had written. I was scared to death but managed to read as slowly as I could from top to bottom. The teacher, Sithong, who we had to address as older brother teacher, was Laotian and very kind. He understood that the Hmong and Lao Theung students learned Lao as their second language. It was difficult for us. I thought my reading was terrible, but a few Lao Theung students read even worse than I did because they had the swinging accent that went up and down. When they said the word horse, it sounded like dog because the tone of the two words were not much different.

After two weeks of attending class, the school officials decided to give the students who failed the final tests in June a second chance by offering the tests again to third, fourth, and fifth grade students. If anyone passed, then they were to go to the next grade. The officials gave me a special condition as a transfer student to be allowed to take the exam. Like many other students, if I could pass the exam, I should be advanced to fourth grade. It was good news, but also a nervous situation. I did not read well and underestimated myself, too. However, my second thought was just to give it a shot to see how much fun or headache the tests would be.

The exam was administered on a Saturday in Chaengsavang, a junior high school comprising the sixth, seventh, and eighth grades, and very close to our elementary school. Walking there in the morning to take the exam was like moving in a daydream. The teachers, the classrooms, the environment were all new to me. Every single test was a written test. While sitting in the classroom taking the test, my heart was racing, my feet were trembling, and my fingers could not manipulate the pen and paper. The teacher had to read a chapter of two pages for spelling. We called it dictation. A perfect spelling earned 10 points total. One mistake then one point was deducted. If you made 10 mistakes, you were done for that test and they gave you one point for your effort. The essay we called composition. It tested how smart you were. We wrote about the human body in under 55 minutes. I could not spell the word gallbladder correctly, so I misspelled it as tearing apart. They did not take away the points, for how I spelled the words. I got 7.5 of total 10 points on that based on how well I explained the content. But I was still laughing two days later when I thought about my spelling. Before seeing the results, I knew I did good on the math, but took a lot of guessing on other subjects. In the end, luckily, my name was posted on the bulletin board with others that I passed the exam and moved up to fourth grade.

On that morning after we finished the math, dictation, and writing analysis, then we came outside into the sun for a break. There was a Lao teacher who had a monkey face. In fact, students actually called him monkey *(liab)* because he had a flat nose and flat face just like a monkey. This teacher told me that I did damn good on my math. It seemed that his eyes were focusing on me. While engaging conversation with him, my broken Lao language was awkward and awfull accent. He then asked me where I was from. At the time I was being too honest and told him the truth that I was from Meuang Saisumboun, which he knew was an area of heavy fighting between the Pathet Lao and Chao Fa. Then right away he said to me, "Oh, so you are one of the Chao Fa children." Suddenly, my body temperature accelerated. My heart beat ten times faster, but I denied to him that I was a child of the Chao Fa. He smiled at me and turned to engage in conversation with one of the Hmong teachers who sat next to him. I was glad the monkey-face teacher did not talk to me very long. Then my body temperature cooled down. After that day, the whole time I attended school there, I never disclosed to anyone in the class where I was from because of the tension between us, the new residents and the old villagers. Two years later when I attended sixth grade there, I heard some students say the monkey-face Lao teacher was transferred to another school in a different town.

Even though we were very poor, I enjoyed my life the most during this three-year period in KM52. As a young boy, I felt I was living in an open society without fear of anything. There were no gangs, no kidnappings or shootings in the village. We could walk at night from one village to the next without any trouble. The bad thing was the political activities from the government level that caused people not to be able to live their normal lives. In school I had a lot of good friends. We all were mature enough to know about care and love for one another. Everything we did together or anywhere we went was always enjoyable despite our poor living conditions. While attending school, I passed all the final tests to be advanced to the next grade level each year. If you failed the final exam, it was so bad to stay in the same class for another year. It was very embarrassing and emotionally painful to see your classmates moved to the next grade. Some teachers used to say, "You worked all year long in the farm and after harvesting your rice into the barn, fire burned your rice stall." There were always some challenges for me because I had less of an educational background and learned the Lao language too. I finished first grade in 1975 and then jumped to fourth grade in 1979, with no schooling in between. It seemed my classmates who had not had any interruption in attending school, read better than I did. So, I had to study harder than they did every day. After two years in Nam Chaeng, meaning Clear Water Elementary School, I passed the final exam to go to sixth grade in Chaengsavang Junior High. It was what every student had always hoped for. By passing the final exam in elementary school to go to junior high, I felt like I grew a couple inches taller when I heard the results.

The junior high was much further walking, about 30 minutes from home. Some students had a bike to ride to school every day. They were perceived as rich or we even see them were like a prince. Most of us were walking with our flip-flops because we were poor. In junior high, students behaved more like adults and respected each other. Likewise, in the classroom we were expected to be not just like students, but more like adults as well. Unfortunately, the politics and socioeconomics constantly changed in the new government system, so I did not have a very long time to be with those good friends as I wished. I attended school in this village from September 1979 to the beginning of September 1982 when I started seventh grade.

After attending school for the first week, I left Laos to Thailand. KM52 was another place I left forever. Soon I ended up on the opposite side of the world and separated from my schoolmates, maybe for the rest of our lives.

At the end of May 1981, after we finished our final tests, our fifth-grade teacher took her whole class of students to help her family plant rice in the fields. It took us almost a half day of walking to get to the teacher's rice fields. On the way, a girl stumbled and fell into a little ditch where the truck tires passed through many times. She could not get up right away because she had a full back basket of things. Without realizing it might have hurt her feelings, I jokingly asked why she wanted to be helped by others, just pretending to fall down, so others would pull her up like she was hurt. She got up and was sort of mad. I thought she was going to send me to hell for saying that to her. Then she said to me why does every boy treat girls the same way. But, I realized she was not really mad at me because girls in those days were very polite. Later in the day she was happy and told me she knew it was only a joke. In fact, she turned out to have a different personality after that. She was a fun person. While we were together as a group in the fields, we took some pictures of the whole class for souvenirs.

Planting rice in the field was a hassle for me because I never had done it before. I was in the middle while some were older and some were younger. We used the old method which our people had used for a century to plant rice. The men used round sticks, the same size as baseball bats and about three yards long, sharpened at one end to poke the ground to make holes. The space of each hole was approximately a foot apart. The ladies carried a sack like a pouch or a bib bowl in front of them, full of seeds. If no sacks were available, some just carried the seeds in big bowls. The ladies kept following and tossing the seeds, about seven to ten grains, into the holes while the men kept poke holes and moving backward. Since I have not done this before, my palms were very soft. After five hours of poking the hard dirt, I got blisters on both of my palms, as did many others. It was a child labor. Since I was the youngest son in the family who was considered as the baby, many girls liked to tease me a lot. Some said, "Today the little darling boy is working too hard and hurt himself so much. Who should his mother blame?" Some of the older girls also teased the younger ones, "If any of you like him, you should go get a cup of water for him to drink, just like Gao Nor brought the cup of water for Nou Shi Long." Then they laughed. No one was angry because it was just the jokes to keep the day short.

Finally, that afternoon was over when the sun left the earth as it disappeared behind the high mountains, but my palms would not heal because it was only one night of rest and would be sore again the next morning when I had to jab the long stick into the hard dirt for the whole day.

The first afternoon, we planted rice almost until dark. The teacher also took a few poses of pictures for souvenir before we returned to the farmhouse. Once we got back in the house, the teacher and six or seven girls cooked dinner for the total of over 20 people to eat. The boys were more tired because we were jabbing the long sticks to the ground all the afternoon. Everyone missed his own bed. The boys were not allowed to do any food preparation, except carry water from the stream a couple blocks away. One young boy was smiling and walking back and forth on the grassy area. He said the cooking was the girls' responsibility to do before they became a housewife. When dinner was ready, it was already too dark. We burned a lot of dried bamboos in two big fire places to give us light. The teacher said to everyone to make our throats steeper. In the culture it meant that we must eat fast and get ready to go sleep for the night. It was fun to work, eat meals, joke, and laugh together as a happy memory of the fifth grade before moving on to sixth grade in a different school. After dinner the teacher separated us. She put the older boys, seven of us, to sleep in another farmhouse in another field high up on the mountain. She allowed a few younger boys to sleep in the house where she was. She feared that some of us who were older might attack the girls at night because four girls were 16 and 17 years old already. One of the older boys, 20 years old, joked that maybe she thought we were like tigers. She was so thoughtful, but she did not think about our safety in the mountain house. If the real tigers ate one or two of us in the night, she might not just lose her job, but was worth less than a human being. Up there, we were thirsty because we had eaten salty foods for dinner. There was no water in the house. Then we had to use the moonlight to walk down to the stream to drink water. What we were scared the most about were snakes and scorpions while walking in the dark. We might step on them at any time. In the KM52 area, there was a type of small, short snake about a half foot long and thumb size, which bit people, and they could die within hours. We were lucky that night, not stepping on any of them. When we got back in the stilt house, we just laid flat in bed without blankets and mosquito nets. We recited folktales for a couple of hours until some people dropped off because we all had worked all day long in tiring labor. It was a peaceful night in this mountain house with the cooling temperature. In the morning the sky was beautiful for the day. We got up and went back to have breakfast in the house down in the valley. After breakfast, we walked back for a half mile to the field to jab the ground again until noon and returned to have lunch.

 The lunch was a long waiting because there was no more meat. So, the ladies had to kill a few chickens, clean them, and cook for lunch. A couple younger boys leaned against a stump with sad faces. The oldest boy in the group asked them what the matter was why they were so sad. They said they wanted to eat fried ice because they were too tired. It was a joke because the ice would be melted away when it was fried. Once lunch was done, we walked back to the field to finish planting and returned home in the late afternoon.

I really felt bad when we got back home and found out the girl, who fell into the ditch, had failed the exam and would not be advanced to sixth grade in September. She must remain in fifth grade for another year while I, along with many others, went into sixth grade. After I left the elementary school of Nam Chaeng to junior high in Chaengsavang, we did not see each other for the entire year.

In September 1982, she came to sixth grade in junior high with us when I was about to leave for Thailand. She saw me on the morning of our first day and was smiling, but said not a word. We were there in the same school for only three days before I left. Four years later when I was in high school in Saint Paul, Minnesota, she sent me a letter from KM52. It was a surprise. I was not sure where she got my 1584 Timberlake Road address, but I believe she got it from my sister, who married into the Lee clan and was still living very close to them at the time. In the letter she said not to remember her or the class, but to remember the pictures we had taken together for memory. It was a sad reminiscence from our past, since each one was now on opposite sides of the globe. I wrote a letter back to her that same month, but it was quiet thereafter. Maybe it flew into the air and then dropped into the vast ocean. A year later my sister who was still in Laos said she got married already. I guessed she must have married after she sent me the letter. The friends, the jokes, and all the places I have lived were gone forever. By now, maybe she is very old and has children and grandchildren already.

The Chaengsavang junior high school was one of the first Hmong schools built by a Hmong gentleman, Ly Tek *(Lis Teeb)*, before the country fell. It was on a beautiful long hill very close to the main road and market. In this junior high we had a mixture of three different ethnic groups. Hmong, Lao, and Lao Theung students came from four villages together to learn one Lao language. The school did not go so well for Hmong students in later years. From elementary to junior high, Hmong students always dominated the top-class rankings. By the time they started senior high, they started to fall behind because they lacked financial support from their parents. They were constantly moving from one place to another and not focusing much on education. The vast majority of parents did not have any educational background or have enough knowledge to support their children and emphasize the importance of education. Most often they let their children struggle through school by themselves. The stronger ones were able to finish some higher levels, but the weaker ones would drop out at some point when they had a difficult time with no help or hope. Maybe about one third dropped out after junior high and went back to work on the farm which repeated the same life cycle of their parents. About one half made it to senior high. A portion of these decided to go to vocational schools after eighth grade, which was another option. For the Lao and Lao Theung, a small portion of these students would drop out during this period to go back to work on the farm. The rest would continue going to high schools. There were almost none who got married at this early stage. One particular reason why the Lao students were more successful was because it was their own society, their culture, and their language. Beyond the lack of financial support, the Hmong and Lao Theung students had a greater disadvantage and challenge to adjust themselves to the school system.

What I wanted the most in those days were a guitar, a bike, and blue jeans. There were many other youths also wanted the same thing as I did. Having a guitar to play was a luxury. Wearing blue jeans was considered to be cool and popular. And having a bike would mean you were rich. Most of Lao students came to school with their bikes while the Hmong and Lao Theung walked.

My classmates and I often walked in the moonlight from our home in KM52 to another place, a few miles down south, to see the Lao party, which they called "boun." This place was called Na Lao ນາລາວ (Lao Rice Terrace). On the way there and returning home, we walked many students together and sang songs. One Lao song I remember was "Separated the other day, but today we meet again" and the Hmong song "Leaving because the time has come, *ncaim mus vim lub caij los txog.*" It was fun and harmonious to sing while the temperature was cooling down and the moon was shining above our heads. Everything was cool when you were in this young stage. There was never any danger in this place. The fun time in those years never diminished from my memory. I wish we could rewind the time to go back again.

The Lao educational system was very slow in progress. Every year students in one grade studied the same math and read the same books. One textbook lasted for many years. In 1975 when I was in first grade I was reading the textbook that my second brother had five or six years before. When I was in school from 1979 to 1982 in KM52, we still did the same thing. In other words, there were no new reading materials published for elementary and junior high. Some students who failed the class many years were tired of reading the same book over and over again. The more they were tired of it, the less likely they would study and more likely they would fail again in the final test. Since we had no textbooks in the classroom, the teacher had to copy everything on the blackboard. Teachers were another factor. In the early 1980s and before, there was a very scarcity of teachers. Thus, many people who completed six and seven grades were recruited to teach first and second, or even third grade. My fourth and fifth grade teachers had only finished junior high school.

My imagination was too big. One time I joked with my two classmates that I wanted to marry a Lao girl because they were beautiful. Actually, I was still too young to know which one was the pretty one. My classmates told me that I would not survive because of our cultural differences and the food we ate. One told me that he did not think I could always eat the sticky rice. I told him that not just the sticky rice, I could even eat the raw ferment fish without any problem. It was just a joke, but I think what they said was right. My hope was that one day I would graduate with a nursing degree or something even bigger like a doctorate degree. I would walk out of the university and marry a wife who graduated with me in the same year from the same school. By then my job would not be working on the farms, but sitting in a nice office. Our fun activities would be touring other countries around the world, holding hands together, walking side by side on some seashore. We would go to see the beautiful Phou Si (mountain) in Luang Prabang. I would build a stilt house close to the forest to keep the temperature cool because we did not have air conditioning yet. At home, when I returned from work, my wife would be home and dinner would be ready on the table. But, my reality turned out to go in the opposite way. The traditional life I had thought about was just an illusion. I ended up being in another different country, marrying a wife with a different level of education, and different way of thinking, too. In the US each one of us works a different shift, so we could take turns babysitting. When I returned home from work, she was leaving for work. Instead of having dinner ready on the table like my thoughts of long ago, I have to clean up the mess and wash the pile of dishes in the sink. Our busy schedule of working was just to earn enough money to pay the bills and buy enough food to feed our children. The young lady I imagined during my youth of how she would look, what she would wear, and the way she would talk to me, does not even exist as a shadow for me to see in these days. All the tours I had hoped for before, I have not gone on one. The high beautiful Phou Si of Laos I have not taken a peek of. What I saw was only a picture from geography. The wish I had 30 years ago, disappeared forever.

While I enjoyed my life very much as a youth, my brother was not very happy about the political activities in the town. It seemed that there were always some troubles coming to him. He had to attend the *samana* so often each month without pay. A few times he was accused of having two heads, which meant he believed half in communism and half in capitalism. Whether he had done anything wrong against the government or not, he was portrayed in that way. In the village where we lived, the government installed a new *taseng* very often. One person held the office for a few months then escaped to Thailand to get away for the political reasons of being accused by the communist government. Once they discover that we had two brothers who had escaped to Thailand, my brother had a harder time of coping with his situation. He was not certain whether he should stay or sneak out like the others had.

One time in late 1979 in KM52, there were three men who were shot dead in the fields by the Kong Lorne soldiers. These soldiers were mostly in the village as security personnel and were never involved in active military duty. The three dead men had returned from Thailand to pick up their wives and children. Security at the time was very tight, so the three men were waiting to see if their families could sneak out to the jungle to be picked up. However, someone disclosed this information to the Kong Lorne. While they were hiding and sleeping in the farmhouse, the soldiers went there and shot them dead. According to the news, one man managed to escape with body injuries because they found blood stains where he escaped. It was a very sad situation for the families to bear. They just buried the men in the woods without funerals. As usual, the new people kept coming from other places each week, but they disappeared again the next few days. They came there to prepare food and leave again. Mostly, they crossed the Mekong River to Thailand. The livelihood was very unstable.

There was a single man from the Khang family who returned to our place after he had fled to Thailand a year earlier. He knew my family since we lived in Xieng Khouang. Late one evening while I was studying with my oil lamp lit in front of me, he whispered to me from outside through the woven bamboo wall. He asked me to tell my brother to bring him some food because he could not go out to buy food in the market. He was hungry and hiding in the woods under a big tree very close to our house. I told my brother after he left our yard. My brother packed some food and went out for a while on that full moon night. I did not ask him what happened when he came back home that night.

Three days later I asked him and he said the man returned to Thailand the same night he got the food. I did not bother to ask for details about his purpose of coming back to KM52. A year later he returned to Laos again and was killed by the Pathet Lao in Na Yao (นายาว), another place to the north. The rumors were that the Pathet Lao caught him and slashed his throat.

One time in the summer of 1981, many of us took some rice to sell in Viang Chan, the capital city of Laos. At first, we planned to return home the same day. After we sold our rice in the late afternoon, we gathered with another group of married people. They persuaded us to stay with them overnight to tour the city and went to visit Wat That Luang because they had kickboxing fights there during the night. We spent the evening in the Wat to see many displays and the kickboxing. At around 12 o'clock midnight, we came out of the Wat and went to get a place to sleep in some relatives' houses which were not far away. The married people said their women were hungry, so let's go find food to eat before going to sleep. Once we got to the marketplace on the side of the street where people were selling food, the Lao people were suspicious about us because we were different. Often, they thought that Hmong people were there to find a way to cross to Thailand. Before we bought our food that night, we were asked by two men some silly questions about why we stayed up so late in the night. After a moment they disappeared. We knew they were going to get security and police to come arrest us. We then ran down every aisle in the open market to get out of there. In a few minutes we heard the Lao people asked each other questions, "Where did they go?" Then we knew for sure they were looking for us. We regrouped and ran like frightened cows running away from tigers on a small muddy road out to the suburb where the relatives lived and we were supposed to stay overnight. It was good we made the move fast enough before we got caught. Otherwise, we could all have been jailed.

Another time in the beginning of November, my sister-in-law, my two sisters, and I each brought ten kilograms of rice to sell in Viang

Chan. When we got half way to the city, the bus was stopped by the security. We were checked and they detained our sacks of rice. We were told that if we returned home, then we could have our rice. If we wanted to go on, they would keep our rice. There were about six or seven Lao business ladies. Some had only baskets of fruits such as papayas, bananas, pineapples, and stripped eggplants. They were fine. I saw two ladies, each one had two big sacks of rice with them. They were from Viang Chan. The two ladies gave up their rice to the security. My sister-in-law decided to take the rice back home. My two sisters and I went to the city for shopping for the day.

In the middle of 1982, my sister-in-law's Vue cousin came back from prison. I did not ask him where they had imprisoned him. When we surrendered to the Pathet Lao in Meuang Orm, they found out that his father was affiliated with the American CIA in the Secret War. Then they tried to arrest his father. The moment they surrounded their house, his father escaped. When they entered their house, the son was there. He was only 16 years old at the time. Since they could not catch his father, they arrested him instead. The Pathet Lao tied and dragged him to their camp. They tied him against a post in the hot sun for three days before they sent him to re-education camp with adult prisoners. After four years, they released him. Then he came to KM52 because his father had escaped to Thailand and resettled in the US by this time. He stopped in our house for a few days and fled to Thailand. He was the first person who I knew was punished on behalf of his father and came back from re-education camp.

In late August 1982, my cousin's brother-in-law, Chia Xa Yang, who was a soldier in the CIA army, wanted to escape to Thailand for his own safety. His concern was that one day they might find out about his previous affiliation with the American CIA. By then he would be in trouble or maybe he was in trouble at that moment already. He had attended a few *samanas* during the year with others, and they were told that they would be sent to Sam Neua to attend the seventh session. What did the Pathet Lao government mean by that? No one knew for sure. However, anyone who was sent to Sam Neua meant either to prison or death. He knew he must escape to a safe place before trouble came to him. Then he secretly searching to make a connection with the people in Viang Chan who were willing to take bribes to send his family cross the Mekong River to Thailand. After searching for a while, he had found a police chief, who often did this business. Brother-in-law shared the information with Father and brother. Before making the final decision, he had to go back to see the police chief one more time. Father and brother thought our family was large, so we could not escape all at one time. However, they were willing to let me go to Thailand with brother-in-law and his family. Then one day we took the bus from KM52 to Viang Chan to meet with the police chief, who was going to send us across the river. The purpose of the second meeting was to see his expression and to make sure he would send us to Thailand, not kill us. It was a very stressful situation because we did not know whether he was honest, telling the truth, and sending us across the river or not. When we arrived in the chief's stilt house in the suburb, the middle age man seemed very calm. He was a slender man with a mustache and a soft voice. He was sitting cross-legged, wearing his boxer shorts, and a police shirt, while chopping some dried leaves which later brother-in-law told me was *sa* leaves, in the Lao Language. In our language, it was the leaves of *maj*, the plants that mother grew in our farm in Sala to make clothes. All we knew was to use the thin bark to make clothes, but this man smoked the leaves. As the conversation went on for 30 minutes in front of his 16-inch television set, the police chief said he needed one silver bar per person for the trip. For some little children, he might take as much as five French 50 cent silver coins for each child. According to brother-in-law, he had done many of these business transactions for a long time. Although he was a police chief, the man was a drug user and did this kind of black-market business without any punishment. He was very rich when comparing him with other people in a poor country like Laos. He had the television then it meant he was rich.

After the conversation ended, he set the time to meet him on September 9, 1982, in the Afternoon Market in Viang Chan. We must be there by 6 o'clock that evening. Then brother-in-law and I returned home. On the way home, we were hungry. We decided to stop at the Sikhai Market to eat Lao noodles. It was also a place we had never been before. So, brother-in-law just wanted to take me there. While we were waiting for our orders, a Lao man was walking around the place with a crowbar. He kept asking people to buy it. He kept saying, "This can lift up nail number one, number two, number three." There was no one interested of buying it. I thought, "Why is he so dumb by walking with that piece of metal? Everyone is here to eat, not to buy something like that. It was just annoying." When we finished eating, we walked all the way back to the bus stop to catch the bus home. As we were on the bus heading home, I could not make up my mind whether to go or stay. There were three reasons that made me feel it was too difficult to decide. First, I feared that the man might not send us to Thailand as he promised because in the past there were many people killed along the river. Some were dumped in the water and drowned. He could not be trusted since he was a police chief. I was very much afraid of death. It might be very hard for my family to cope with the grief if I was killed. Second, I did not want to lose my friends in school. I was close to them very much like family. Thirdly, we kept moving all the time in our lives. So how many more times did we have to move before we settled in one place. All these three thoughts made me feel like I was going to lose a lot of everything. On the other hand, my goal was to get a higher education after I finished high school. If I studied hard and did well in the class, I could possibly go to the university some day. Nevertheless, I was thinking about my brother who had no peace of mind. Anything he did was always difficult because of the political pressure. That was why brother-in-law was searching for a way to leave the country because he no longer felt safe at home. That was why I was on the bus with him on that day. Thus, it changed my thoughts a bit when all these negative things came through my head while on the bus home. Now, if I did have a chance to go to Thailand, I had to go. Soon we arrived at the KM52 market where the bus supposed to stop. Before we got off the bus, I asked brother-in-law again how much he trusted the policeman.

He said he knew the policeman had done this kind of business for a long time, helping many people to cross the Mekong River to Thailand. It should be safe to go with him. After he assured me for the second time, I felt like his answer reduced my fears.

September 9, 1982, was during our first week in school. My mind was unsettled because it was time to leave. It was a Thursday in school and we were supposed to have our first test on Friday. Some of my close friends asked me if I was ready for the test. My response was not very strong because I hid everything inside me, not to let them know about my leaving. I told them it was only the first test to refresh our studies from last year. We should not have to worry too much whether we did good or bad. I went to class in the morning and returned for lunch at home as was the usual routine. On the way home when we were close to the dividing path where we were supposed to go on our separate ways, I told my cousin Soua Thao, whose house was about a half block away from ours, that I was leaving with his brother-in-law and family to Thailand in the next couple of hours. The moment I told him, my cousin was sort of startled or even shocked. All this time he knew his brother-in-law was leaving, but he never thought I was leaving with him. He said if I did go to Thailand with his brother-in-law, then he should go with us, too. He no longer wanted to stay any more. Life was going to be sad if he stayed behind. I told him that the plan was to gather in the Morning Market in Viang Chan late that afternoon, then go to meet the police in the evening in the Afternoon Market. After the quick discussion, we went home for lunch as calm as usual.

With only one hour of lunchtime, I did not pack many things other than putting a notebook and one extra pair of clothes in my school bag. My mind was not clear for the unforeseen situation lying ahead. I was thinking about the day brother-in-law and I returned from Viang Chan, he told me to give away my watch to my brother before we left. The bad imagination of my trip had already haunted me. People who crossed the Mekong River to Thailand would be robbed of all their valuable belongings, including watches and jewelry, and females being raped by Thai gangsters. Would we be robbed like those who crossed before us? Many questions kept coming to my head. We were to resume our afternoon class session by one o'clock. So, in order not to be noticed, I left home at 12:30 PM, pretending that I was going back to school. Father did not say much while sitting on the guest bed with legs hanging down under. The more you talked the more sounds would travel to strangers' ears. Then you screwed up your plan. That was what we believed. What I heard from him was, "*Ceev faj thiab saib tej yam yus tsis paub tom ntej.*" Translated, "Be careful and watch out for unexpected things." It sounded like Father signaled to me that it was the time I was on my own. He would no longer be with me to protect me as before. As usual when we ventured to a dangerous place, Father always called the spirits of grandpa and grandma in heaven to come down to protect us. This time in the late evening before Father had already burned five incense sticks, standing outside on the flat dirt backyard, asking for help. A moment before my departure, Father also lit three incence sticks at the little altar *(xwm kab)* attached to the wall, asking for the house spirits to look after me and give me protection.

Now her skinny little boy with baby face was leaving for another country. Skinny? Yes, when three months earlier the graduated nurses from Viang Chan came to do their training in our village, all the girls called me, "The skinny darling." They teased me a lot when we played woven rattan ball *(kataw)* in the courtyard. As I left home, Mother followed me on the way for about a block with tears in her eyes. Before I crossed the little wooden bridge over the canal where I could no longer see our home behind the thick bamboo trees, I turned back to tell Mother to go home. I could see her facial expression of fear, which indicated to me that she was afraid I might not make it to Ban Vinai Refugee Camp in Thailand. However, in my mind I thought if I were to die, I would have died a long time ago when I was about eight or nine years old, about three feet tall, and lived in the cornfield by myself. I did not say it out loud to Mother, but in my mind, I said, "Mother, I will not die. You are honest throughout your life. God won't allow any bad species to pull your baby son's feet to the ground." My emotions must not be shown to make her unhappy again. But, that day it was too stressful for Mother to go back to see the house without me. Her son who used to return home from school for lunch, from this day on he would never show up again when lunch was ready on the table. In that late afternoon when the sun was leaving the earth, we said, "The sun tilts *(hnub qaij)*", she would only see the neighbors' kids scuffle their feet on the dirt path with joy and laughter. Not her own son. I crossed the little bridge and turned back again, watching Mother wipe away her tears while standing at the other end of the bridge. She stood there pinching her fingers, watching me for a few minutes, and then turned around, heading back home. In my last wish was, "Mother, return home. I will not die." I stood by the side of the stream and looked at the big tree in front of our house for a last time for my memory while mother disappeared down the crooked path under the thick forest between me and our home. It was the moment I abandoned my bamboo walls and thatch roof house. The house which my brother had built for us two years earlier. It was not the end of my trip, though. There was still a vast distance I had to pass before I could get away from Lao soil. But it was the last moment I had to remember my home in Laos. Then I turned around and headed east to the bus stop on the main road, but also pretending I was walking normally like I was going back to class. Without mentioning anything, I indeed missed the house, the dirt yard I used to walk on, the starfruit trees I had planted, and above all, my family. From this afternoon on I would never again meet the people, old and young, men, women, and children, from my home to the main road as I did before when I walked to school in the morning and came back from school in the afternoon. My heart was torn about my journey.

When I got to the KM52 Market on the side of the main road waiting for the bus, three of my classmates met me there. They were on their way to school, but stopped to buy some school supplies. They asked me where I was going because it did not look like I was going back to school. I told them that I had a cousin, who was from Xieng Khouang, attending school in Dongdok. He was sick and stayed in the hospital in Viang Chan. I was off to see him. I would be very appreciative if they were kind enough to let me see their Thursday and Friday lecture notes before next Monday. The three teenage girls did not say much, but one girl said, "Whatever you want." I thought, "Was it a joke or what?" I lied to them because I never returned home and borrowed their lecture notes. In my thought was, "I will be gone forever and won't see your faces any more, girls." I guess they would be surprised the week after when they found out my cousin and I had escaped to Thailand. It was the last time I saw their smiling faces. They might now be very old, have many children, and even have become grandmas already.

In the market while waiting for the bus, I met my cousin's sister with two little children. Her husband, who was my cousin's brother-in-law, had left early in the day to Viang Chan with two children. As we waited for the bus to arrive, my cousin came. I wandered back and forth in the market place with no purpose. Some people were watching my movements suspiciously. At about 2 PM, the bus from Viang Chan arrived. We rushed to board the bus before it departed. I don't remember exactly, but it seemed we paid 15 kip for one way because the Pathet Lao had just exchanged for a new currency two years earlier. The inflation rate was not high at the time. The paper money had only one-kip bills, not five or ten yet. The bills were about two inches wide and four inches long. While sitting on the bus, I started to think about my family and how would they cope with the situation of missing me in the house. Soon the bus started to turn around heading south again on the single lane road, which was still wide enough for two cars, one in each direction. The road had no yellow line divided the center. When another car came from the other direction, this one just moved to the side a bit. At the crooked road where the driver could not see very far ahead, he just honked the horn very often. This was a signal to other cars coming from the other direction to be cautious. It seemed every building was running in the opposite direction as the bus was moving forward. My heart was torn, but I showed no signs of emotion. In the late afternoon trip like this one, most of the passengers were Lao people who were going home to Viang Chan. The bus was not as crowded as the trip in the morning. It was the last moment to remember this place, no matter how bad or good it was. I thought there was no chance that I would ever return to see it in the future. Would there be any of my friends who even noticed that I was missing in the classroom? I wished I could say some words to those who I cared about and to hear that they cared about me before I left. But, my trip was a real secret which should not be revealed to anyone. Looking at the landscape of Lao stilt houses hidden deep under the coconut trees along the road, I thought they would be gone forever and only exist in my memory. I questioned myself, "Why do I have to leave this beautiful place?" Every moment as the bus was moving, I looked through the windows to see the afternoon bright in sunshine on the green landscape, and it made me feel like I wanted to cry. My throat had a lump in it and became tight. As we were further somewhere down south, along the road peasants let their herds of water buffaloes to graze in the pastures. I thought, "Very soon as the sun goes down, those animals are going home. But where will my home be tonight? Maybe in the ditch or I probably will just turn myself to the police to butcher me. Or maybe he might just throw me in jail tonight." The bus stopped very often for people to get on and get off. Even though the bus was running at its usual speed, it seemed it was running faster from KM52 to Viang Chan this time. I did not remember exactly, but it seemed it took one hour and twenty minutes or less than that from KM52 to the Morning Market. Soon I saw the three-elephant head statue on the side of the road, which indicated to me we were now close to the Morning Market, the place we would have to get out in a few minutes.

Upon arriving in the Morning Market (Talat Sao), we searched everywhere, but could not find brother-in-law. To be unnoticed, we separated from each other and planned to meet again in the front store at 6 PM. After we separated, I wandered the store like I was looking for clothes by going through every aisle in the building. It was a way I just did to kill time and not be noticed. While walking around without a purpose, I met four men from Nam Po, a village in the high mountain above the Ngeum Reservoir. They asked me where I was from. I told them that I was from KM52 and would spend the night here. My heart was beating fast while talking to those men, but I showed no sign of emotion. Without asking any further question, they just went on their way. But, time was flying. Soon the sun left the earth as we used to say in the old days, the sky is dead (*tu ntuj siav*), meaning, darkness is taking place. Some shop owners started to close their business sections inside the building. Then it was time to come back to the front to meet my cousin and his sister.

Once we had re-grouped in front of the Morning Market, brother-in-law was still missing. Whatever the circumstance, I had to decide what to do at the time. I told cousin and his sister that we must go to the place the chief told us before. We ran fast across the street to catch a taxi going to the Afternoon Market, hoping that he would be there, too. When reaching the other side of the street, we met a man, who was not a taxi driver, but who drove a silver Mercedes Benz. He was just off work and heading home at the time. I asked him if he could take us to the Afternoon Market. He was okay with this and opened the doors to let the five of us get inside. He did not ask any questions while we were in the car, but drove us fast to the place where we wanted to go. He made a few turns and stopped where I had told him before. We got out. I now don't remember how much we gave that driver, but remember I gave him some money. There was a water well with a muddy and trashy area surrounding it and with cars passing through steadily on the roads that ran in a circle around it. This was in the Afternoon Market (Talat Laeng) territory, but we were not very close yet. We were in the right spot the police chief had designated for us. Once we got out, people were running everywhere in the dark while cars were passing around one after another. In a couple of minutes, it became even darker because the area did not have street lights. Brother-in-law was not there to guide us. The police chief, who was supposed to pick us up, was not there either.

The Long Journey

It was so obvious to spectators who noticed us what our plans were. We were freaking out and scared to death because of fear that soon someone might come up to question us about what was going on. Even though the people did not bother to say anything to us, it was an anxious time. After about 20 minutes, when it was completely dark and you could not see people beyond a few yards, an old white truck pulled up in front of us. Brother-in-law and his two children were in the truck. We were relieved. I thought the only person who might arrest us now was the police chief. We rushed into the truck and the policeman drove us back to his house. We were like captive birds in his cage. He drove his truck around so many streets in the dark, so I did not recognize which direction he was taking us. After about ten minutes we arrived under his stilt house. He unloaded us to go into his house on the upper level. He left the house again for a while and returned with the Lor family. Now we were scared and powerless people. All the young children did not even make any noise.

Inside the house on the second floor, we were either sitting or lying down, huddled together like a herd of pigs. None of the chief's people were in the house. It was quiet, too. I thought why in the world had I forced myself to do this kind of a nonsense. We were put in a position of powerlessness where we should not talk, or else we all might be killed. If the guy just robbed us for our money in the night and sent us to be killed some other place, there was nothing we could do. In the house, brother-in-law told the police chief that we had one extra person, who was his wife's brother, with us. He was negotiating with the police that we must not leave him behind. However, we might not be able to pay him one silver bar for the extra person like we paid for everyone else because we were short of silver bars. Then he told brother-in-law to collect everything as much as we could and give it to him. He would be okay with that. Brother-in-law came to me and said that since I had some paper money left, we should add it to my cousin's silver coins and give it to the police chief to see what he would say about it. I had over 300 kips at the time. I thought after we crossed to Thailand, that amount of money might not be worth very many Thai baht anyway. Then I gave my paper money to brother-in-law. He brought it along with my cousin's silver coins to the police. He accepted what we had. The deal was done.

The night was not very long at all, but it was a very different night. The police put my cousin and me in a bedroom without a mosquito net in the lower level. It was a quiet night, but I could not go to sleep. I felt there had been only a few hours in the night, but it was 3 AM in the morning already. The police chief woke us up and rushed everyone into his truck again. It was very dark outside. My heart was pumping fast, nervous, and even thrilling. "Are we going to hell or going to Thailand?" in my thoughts. The children were asleep still. No one made any noise, not even whispered to each other. He drove us along the Mekong River on a bumpy dirt road, going up north for one and a half hours. The cooling wind brushing against my face made me feel like it penetrated to my bones. If the chief wanted to kill us, it would be either bullets or knives, or put us in the boat to drop us off in the middle of the river. Once we reached our destination, he stopped the truck to shovel us out. We all got out on the side of the road in the dark morning. He told us to move down to the river and wait for another guy to come to pick us up in the next couple of hours. Whether this was true or not, we proceeded as he directed. This might save our lives and not be killed. Whether there were snakes, scorpions, or anything else, we just stepped over them now. We rushed down the bank of the Mekong while the man sped his truck away. We pushed ourselves through the thick bushes for about ten yards and then the water was there. We stopped.

Along the side of the river, we hid under the tall elephant grass, about a couple yards away from the water. We waited for one hour, then two hours, and the sky was clearing where the sun would rise. There was still no one who showed up yet. We waited for another hour until after 6 o'clock when the color of clouds in the sky in the east turned orange. The little birds flew over our heads. We saw people paddling their small boats from the north down the Mekong River for fishing or to do their usual daily work. It indicated that dawn was over, but no one came. It was another frightening moment of hopeless. It was the time to worry that maybe there would not be any one to come at all. Our thoughts were that the police chief had betrayed us for sure. Soon the birds sang, the sky was completely clear, the sun rose, and the rays hit directly on us. No one had showed up anywhere yet, except more people were paddling their boats along the river. We were exposed to those people because we had nothing to hide behind. Parents cuddled their little ones and whispered to them to be quiet. All we did was sit motionless, hoping someone would come to take us as we had been told. Sai Khue Lor told us to move back up to the road where the bushes were much thicker. Brother-in-law, who used to be in the army, knew what was safe and what was not safe. So he said, "No. Whether we are dead or alive, we must not move away from where we are."

We waited and waited until the sun rose about a yard above the horizon, then the sound of a boat engine came very faint from the south. We knew that it must be someone coming, but were not so sure if it was the right guy or not. At this moment it passed the time business people paddling boats along the river to go sell their goods in the market. So, there were no more boats coming from the north. It was quiet. In about five minutes or so we saw the boat was moving to the side of the river, coming toward us. The man was looking for us alongside the river. That's why he came so close to the shore rather than went out in the middle of the river. As we kept watching the boat, it came directly to us. In a few minutes when he saw us, he pushed the bow of his boat against the sand with the engine running. Then we knew that he was the man. He told us to jump in quickly. However, we still were not sure where he would take us, once we got into his boat. We also were scared to death because his boat was only about three feet wide and eight feet long. After everyone jumped in, the top of the boat was only about three inches above the water. He pulled the boat back and made a diagonal, cutting across the river toward Thailand. We knew he would take us to Thailand for sure. But, if the boat swamped or tipped over, we would all be going into the water. We did not even have any rubber inner tubes with us. After a few minutes the boat hit the shore of Thailand in an area with high banks above us. Above the river banks, the bushes were mostly prickly thorns. He rushed us out of his boat as fast as possible before he returned to Laos. We jumped, ran, and dragged children through deep mud as our feet sank down about six inches. Some people who wore only Lao flip-flops could not pull them out from the mud. Instead, they would rather run away without them. My white Thai tennis shoes were filled with mud. We climbed up the high river banks through a little channel-like animal trail with the thick prickly bushes above our heads, which scratched our bodies everywhere.

In a few seconds everyone was up in the flat grassland above the river in Thailand. We knew that we were away from the dangers in Laos, but unexpected bad things could still happen to us at any moment. Even if we were on Thai soil, there was a gut feeling we knew so well from before. The unknown situation of our trip was lying ahead of us. In the past some of the small groups of Hmong people crossing the river had been robbed of their money by Thai gangsters; and then police and soldiers raped the young girls and women afterwards. They just came to take any females they wanted with them for days and nights. By the time the women were released, they hurt as much as a woman who had given birth to a baby. We used to say that you escape from the snake, but you meet the tiger. *Khiav nab, tab sis ntsib tsov.*

Later, I met a man in the refugee camp. He said his group arrived on the river bank on the Thai side the night before. There were about 50 people in his group. They had knives and axes, but only one M-16 rifle with them. Early the next morning, a group of Thai soldiers marched up and surrounded them. There were a total of about ten soldiers. They seized that man's gun and put their knives into a pile on one side and then gathered the people in one place. They grasped the man who had the gun and dragged him to the river. Two soldiers held the man's arms and another soldier shot him in the back of his head, one shot. After he fell down, the two soldiers hauled him to toss into the Mekong River.

It was his end. The soldiers came back to rob the refugees of jewelry and silver bars. After they had been robbed, they were chased to run on a narrow path toward Pak Chom (อ. ปากชม). On the way the soldiers shot to the side of the people to scare them. One man was shot in the leg and another man got wounded in the upper arm before they arrived in the Thai soldiers' headquarters in Pak Chom. The informant said he was just a young boy when he crossed the Mekong River. After he saw the soldiers kill his cousin and throw him into the water, it hurt him for life. This type of abuse had happened time after time, but no one ever documented the situation for their records, or never wanted to reveal it to the public. They believed it was better to hide it than disclose it and cause further detriment to the victim's future life.

We walked for about a block to reach the road. There was a private *songthaew* (สองแถว), coming from the south and going up north. Once the driver's assistant saw many of us on the side of the road, he yelled to the driver to stop the pickup. He asked, "Are you Meo?" Brother-in-law said, "Yes, we are Meo and want to go to Ban Vinai Refugee Camp." The Thai man told brother-in-law that Ban Vinai was too far away, but they could take us to the police station in Sri Chiangmai (ศรีเชียงใหม่), which was very close. The driver turned his *songthaew* toward the south and let us, a total of 16 people, climb in. He drove us directly to the police station without any delay. Within ten minutes, he stopped inside the station which was next to the road. He pushed everyone out of his *songthaew*. He drove off up the road again and disappeared as the orange cloud of dust behind his vehicle rose up. Suddenly, the Thai police chief and five other police in light grey uniforms came out of their quarters with M-16 rifles pointing at us. The chief yelled very loud in Thai language, asking why we came to his place. We dropped our stuff on the ground. I was not afraid of them anymore because my fear was over after we crossed the river. As I looked at the others, they were not nervous either. Some of the young children looked at him like he was nuts. They did not understand a Thai word. But they probably wondered what the hell the tall man was yelling about. He said there was no food, no nothing to feed us. Why did we come to their country? In response, brother-in-law said softly to him that we did not just want to come to his police station or his country. We came there because of the communist regime's oppression. We had tried to live with them for seven years but could not endure the system anymore. The chief then asked what the real problem was. Brother-in-law told the chief that he lived with a terrified life all those years because he was a soldier of the American CIA. The moment brother-in-law told him this, it appeased the chief's anger and calmed him down. He then asked brother-in-law what battalion he was in. He said he was in the 21st Battalion. When he heard this kind of explanation, he seemed to change his attitude to be a different personality. It was the end of his anger. What a jerk! He told brother-in-law he knew all about the 21st Battalion. He said he went to stay quite some time in Long Cheng. Once the chief calmed down, so did his five fellow policemen. They dropped their rifle butts to the ground, relaxed, and watching the chief talk. What I thought was that they were nothing but jerks. He then instructed us in a few words in Hmong language not to pee or poop in the area, except in the restrooms. He told us to take everything to a tin roof building without walls next to the station. It was also next to a couple's house with some coconut trees in the yard. Before he left, he asked us if we had any money to buy food. Sai Khue, the father of the Lor family, pulled out a stack of paper money about one and a half inches thick and showed it to the chief. It was the paper money from the era of King Sisavang Vathana before the communists took over Laos. But the police chief joked with Mr. Lor that the money was from the era of King Anou. Actually, King Anou was the ruler back in the 1700s. He said the paper money could not be exchanged for Thai currency now. Then the police went back to their quarters.

It was 9 o'clock on the sunny day. The weather in Sri Chiangmai was not different from Viang Chan. The place where we were at the time and Viang Chan were still in the same geographical location, except the Mekong River divided the land. There were many mango, coconut, and longan trees, just like home. We knew that the Esan people spoke a language similar to Lao. Their stilt houses were sunken under the fruit trees the same as in Laos. I was thinking about my family in KM52 and wondering how they were doing now. If I had not left my home, I would be taking the tests in school by then. My second thought was that it was too late to think about my school, but it was not too late to think about Ban Vinai Refugee Camp. I hoped one day soon I might see my brother and cousins in the refugee camp. On the other hand, maybe my family was thinking either I had crossed the Mekong River successfully to Thailand, or I was dead in the river. They would be trembling one day when they heard that I was still alive. Even though it was a beautiful sunny day, my mind was not clear. Maybe the unexpected situation of being raped, robbed or tortured by Thai people was over, but there could be other bad things to come. I had no money with me. The only thing I had were two pairs of clothes and a pair of shoes. Without any help, the entire group would go hungry soon. I kept everything inside me, not to express my feelings to anyone because I thought the group may feel the same way as I did. After a while, the second oldest of the Lor girls, about 16 years old, went to turn on the water hose next to the restroom to wash her clothes and take a bath. It seemed she had no fear or worries about anything once we were in Thailand, which was what we had hoped for. She was also sort of happy, but not me. After she was done, my cousin and I went there next to wash ourselves. Cousin was still smiling when we talked. I thought it was good that he was not depressed yet. We took a bath and cleaned our dirty feet, which were stained with mud from the river. We washed our clothes and hung them to dry on the clotheslines. My white Thai made tennis shoes were filled with lots of mud. I needed to wash and dry them before the sun went down. Without anything to do, we just walked back and forth on the grassy area for a while before we came back to the house. Unlike when we were in the jungle, this was a time without home and family, and also living in another country. Now we were living in a building with a concrete floor without walls. It became our home.

Later in the day, a Thai man in civilian clothes came to interview us about the Russian built antenna on the high hill in Ek Xang, a place close to our KM52 village. He said people told the Thai intelligence in the past that it was built by the Russians. It seemed the Thai government still disliked the Russian government, even though they were friends with Communist China at the time. My cousin and I told him that we saw the antenna was there, but we were not sure what its purpose was. This was so true that we did not even know about such things because we were too young to know. Then the man left.

A few hours later another middle age Thai man in civilian clothes came on a motorcycle to ask if we had any silver. Since we did not have any food and the children were hungry, Sai Khue Lor again, pulled a handful of old French 20 cent silver coins to show to the man. The man told Mr. Lor he did not have any Thai baht with him, but he would be willing to take the silver to exchange for paper baht in the bank and bring the baht back. Unaware of the century old Thai number one robbery and bribery, Mr. Lor handed the silver coins to the man. Instead of thinking he might be just a thief, Sai Khue Lor thought the man would bring a handful of paper money to him within a couple hours. The Thai man put the coins in a little sack, jumped back on his motorcycle, turned on the engine, and took off. The bloodsucker devil flew away and never brought the money back to Mr. Lor. Finally, at dusk Sai Khue Lor learned his lesson that the man was a thief who intentionally took advantage of others. Obviously, we had heard more than enough before we came to Thailand, but he just lacked self preservation instincts. Since there was no paper money returned by the Thai man, there was no food for dinner, and his children were hungry for the night.

My cousin and I came there with empty hands, except each one of us had an extra pair of clothes to cover ourselves. Only one night and life had turned out to be hell. In that first day we just shared the rice we had with us from Laos which amounted to about a fist size for each person. When night fell, the concrete house without walls was our place. Hopefully, there would be no one come to rob us in the night because we were close to the police station. In the night I put my school bag with the clothes in it under my head to sleep. I laid my butt on the concrete floor and exposed my body to feed the mighty mosquitoes. We were crowded on the floor like a whole litter of pigs again. Life seemed ended here.

On the second day we were told by the chief to go to the temple very close by to beg for food when the Thai villagers served food to the monks at noon. The first morning I did not go to the temple with brother-in-law and cousin. By one o'clock they came back with some sticky rice and soup of bamboo shoots. The monks never eat meat. It was the leftovers after the monks had lunch. We had one meal for that day. On the third day I thought I had to go to the temple with cousin and brother-in-law to beg for food. It was the first time I had ever been to a Buddhist temple. Before entering the room, we had to take off our shoes in the shoe area because the floor was covered with mats. The monks sat on the side next to the statues while all the villagers sat on the outer side next to the entrance. Most of the people who came to serve food there were females. We were told to sit down with crossed legs next to the villagers. It was not easy to get used to this position and I could not cross my legs flat on the floor like everyone else. No matter how hard I tried to press my legs down, my knees were still about half a foot above the floor. Besides that, I wore tight pants. No one said anything, but the master said I was not respectful to their Sasana Phouk, meaning their religious belief of Buddhism. I knew he was just joking because he saw me try hard enough to flatten my knees. Before the lunch was served exactly at noon, they had to chant a long song. We did not sing with them, but sort of understood some words in it because the Lao and Thai languages are very similar. A version of the song the monks chanted we used to sing in Lao before class started before 1975, except they chanted in Thai. Also, the people who lived along the Mekong River were Esan, the Lao people who had been seized by the Thai government during the war centuries ago. This area used to be Lao territory, so the people spoke a mixed language, half Lao and half Thai. After lunch, they gave all the leftover food to us again. It was my first and our last time begging for food.

During the day the children were hungry. The two Lor girls went to see the couple next door. The wife was pious enough to give them some fresh young coconuts from their palm trees. She chopped them open in half and gave them to the two girls. The girls and young children drank the juice and chewed the flesh inside like starving animals. Because they were so hungry, they fought for the coconut juice that they had never tasted before.

It was the weekend, so the police stopped working. There was no way to know whether we would be sent to nearby Nong Khai (หนองคาย) or distant Ban Vinai Refugee Camp. Until the next Monday morning, on September 13, 1982, we did not have anything to eat. We were very weak and tired. Since the children were too hungry, they no longer cried. It was a hopeless situation. We thought maybe the police just let us stay there until we all died of hunger. Without any help, soon we might have to search for food in the trash cans, but there were no trash cans anywhere around either. At ten o'clock a Thai man wearing a brown grey uniform drove an old Japanese made truck to the station to see us. We thought it must be good news. He said he was going to take us to Nong Khai Camp, but in our thoughts, this was not the place where we wanted to go because they had transferred all the Hmong to Ban Vinai. He was a nicer man than the other Thai men. He was very calm when he spoke. We wondered if we could request to go to Ban Vinai instead. In truth, it was their choice. There must be no questions asked. Therefore, we could not refuse to do anything, but had to follow whatever the Thai police instructed us. We packed everything and climbed into the truck. The man drove us for about five minutes on a few crooked, dusty roads. Finally, he stopped in a building looking down on the Mekong River. He pulled the truck under the building's stilts to unload us. Then he told us to go upstairs to do some paperwork. Once we got up to the second floor, he disappeared inside the house.

About ten minutes later, he cameback with some papers, a stamp, plastic plate, and dirty black ink. Then he did some paperwork for us before he did our fingerprints. When he did my fingerprints, he told me that once we arrived in Nong Khai Camp, we should not attempt to escape to Ban Vinai. In the past they sent some refugees down there, but some Thai people got paid to take them to Ban Vinai Refugee Camp. I was silent for a while then replied to him, "Yes", meaning, we would not try to escape to Ban Vinai. I was not sure if he told everyone the same thing or only me.

It was a slow process. We were hungry, but there were 16 of us for only one man to process the paperwork. By 1 PM, he had finished up everything for us. He pushed us back onto his truck again. He drove along the Mekong River for a few minutes and then went back to the main road going southeast. After a while on the road before arrived in the camp, he stopped on the way again, where there were many big buildings. The man told us to stay in the truck while he was making a report to the officials there. He went inside one of those big buildings alongside the river. In this place we could see houses on the other side in Viang Chan. It was sad to see the place where we used to walk around. After 20 minutes, he came out of the building, opened the door, and jumped in to start the engine. He drove off to the main road for a short time then reached a gate with two men with grey uniforms standing next to it. Once we approached the gate, the arm rose up. He said a few words to those two men before he drove past the gate to go inside the camp. He pulled his truck on a large dirt area and turned off the engine. Then he told us to get out because we were in Nong Khai Refugee Camp.

After we all got out of the truck, a man came to see us. He was a small guy, even shorter than I was, but physically strong, and with a very calm manner. He told brother-in-law that he was from Laos as a refugee, too. He was managing everything for people in the camp. Without much discussion, he moved us to an empty building. When we were all in a bad situation like this, no matter what ethnic group we came from, it seemed we cared for and loved each other. The man did not seem to care whether we were Hmong or Lao. He tried to do anything he possibly could for us. It was not like in Laos where the Lao tried to push us up to the tip of the mountains. After we moved into the building, he left the scene for thirty minutes or so. Then he came back with pots, pans and utensils for cooking, blankets for sleeping, and nets to protect us from mosquito bites. We also received some cooked rice and egg soup with bean sprouts for dinner. At the time I though if we were to die, we might die for some other reasons, but not for lack of food anymore. However, the food portions were very small. It was just enough to keep us alive. They distributed cooked food twice a day for the first two days. Then we received uncooked rice and raw eggs thereafter.

It was an old place. The buildings were built with concrete floors, wooden walls, and tin roofs, some of which had become rusted and turned brown already. Some buildings were empty. When anything fell apart, never were any repairs made. There was a running water hose in the back area of the building for bathing. Inside the restroom there also was running and flushing water. The camp was a locked place with a high fence surrounding it and nowhere else to go. Without expressing my feelings to anyone, I thought we had come at the wrong time to end up in this wrong place. I don't have much memory of how big the camp was and how many buildings there were because we stayed for only a short time. Also, I was worried more about my future than interested in trying to explore the place. Later in the month when I arrived in Ban Vinai Camp, I could see that it was a civilized place like a Thai village, Nong Khai was a ghost place.

While living in Nong Khai Refugee Camp, we met one young Lao couple who lived in the next building. He had the same t-shirt and boxer shorts on every day. My cousin and I asked him one morning while he was steaming rice outside his building why they were there. He said his uncle was in the army and left Laos in 1975. At the time he resided in France. He and his wife crossed the Mekong River to Thailand a month earlier. When they crossed the river by swimming with rubber tubes, they lost all their belongings. Once they arrived in Thailand, he had the boxer shorts and wet underwear left. His wife had her bra, one skirt, and underwear she wore while swimming across the river. Inside the camp they hired him to teach a class for a few children, so he earned a little money to buy the t-shirt. That's why he had the same t-shirt on every day. When they got to the camp it seemed they had no way to go to France to be re-united with his uncle. As we discussed further, he said they might be transferred to Na Pho some day in the future because Nong Khai Camp was going to be closed soon. We did not ask him how many Lao families lived in the camp at the time either.

A few days later, the Lao guy who distributed supplies to us the first day told brother-in-law about the closing of Nong Khai Camp. It was already closed with one exceptional condition for temporary refugee people. He might be transferred to Na Pho Camp because he was not ready to be resettled in a third country yet. At the last minute if there was nowhere special he liked to go, he might as well go anywhere in the world. The United Nations would make the decision for all the refugees. His storytelling scared us all big time. Once brother-in-law heard this news, he was very concerned about our future. We felt it was a dead-end route for us. Our hope was to go to Ban Vinai Refugee Camp, but we ended up in the wrong place.

On September 19, 1982, at about 11 o'clock in the hot sunny morning while I was washing my clothes, brother-in-law called me to come back to the building. He told me he had talked to two Thai men who would be willing to take us to Ban Vinai Refugee Camp. He said the men wanted to know if we had anyone in the camp responsible for the payment once they took us there. Then he took me to see the two Thai men face to face, one was in his early twenties and the other in his late thirties. Brother-in-law told the two men he would like to let me go with them on their motorcycle to Ban Vinai to negotiate the cost with our relatives before they took everyone there. When we got to the camp, if my brother Qhua and Uncle Blia Cha, who lived there did not have money to pay them for the cost of taking everyone, then they would just pay for the cost of my trip only. The rest would just stay in Nong Khai Camp. At the time he told them that they must take me to Ban Vinai Camp, otherwise they would never get any money for the trip. Without having any experience with Thai people before, we assumed they were decent and honest. We hoped they would not do any harm to me after we left the camp on their motorcycle. However, my heart was beating fast again because I thought things might go the opposite way. They might just slash my throat any time on the way.

Once we ended the conversation with the Thai men, I jumped on their motorcycle in between them without anything with me and not even remember to turn back to wave my hand to brother-in-law and family behind. I left my wet clothes hang on the clothes line and my school bag with brother-in-law. From Nong Khai to Ban Vinai, in Pak Chom Minicipality, were many gates on the road at which the police searched travelers for illegal items. It was their policy or their traditional way. On the way they told me if we were asked where we were going, just tell the gatekeepers that we were going to investigate some opium cases in the north. I was panicked, but they were acting like some undercover agents who were on duty. They told me the trip was going to be four hours from Nong Khai to Ban Vinai.

In about 30 minutes, we arrived at their house. We went under the stilts; the ground level was an empty space. He parked the motorcycle, shut off the engine, and we got off. The real house was on the upper level. We climbed up stairs to the wooden second floor. There was one old man in his 40s, one beautiful young light-skin lady, and one little girl about two years old in the house. The young lady was the wife of the older guy who was taking me to Ban Vinai. The little girl was their daughter. The older man in the house was their older brother.

While we were at their house, there was a lot of discussion between the three men. They spoke half Thai mixed with half Lao because they were the Thai Esan. The older man asked me if I was hungry at the time. Even though I was hungry, I was sort of shy and afraid of being poisoned, so I told him I was not hungry. However, in the meantime, if they wanted to butcher me, they still could and there was nothing I could do. I tried to listen very carefully to their conversation to see what was going on. At one point I heard the old man tell them that they must be crazy to take people from Nong Khai to Ban Vinai for 700 baht per person. And what if when we got to the camp, my relatives did not have money to pay them, what would they do? As they debated on and on, the two younger men assured the old man that the people in the camp must certainly have the money to pay them. It seemed they did not agree with each other, but the two young men decided to go anyway. After the long conversation was over, the lady poked and pinched her husband in the ribcage a lot before we left the house. They both were smiling while pinching one another. She grabbed his arm and held him tight, not letting him go even when we were ready. Then he told her he was coming back as soon as possible. The lady let his arm free and went to the bedroom. The older man went downstairs. The man who was married looked at an eight by ten-inch mirror hung on the wall to clean his face. He said he should have many children already. He probably thought that he was old.

We went downstairs together to get on the motorcycle again. It was about 1 o'clock. Back on the road, every checkpoint we had been through had no gatekeepers because it was Sunday. On the weekends, guards tended to be lax on watching the travelers. After one hour driving on the road, the man drove us up to a high mountain on the left side of the road. It was a park where people were coming to gather for fun on the weekend. Once we got up to the park, the man turned off the engine and parked the motorcycle. They took me to tour the place for a while, and we stretch our bodies. Up there the business people grilled chicken on small bamboo sticks, fried bananas, and many other foods for sale. I did not see any foreigners, but many Thai people had stopped by on their tours. The younger man bought some fried bananas. He divided three pieces for each of us. After we finished eating the fried bananas, we walked back to the motorcycle to start our trip again. From that point on, the road was closer to the Mekong River. It passed along the foot of every high mountain along the river. Occasionally, we saw the water flowing very close to the road. Some areas were cool since there was less sun exposure under the high mountains. After a few hours on the road my face was numbed because I did not wear a helmet. We kept going without stopping. By sundown we got to an area which had a few houses on each side of the road. It was a small village, I guess. At this point there was a small dirt road on the left side perpendicular to the big one we were on. The man slowed down his motorcycle to make a turn onto that small road on the left, which went southward. Without asking where we were going, my heart was beating fast and I thought that either we were going to the camp or else they might just throw me in the cold forest. My second thought was that I should be confident and trust in them because they took me there for only one reason. It was that they needed the money. If they wanted to kill me, they would have done it at the beginning. That's why they drove me on the road for half a day. Whatever the circumstances were, I had to wait until the end.

After a while on the bumpy dirt road, we got to a huge village in a mountainous area. It had a mixture of tin and thatch roof buildings. The two men told me it was the camp. He did not follow either one of the two diverging roads, with one going southwest and the other going south, straight into the camp. Instead, he took us through a small pathway like a goat trail in between them, going toward three long buildings on the side of the hill. I later found out those were the school buildings for the camp. They asked me if I knew where my relatives were. I told them I did not know where they lived. But, if this was a Hmong place, we should be able to find them. We went past the buildings and up further on the hill where it almost went down to the other side. He shut off the motorcycle. We got off. At this moment we were inside the camp already. One of the things about Ban Vinai Camp was different from Nong Khai was that there was no fence surround it at all. We walked along the dirt pathway going down the hill back to the main road that came from outside the camp again. It was getting dark.

They were behind me all the time at this point because they were sort of nervous too. Thai people were not allowed to be inside the camp on a dark night like this. It got to the point that we did not know where to go, except we must ask people in those houses. Fortunately, we met a young man who came up from below the road. I asked him if he knew where my Uncle Blia Cha Thao was living. He said he did not know because the camp was too huge to know everyone. However, he had just met another Blia Cha Vang, who lived very close to this area, and who went to get water in the well in the canal down below. If we wanted to meet that Blia Cha Vang, he would be glad to take us down there. Then I thought we might just get shot at by running quickly down to the well if he was still there. Once we got down there, Blia Cha Vang was next to the well with two pails of water. He happened to be our Vang cousin who lived with us on the farm in Pha Hoi. They came to Thailand in 1979 after we separated in the jungle in Meuang Orm. We recognized each other very quickly. I told him I had just come from Nong Khai with these two Thai men. I wanted to go see my brother Qhua and Uncle Blia Cha Thao. Once we met each other, the young man who took us down there left the scene before I remembered to thank him for his help. Then cousin Blia Cha grabbed his bamboo pole to hang a pail on each end and put the stick on his shoulder to walk home up above the road where we came from. We followed him to his home. He dropped the buckets in front of the house on the dirt courtyard. Then he took us down to the main road below his home again. It was very dark and the people we saw walking were like shadows by now.

We walked over two bridges crossing small streams, and then passed a large dirt area. He told me this was a soccer field. I thought it was funny because the soccer field was on hard dirt without grass. When we passed the soccer field, there were still some people selling some small blue plastic bags of a liquid, hanging from stands alongside the street in the dark evening. He pointed out to me that those little bags were diesel fuel for sale. Buyers used it for their lamps at night. While walking he also said that at night Thai police frequently patrolled the streets. They just arrested anybody and put them in jail for no reason. Therefore, whenever people approached the police, they ran for their lives to get away from them to avoid being arrested. It seemed we had only walked for 15 minutes from his home to the west side of the camp. Then we went up an alley, passing three long buildings. When we got to number four building, he took us inside the fence to step into the front door. This was the building where my brother and uncle lived. *It was Center 4, Quarter 2, Building 4, and room 2.* The two Thai men were still behind us there. At the door of the kitchen house behind the main building, cousin Vang bent his head to look inside, and called for my brother Qhua to come out because I had just come from Laos. It was a big surprise for them. My brother came out. Everyone came out to welcome me. I was home.

My Vang cousin said he must return to his home because it was very dark already. It was also the time the Thai police began to patrol the camp. He left us for the night. I had survived from my trip from Nong Khai to Ban Vinai. I had hoped I would not die and soon be able to send some letters to tell my parents in Laos that their son had survived on his long dangerous journey. This was the place where I spent my next two years in unsanitary conditions to endure physical and mental illnesses.

Inside the kitchen which we called, "The cooking house, *tsev ua mov*" people looked at me like a stranger. The fireplace gave us a little light to see each other. They never thought that one day I might show up at their front door like I did now. I was surprised that their two younger sons grew up to be teenager like I was already. Aunty Blia Cha Thao told one of them to go buy a few packs of Thai noodles in the store, where a neighbor in the next building sold them, for our dinner. I told the two Thai men not to worry because we were safe. Once the teenager returned with the packs of noodles, they cooked and the two Thai men stayed with us to have dinner together. They told me to explain the situation to my brother and uncle how they would go back to Nong Khai to pick up brother-in-law and family. They said their price would be at least 700 baht per person. When I told them, as I was the interpreter, brother and uncle told the Thai men that they would like to talk to some of the Lor families about this matter the next morning to come up with some money because there was also a Lor family in Nong Khai as well. Uncle praised them for taking me up here to find them in the camp. No matter what happened, they were going to find money to pay them to go back to get brother-in-law and family in Nong Khai Camp the next day.

After dinner, they left the camp, but they did not tell us where they went to stay during the night. I was in a safe place, but throughout the night in my uncle's house, I just could not fall asleep at all. I did not know why either because I was not thinking much about anything. Finally, at 3 AM early the next morning, I fell asleep for a while.

At dawn that same morning, brother-in-law and his family arrived in the building, too. It was another surprise for me and the others again. Brother-in-law said after I left Nong Khai, another group of Thai people went there. They decided to go with that group instead of waiting for the two men who took me to Ban Vinai the day before. At 7 AM the men who took me there the night before came back into the camp. Once they arrived, they saw brother-in-law was in the house already. They were shocked and also wondered how the hell brother-in-law got there. They were not very happy that brother-in-law did not wait for them to go pick him up. They felt they were being betrayed and demanded their money. We knew trouble was coming to us for sure. My brother handed 750 baht in payment of my portion. Uncle Blia Cha told brother-in-law to walk out of the house and go someplace else for a while. Once he left, uncle told the Thai men he could not pay them since they were not the ones who brought brother-in-law's family into the camp. They had to pay the people who brought the family in. After a while the men could not do anything about it and left the building. It was the end of that ordeal.

10

THE REFUGEE CAMP

*"Lub yeej Vib **Nais** yog lub chaw lom zem rau ib tsoom tub **ntxhais**. Cov nquag ces mus khwv **nyiaj**, cov nkees ces mus twv **txiaj**. Thaum kawg ces ib cov nyob los ib cov yuav **mus**. Thaum twg puav lub neej dai taw mam nyob **tus**. Thaum Hmoob tawg mus nyob thoob qab **ntuj**, luag yuav saib hmoob tsis tsim **nuj** thiab luag yuav rhuav kom hmoob tsis nrog luag muaj **txuj**. Thaum Hmoob tej tub ki tsis paub hais hmoob cov **lus** ces Hmoob lub npe ploj mus **zuj zus**."*

Ban Vinai Refugee Camp, the place the elders loved to live while the youngsters had entertainment. As the sun rose in a clear sky, smoke rose everywhere in the huge mountainous camp. Since it had already been established for seven years, coconut and mango trees had grown taller than the tin roof stilt buildings. The one-story buildings, constructed by the United Nations, were hidden down below the fruit trees. It looked like a very civilized village rather than a refugee camp.

The camp was divided into eight centers at the beginning and later in 1984, the United Nations built another center, Center 9. Each center was also divided into quarters from one to eight. And each quarter had at least 10 buildings with one building divided into eight rooms for eight families. There was one camp leader appointed to oversee the nine center leaders. Then each center would have a leader to preside over the eight quarter leaders who would oversee those building leaders. Since it was only a refugee camp in which people did not reside permanently, leaders were replaced often. Whenever a leader left the camp to resettle in another country, he gave up his position, and a new leader took his place. It was the same for the school system. A principal for the elementary school of first to sixth grades was replaced every one or two years.

This camp was where I spent my two years without any fun. I was very poor, as were others. Everyone in the camp received some United Nations food assistance from month to month. However, the portion was too little, or just enough to keep us alive. They distributed rice and charcoal once a month. Other foods such as chicken, fish, and vegetables were distributed every two weeks. In our family we had a total of eleven people, including, uncle, aunty, their three sons, one cousin who just arrived from Laos, my brother, his wife, their two little children, and me. Sometimes we ran out of rice before we received the next month's distribution. It was good that Aunty Blia Cha was able to go get some extra rice for us from her close relatives. The Thai business people also sold a lot of food in the market, but we did not have money to buy their food. Those people who had more rice left at the end of the month were those who had money to buy better rice from the market to feed their families.

In the refugee camp, people mainly got money from their relatives who lived overseas in the United States, Canada, Australia, France, and elsewhere. Some people who had large families resettled in those countries could send some little money of their own to support their people in the camp each month. They also did business to earn money by sending jewelry made in the camp, herbal medicines, or any needle goods for their relatives overseas to sell. I did not have this kind of support. My married brother at the time had two little children. He was as poor as I was and waiting for food from the UN each month to feed his children and wife. My fourth brother, who arrived in Thailand

1979, came to the United States in 1980. He was in his first year in college at the time. When I arrived in the camp, he sent me $50 to pay my debt my brother borrowed to pay to the Thai men who brought me from Nong Khai. He did not have money to send to me each month like others. To earn money, we had to do heavy labor jobs by picking and planting crops for Thai farmers in the surrounding villages. We earned as little as 20 baht per day plus our lunch if we did heavy work. By doing this, we still only took a chance to be lucky. Sometimes at the end of the day, the farmer paid his workers, but then some gangs would rob them when they were on their way home. This robbing of refugee workers occurred very often after Hmong people arrived in Thailand and still continued to the people who went to live in Wat Tham Krabok. Even though it happened time after time, we could not do much to prevent it in our refugee status.

The scenery of the camp was beautiful by looking down from the mountaintops. Comparing it to a Hmong village in Laos or Thailand, the camp's area was huge, too. It was well established. Since there was always an influx of new people into the camp, more than the buildings could hold, more special small houses were built in every corner space next to the main buildings. Soon it became very crowded. The sanitary condition was very bad. There were six non-flushing squat little toilets in a row. But, six to eight families shared one of those six little toilets. Each toilet had its underground cesspool. The UN provided only one truck to drain the cesspools in the entire camp. The underground containers filled up very fast due to the large number of people using them. And the truck was over-used from dawn to dusk, but still not able to keep up to empty the underground tanks. The toilets smelled horrible when you entered them, and the air when the wind blew. I did not use the toilet very much. Sometimes I waited until dark and sneaked out to the forest outside the camp to get rid of the waste.

Up in the hills on the southside of the camp, the United Nations built three huge pools for dumping the waste. The first one was very bubbly on the surface with a dark marshy color. The second pool had no solids floating on the surface, but the liquid was dark green. The last one was clear with light green color like auto coolant because the liquid had been filtrated through two filters already. A lot of coconut and mango trees were planted around the pools. The green water was irrigated to nourish the trees. They were growing very well. Next to the three large pools was the trash landfill. Even though the fire was continuously burning the heap 24 hours a day, it kept rising higher each day.

The Thai people's businesses were amazingly blooming. They had the luxury of doing great business by bringing in more food and livestock to sell to the refugees. It made them prosper while their goods helped the refugees survive. Besides the food and animals, they brought in extra materials to sell to the refugees for building new houses. Most of the materials were reeds for making thatch for the roof, bamboo for the walls, and logs for the framework of the houses. Within the seven years after the refugee camp was established, the surrounding Thai villagers became prosperous because of the refugees. Those poor farmers, who used to live inside their little bamboo walls and thatch-roof houses, were able to afford to build cement or brick houses from their business profits because of the strong US dollars mailed from the oversea relatives to the refugees in the camp. For this reason, the local Thai people, farmers and business people as well, never thought some day the refugees might vanish. They hated the refugees, but also wished they would be confined in this crowded camp forever, so they would continue to bring them prosperity. They never realized one day their business would dry up like a drought without rainfall. The refugees were there only like a quick gust of wind. The Thai government could not keep them in this place forever. They had to go. Soon, not only the people, but all their buildings disappeared too. The entire camp would grow up in weeds, and later into farms.

The Thai market outside the camp alongside the main road going north toward Amper Pak Chom (city) used to be crowded with shoppers and traders under the orange dusty clouds from sunrise to sunset. Every morning when people inside the camp were pushing to the gate, waiting for it to be opened, we saw nothing but the thick orange color of the dust cloud rising up above the shoppers. Even though it was not a healthy condition, it was their way of earning a living. The dust particles fell like shaking powder in front of your face in the early bright sunrays. During the day the dust rose up as people walked or cars sped past and blew through. At night, as we could see the moon light through the road, the dust settled down on the ground as people left the area, creating a clear atmosphere again. Inside the camp, along each side of the dirt road, were tables and booths of flea markets selling food, livestock, clothing, and household goods. The old and young people were jamming the road along with bicycles, motorcycles, and occasionally some cars, leaving almost no space to go in any direction. It seemed that these people did not know where their future would be. All they did was to stay there to maintain their bad living conditions, endure the Thai oppression, and shop in the prosperous Thai businesses.

Another business the Thai people did with the refugees was the postal service in the camp. The postal owners deducted at least seven to ten percent from every single check from overseas while each post office received hundreds of checks each day. Soon they all became millionaires. They did so well because they paid no tax, paid no rent, and no electricity bill. But not too long afterwards, their business went dry. In the early 1990s, the camp was forced to close completely. It was unfortunate for those Thai business people, when most refugees were resettled overseas. Some of them were transferred to other refugee camps, while others who were not sick and tired of the Thai police yet, sneaked out to settle temporarily in Hmong Thai villages in other parts of the country. The foreign checks no longer flowed into the postal service as before. Not only did the postal services close, but the Thai farmers were no longer able to sell their sick pigs and chickens. The economic drought finally had arrived. The police had no more jobs of chasing people and extorting money from the refugees when the camp became cold. All they did maybe was chasing ghosts and rats. After the camp was closed, the buildings were demolished, burned, or shattered.

Farmers moved in to cultivate the camp and grew corn one spot here and one spot there under the dead fruit trees. It was the end of the Thai business with the Hmong in Ban Vinai Camp.

One informant, Chou Yang, said that even though their business died in Ban Vinai Camp, the merchants did not stop there. They continued to chase the Hmong refugees, who were from Laos, to wherever they moved because of the overseas checks. They did not do business with the Hmong-Thai people who had lived there for centuries because they did not have relatives in other countries who sent them money. After Ban Vinai Camp was closed, the same group of Thai businesses next move was to Wat Tham Krabok in Saraburi province, a place that continued to receive refugees. Those refugees who were unwilling to resettle in another country, entered the Wat to live near the drug treatment people. This was the institution that provided the largest drug treatment center to addicts in the area. Once the refugees moved into the Wat, they were considered as people seeking drug treatment. Here the Thai people had a good life once again by doing the same business as they had done in Ban Vinai. Their postal services were established to control the refugees' checks from foreign countries. The business of selling livestock and food items started to bloom again. They must have thanked the gods for sending the Hmong there to help their business grow and bring prosperity to their lives one more time.

At some point the postal owners played tricks on the illiterated elder refugees. The informant said there were many instances of people being accused. Sometimes, one elder had only one check in the Thai mail box, but he was told he had two checks by giving someone else's check to him, too. The man could not read and he just cashed the check for him. Later, they accused him of stealing someone else's check. Then the Thai people punished the man, forcing him to pay for the crime, with the principal plus interest. Even though this happened very often to many individuals, the elders never got the message across to each other in the community to be aware of it. Until the early 2000s, the refugees finally brought the dispute up to the monastery head, who was

Luang Por, the man who oversaw the people there. They fought and won the case. The refugees were allowed to establish their own postal service. The refugee postal service owners charged 25 baht per check. Once the Thai postal services did not have any more mail coming to their box, they complained to the army which was in control of the Wat at the time. The soldiers were having headaches and angry from these lousy complaints. Then they demolished all the Thai business buildings there. The Thai businesses disappeared. After ten years, these leftover refugees were sent to America in 2004 and thereafter. The gods must have changed their minds by not keeping the Hmong there for the Thai business. Soon the crowded houses in the flat valley, adjacent to Wat Tham Krabok, were empty one after another and demolished. Their chickens, pigs, cows, and buffaloes, waiting for US dollars from the refugees to buy them, were dead in the hot sun because no more captive hungry people bought and ate them. Not only the animals were wasted, but also bowls of noodles and green vegetables were just exposed to flies and dried in the hot sun. Their businesses died as the economic drought arrived for a second time.

The parents in the camp still had the memories of the good climate in Laos. Even though they have been through the artillery shell explosions, ripping up their houses, and bursting them into flames during the war, some of them still wanted to return home because it was their birthplace. The things that came into their heads, day and night, were their old homes in Laos. It was their normal way of life. However, their children, who were carried from Laos at a very young age and those who were born in the camp, had no memories of the loud, horrific sound of artillery shell explosions or how wide the Mekong River was that their parents had crossed. They heard their parents mention the danger, the hunger, deprivation, and what they suffered from the war, but the children had never been exposed to it, or felt what it was like. Growing up in the refugee camp, what they knew was to sleep at night in the stilt buildings and eat their meals in the dirt floor kitchen. Their boundary was never to cross the perimeter of the refugee camp. The danger they saw was when Thai police beat the crap out of refugees with their sticks when caught sneaking out of the camp. When the parents taught them about family values, the lessons never sank into the children's ears. This refugee camp generation spoke another strange new language which was a mixture of Lao, Thai, and Hmong together. It was cool youth talk, but living as a captive. There was nowhere to go in this new life.

In the refugee camp, youths became such a crazy generation from1976 to the time the camp was forced to close in the early 1990s. Their lifestyle had changed from working on the farms to waiting for food assistance from the United Nations. The need of financial support was the main thing in their daily life in the camp. They did every possible thing they could to earn a living in addition to the meager food assistance. The young males started to learn how to sew embroidery pieces *(paj ntaub)*, which used to be done only by females. They were like male transgenders. These males no longer cared much about the traditional gender roles of only doing what was appropriate for them. The old lifestyle of sons working in the fields, chopping wood, and many other things with their fathers while daughters were helping mothers at home to take care of the younger siblings and cook meals diminished in the camp. It was a period of people accepting the change of responsibilities in the family. This was one of the groups of males who did female work. The second group was those older children who could afford to take private English classes, month to month, which were taught mainly by Hmong instructors. These classes cost about five to ten baht per student per month, depending on the level. This group was able to pay private classes because they had more relatives in other countries who sent money to support them, or those who did good business inside the camp. The third group was those who could not afford to pay for English school or had no desire to learn. They carried the Japanese made tape recorders, which was the most popular type, listened to the first Hmong produced classic music, and chased girls or guys around the camp day after day. This group had the most fun without any worries about whatever might happen in their future. They were crazy enough to do wild things by saving their Thai baht coins to go see adult movies in the Thai theater outside the camp, which their parents considered as the most disgusting thing to do. The Thai businesses did not care about legal age because the watchers were only refugees and money was what the owner's needed. The fourth group was those who were brave and strong. Letting their hair grow long was their most desired style. They imitated Jackie Chan's Kungfu style and practiced in the forest without exposing themselves to public view. Young men carried Chinese flipping fans and flipped them constantly in front of young girls. They thought it was cool. The black Chinese Kungfu style clothes and shoes were very popular among them. They believed that the Hmong used to be good in martial arts before they lost their land to the Chinese people and migrated to Southeast Asia. They should go back to follow their ancestors' footsteps which had been lost in China. Yeah, it was very cool, but if you made a little misstepped then you broke your neck. It was the end of one life. This unsuccessful Kungfu style became very popular for a short period. In the end, their hopes faded and they did not get what their ancestors left in China. The refugee camp was closed. They landed on US soil instead. They left their training camp in the forest in Thailand. The master and the disciples each resettled in a different part in the United States, without communication. The martial arts were lost forever because they became busy with their new lives in America, by pursuing industrial jobs. It was the beginning of their American Dream to earn a living in America. The fifth group was first ever to learn how to play western musical instruments such as acoustic guitars. This replaced the Hmong bamboo flute *(raj blaim)*, double string violin *(raj phlauj taub)*, mouth harmonica *(ncas)*, and the mouth pipe organ *(qeej)*. Some young men carried their acoustic guitars on their shoulders wherever they went or sat on the porch on the hot days, brushing up and down the basic notes. Instead of hearing the sound of the Hmong bamboo flute at night like in Laos, the sound of guitars was striking for entertainment. The last group was those who loved to practice sports, especially soccer. The dirt soccer field was full of people from sunrise to sunset. They played games to earn Thai baht. They bet one to five bahts per person per game. It was a societal change, or maybe it was the era of youth culture. They wore soccer shoes and sport shorts or elastic trousers wherever they went in the hot sun, pretending to be cool every day as though they were in practice games for an important tournament. I thought they were brainwashed. Why would young girls put socks and sandals on their feet while walking on the dusty road with temperatures of 90 to100 degrees? It was weird. I thought my T-shirt, boxer shorts, and flip-flops were more appreciated. It was like ocean waves pushing on to the shore as the year went by. Some waves were bigger than others. One person did one thing then soon everyone copied it. Each group did things differently whether it was right or wrong. They believed what they did was cool, but, above all, everything was away from the Hmong traditional village way of life.

The refugee camp was a safe haven for people from Laos, but was also a heaven. Another group started to watch cockfights. This was very popular with the Thai people. Then gambling started as the wind blew the smell around the camp. One Saturday morning in 1983, one of my cousins and I went to see cockfighting outside the camp. It was usually held inside the camp. On this particular day they said it was moved to a Thai farmer's house outside the camp, about a half mile away. When we got there, all the people had brought their roosters in. All the spectators were refugees. We did not realize that the Thai people might play a trick on us by luring people into their territory like we had lured animals into our cages. Suddenly, a truck with five policemen pulled up in front of everybody. They jumped off the vehicle with M-16 rifles aiming at us and gave the command not to move. Some shot into the sky. Others shot into the ground to apprehend the people. The farmer, who arranged the game, stood quietly against the pole next to the ring, watching us. The police yelled in Thai language why people had a cockfight. It was illegal gambling. I thought it was such a big lie and ridiculous, but I was very nervous too. They had cockfighting every single weekend all over the country and also bullfights in a ring about a quarter the size of a soccer field. Many bulls and roosters died each day as the games were taking place. The Thai people were the number one gamblers, but now they could punish the refugees for cash. Then my cousin and I were scared to dead for fear of being arrested and sent to jail. My cousin said he wished he could transform himself like magic and disappear from the scene. It was only his wish. After a while the police decided to release the minors. My cousin and I along with other younger ones were pulled out from the crowd to go home. We were just lucky that day. As soon as we left the area, a bigger truck arrived in the place to load up the men. They were sent to Meuang Loei for charging. Two days later they all were released, but each person had paid a 3,000 baht fine. Then we knew that the policemen and the farmer were the real criminals and conspirators to arrange such a game to solicit cash because they knew the refugees had money even though they were refugees. It was their traditional way of gambling. We gambled with cockfights, but they gambled by pressing charge against people for large amounts of cash. Some people said the middle fish ate the little ones until his stomach was full, then a bigger one just ate the middle one. This way he does not have to chase too much to catch the little ones to fill his own stomach. That's why the one Thai farmer lured everyone into his stilt house, and then the Thai police took over from there.

Sometime earlier in 1982, two American women visited us in the camp. In the first time they met us, one lady told me to speak English. I wondered why the American woman told me to speak English instead of speaking American. She did not even realize that I was in the camp for only a few months and had not learned any English. That was a moment I felt funny when she said, "Speak English, Speak English," but I could not respond. Each day when they returned to our building from visiting other people in the camp, they were sweating and saying it was too hot. For us, it was just fine. The woman who told me to speak English said, *Kub heev kuv yuav tuag,* meaning "Too hot I will die".

One day my young cousin and I went with them to visit brother-in-law who came with me from Laos. On our way back home when we got to the flea market, where people sold a lot of chicken, pork, beef, and vegetables, that women asked me what we and mother wanted to eat. By mentioning mother, she meant Aunty Blia Cha. I saw many flies on the meat, so I pointed to the vegetables rather than the meats and said, "We eat those." She was laughing and saying she ate meat, but I wanted to eat vegetables. She bought neither the vegetables nor the meat. Because of the hot weather, I was not sure how they could cope with life in the camp and how could they sustain the mighty orange dust clouds that rose up on the road when a car drove by.

Among other things, the climate in Ban Vinai was a different matter. The weather was even hotter than my last Lao hometown of KM52. In the summer the temperature rose up to 106 Fahrenheit degrees. I was not used to it, or maybe I suffered from the mosquito bites too much while I was in Sri Chiangmai, our first stop, and Nong Khai Refugee Camp. After two months in the camp, I had an ear infection with a very high fever for many days. I used to have ear infections when I was about six or seven years old. My left ear collected a wax ball about the size of a corn kernel inside the auditory canal. It was the mixture of wax and the infectious crust combined. When I was little, my parents tried to dig it out, but they could not because it was stuck and too painful. It stayed in my ear until 1990 when I was in the US Navy and one Hospital Corpsman on the ship was able to flush it out.

For some reason after the illness affected me in the camp, my right leg became numb, and in the end, it was paralyzed. I was pale, weak, and had to visit the hospital almost every week for treatment of my illness. All my classmates from Laos, who came to the camp after me, were healthy. They had fun every day by playing soccer in the field or chasing girls everywhere in the camp while I was walking like a crippled man. I used to be physically and emotionally strong before I crossed to Thailand. Now I was weak and was like a three-year-old again, waiting for help because sometimes I was not even able to bath myself and wash my clothes. It was very degrading for me. The life of a refugee no one ever knows unless that person has been through the situation. You felt like you were the lowest quality human being. My parents were still in Laos, so I feared that some day I might die without ever seeing them again. I wished I never had escaped from my home in KM52 in Laos. I took a picture with my cousin. It turned out very blurry. My brother sent that picture to my family in Laos. Father sent a letter to us, asking what happened to his darling son because the picture was like he had lost both of his eyes. He worried so much about me. It was too bad that I was out of luck.

While living in the refugee camp, my imagination about the US was huge. My brother who resettled in the United States and his American friend sent me a postcard with the blooming summer flowers. Without asking them for further information, I thought everywhere in America was the same as what I saw in the postcard I received. In my thoughts, this place must be beautiful all year-around. Every side of the road in America would be fenced or decorated with silver and gold. In addition to that, while visiting the hospital inside the camp, I saw many white people. They talked very soft to the point they almost whispered to each other. I thought maybe in America no one yelled at each other. Even though I was very sick at the time, I still had the hope one day I was going to be better in a nice place like I saw in the postcard. We also had experienced the oppression and brutal treatment by the Thai police so much while we were there. Someday, I hope I would be living with only nice people with no worries of being oppressed again.

In December 1982, my brother's American friend, Marlin Heise, came to the camp and visited me. He joked with me through the interpreter that he wished he could put me in his large suitcase when he returned to Minnesota. It was just a good joke. After a couple weeks of visiting many families, he left the refugee camp without me in his large suitcase. Instead, it was full of clothes and many silver gifts to relatives in the US from people whom he has visited. His suitcase was much heavier than if my body were in it. My illness continued after the American friend left.

After Marlin Heise left the camp, I thought I should try to learn English. I tried to prepare myself in case I have a chance to resettle in the US. I had nothing to do other than walking around in the camp, laying down under the trees, and watching the blue sky. I was poor but tried to attend some private English classes since the cost was about five to ten bahts per person a month. It was not very successful for me. I was sick and weak and able to attend the class for only two or three days per week while they were taught five days a week. Although I had studied English for two years, I have not learned very much before I came to Minnesota.

Lee Chai built a temple for worship and taught Pahawh script. He was the host of his band. They improvised their own music, wrote their own songs and poems. The songs they sang, the poems they recited, and the comedy skits they played were very deep in meaning and tied very much to our culture. Their poems were about how Hmong people suffered from their hardship life during the war and when people were rushing to board the C-130 in Long Cheng. They recited the poems of the new life in the refugee camp where people became alcoholics and gamblers. Sometimes it was more about comedy. It was a prediction that Hmong youth were moving toward gang activities. It recited how teenagers have nothing to do, but saved Thai baht coins to go see adult movies in Thai theaters, and so on, etc. The nonstop singing of songs, the poems, and skits one after another from 8 o'clock in the morning to 4 o'clock in the afternoon had inspired the crowded audience, old and young, that was packed into the half block dirt area. They enjoyed and laughed all day long as the non-stop music pumped into their ears. The people did not seem to feel hungry at all or they did not want to leave the area because they might miss the good stuff. The sound of music and comedy on stage were too fun to listen to so some ladies did not realize their babies were on their backs under the hot sun of over 90 degrees. The men and women, old and young, were snapping their cameras every second to capture the movement on stage. The clicking sound of tape recorders to record the music and the poems followed as each began and ended. The talking voices of people rose up soon after the sound of music faded away, but it became quiet again as the next one was taking place. I noticed that some other centers also set up their own stages for playing musical entertainment during the new year. Some had marching bands, but sang the old Lao songs which I heard a long time ago when I was in first grade school in Laos. They did really good on their performances.

However, it was embarrasing when the Thai police officers were watching. They were laughing that Hmong were using Lao ideas. It was a Hmong refugee camp but practicing Lao culture. The one word to describe it was, "Copy." By comparing Lee Chai's band to others, his was more Hmong, emotionally touching from beginning to end. It was also reminiscent of our history from bad to good.

We faced one problem after another. In April 1984, while the United Nations started to clear up the cemetery outside the camp to build Center 9, additional to the eight original centers, for transferring refugees from Camp Nam Yao, our building in Center 4, burned down to the ground. The fire started in the last building on the top of the hill, building number 9. No one could tell exactly how the fire started. Someone said an opium man left his oil lamp on after he finished smoking and it burned his mosquito net, then spread to the walls before they could stop it. When the fire broke out, I told my brother that we must move out all the household items to a safe place before it got to our building in case the fire did not die out. We just dragged everything we could, blankets, kitchen utensils, rice, and water jugs, to a sugarcane garden a few hundred feet away which we believed the fire would not spread to. My brother and I made several trips back and forth while sister-in-law and the two children waited and watched everything we dropped in the sugarcane garden. As we watched, the people did not cooperate to put out the fire. No one even tried to use the water in the water tanks in each end of the buildings to spray on the fire or on other unburned buildings. The people who lived in the burning buildings were running to save their lives, so they would not get burned. Others stepped back, watching to see how fast the fire would spread. The weather was super hot with temperatures as high as 90 to 100 degrees Fahrenheit. During this time of the year there was no rainfall yet, so everything was very dry. They kept watching and hoping that the fire would die out by itself at some point. It did not stop at all. The main buildings were built with tin roofs and wooden walls. The walls were from trees with resin like the pine trees which were penetrated by fire very easily. The kitchens behind the main buildings were built with reed thatch roofs and bamboo walls, which fire also penetrated like magic. Everything was burning so fast, like pouring oil on it. The flames continued to blast and lick from one building to the next, down the steep slope. The gushing spiral of black smoke shot up into the sky, forming dark clouds blocking the afternoon sun. Within 30 minutes or less, two-third of the main buildings in the row disappeared, leaving behind red-hot charcoal and ashes on the ground. By the time the fire truck arrived at the scene, there were only three buildings left. The building number 4 we lived in was gone, too. It had burned so fast that those people living in the building where it started did not have time to move out any of their belongings. They cried, with their palms covering up their faces because they had no home for the night. Those people who decided not to move anything out had nothing left after the fire, except the clothes that covered their butts. Children gathered in some empty spaces in the corners, making hand salutes, watching the empty spots of hot ashes of their homes, and wondering what had happened within the last 30 minutes.

We were homeless again. All the residents in those buildings had to seek refuge with relatives within the camp. That evening we had nowhere to go, so we moved to an uncle's house that was very close by to stay temporarily, waiting to see if the United Nations would rebuild new buildings in the old spaces. It was a slow process because the UN was just in the process of clearing up the cemetery to build more buildings for the refugees from Camp Nam Yao. I had no place to sleep. We lived in one house, but at night I had to go sleep in another uncle's house. We were poor before, but this time we became even poorer. This is exactly what elder people said about a bat without a nest. That was why he hangs his head down.

Three months went by, the UN had not started to rebuild the burned buildings yet. They completed all the new buildings in the cemetery area, which was called Center 9, to receive the people from Nam Yao as planned. The camp officials were considering the transfer of all the residents from the burned buildings to some of the new buildings in the new center, but my brother, along with other people, hesitated to move into those new buildings. First, the new center was built on top of the graves, so people did not feel comfortable living there. In Hmong history or even Asian history, there were never houses built on top of a cemetery. This time they were built on top of graves for people to sleep on them. On earth, there was nothing worse than this. There were a few buildings built next to the toilet waste pools and trash landfill. Those residents who lived in those buildings had to breathe in the odor from the pools every minute. Second, they thought that they might not be allowed to move back to Center 4 once the buildings were rebuilt. Therefore, we would rather stay with relatives as we were and see what would happen.

It seemed the Hmong people in Laos had trouble all the time. One morning while returning from English class, I met our *taseng* from KM52 in Center 4 where we had lived. I did not talk to him long enough to find out when he arrived and why he came. All I did was to tell him that I was happy to see him again and I went home afterwards. But the one thing I knew, without asking, was that he must be accused of something and could not stay in Laos anymore. That's why he was in the refugee camp with us now. My family in Laos also faced a tougher situation at the time. After I left Laos, my third brother and Father thought maybe they made the wrong decision by letting me escape to Thailand. The officials in the village were even more suspicious of my brother. They were watching him closely for his activities, although he did not do anything wrong, except worked as an ordinary peasant.

One day my brother received a letter from the city requesting him to go for training. He knew they were playing a trick on him in order to get him arrested because the letter did not specify what kind of training. Usually when they called people to go to attend a seminar, his friends also received the notification because the Pathet Lao often required several people to go for training each year. Therefore, the letter he received was to call him to the city and be arrested soon thereafter. He did not bother to show up. Instead, he returned the letter to the council to respond to the city. He believed if he stayed in the house, he either would be arrested or even killed. In June 1984, he took my family and three others and crossed to Thailand.

As I observed the living situation in the camp, the refugees lost track of their future. They did not know whether to go to other countries or stay in the camp for the rest of their lives. They were divided into many groups due to the political and ideological beliefs of each group. The majority decided to go to resettle in many other countries, based on how many people the host countries would accept. A small portion of the refugees who still had relatives in Laos wanted to return to their home country. Another group was waiting for the return of Vang Pao. Some families of this group stayed in the camp for the longest time until the camp was closed in the early 1990s. The very last group joined Pa Kao Her. "When the Pathet Lao chased the jungle Hmong in the Phou Bia area of Laos in 1979, Pa Kao escaped and crossed to Thailand. Once in Thailand, he went to visit Wat Tham Krabok in Saraburi province. When he arrived there, Luang Por, who was succeeding to be the head of the Wat, did not have much to offer to Pa Kao, but provided him and his followers refuge" (Chou Yang, etal). Then he moved to settle and build his temple for worship in Nam Tuan Village, at the Lao-Thai border. He named his temple, *Yaj Ces Teb Tsim Meej*, according to Yee Vang. In there he played a strong key leader to lead his followers.

One activity I saw in the camp from when I arrived in 1982 until I left in 1984 was that many men kept going back to Laos. There was a young man living in the building above ours. He disappeared for a few months, then showed up again. Each year he went back to Laos three or four times. He, along with others called themselves the, "Team." He said they were sent to Laos for duty to gather information for the Neo Hom. It seemed they never had enough war. What these people believed was that one day they would have a piece of land of their own. But in truth they were kept ignorant and blind. They felt like they were honored to do the job and had high priviledge from their boss. They did not realize that the potatoes their leaders baked in the fireplace for them to watch for many years were only rocks. One informant said they went all the way to Bouam Blong, one of the former Hmong Army sites in Laos. Some went to linger in Na Yao (Long Rice Terrace), a territory north of Viang Chan, and the place that was most commonly assigned. Some went there because they wanted to, even without any specific assignments. Some of them never came back because they had been killed in gun battles or some just did not want to come back to the refugee camp. By returning to the camp, they felt they were coming back to prison. Even though they lived in the jungles in Laos for many years, it felt more like home with less stress. Their lives in nature were better and more peaceful in some ways.

One day a group of men, about ten, were sitting under Uncle Blia Cha's stilt house, discussing their duty on the other side of the Mekong River. A middle age man from the Thao clan, knew their conversation was of no use. He verbally blasted the group that their purpose of going back to Laos was only to go shoot monkeys and squirrels. He called them such liars because he knew people who were on duty to fight a war were different. The group knew that man got on their nerves, so they all became quiet for a while and slowly left the area one by one. It was a well-done job.

In early 2003 I met a man in Saint Paul, Minnesota, who came to the US in 1994. He said he went to Laos many times since 1976. He went there as a "Team" member. In late 1993, he returned to Ban Vinai Refugee Camp. The place had already become cold and empty. The coconut trees had been cut down and the pulps had been chopped for food. Once he saw this with his own eyes, he knew it was the end. He was too blind to see the stone potatoes in the ashes of the fireplace. They were only rocks. The time he spent going back to Laos all those years, when he was a young man until he started to have grey hair, meant nothing. His children born in the camp were married and had their own children. They learned nothing in life except producing another generation of their own offsprings. His friends, who decided to resettle in another country in 1976, had children who received their bachelor's and master's degrees already. But his children were walking around and kicking up dust in the camp for 16 years. He then rushed to Phanat Nikhom to interview for coming to the United States before the United Nations closed the camp. He believed this was his luck and his last chance.

It was one of the lessons from our past needs to be learned for our future and hopefully we will not walk on the same path again. Within the refugee camp, people pre-established their own official positions for future government jobs. They elected their future officials such as *taseng*, mayors, and governors for each district, city, and province, respectively. They hoped that someday in the future if they had a piece of land, those who were pre-elected would sit in those positions in the new land. It was like we had just built the cars, but we did not build the parking spaces. Although we had a whole bunch of cars, we have no lots to put them in. Without realizing how politics, economics, society, and ideology have changed around the globe, and that the old era was diminishing while a new one was emerging, they had hopes for their pre-establishment future positions. The younger generation, however, argued that an illiterate person could not sit in that position anymore in this new era. We are living in a generation where televisions and computers are working like magic while the pre-appointed elder officials had not caught up with the education they needed to rule the younger ones. Besides the lack of education, we fought too much among ourselves. The old knives should be kept in a good place for souvenirs and it was time to use the new ones. They believed in the political and idealogical influence only, but in reality, a minority group of people cannot rule the majority people. In translation, it would not be possible for the Hmong, a tiny ethnic group, to rule the entire population of Laos.

Secondly, we were not ready to have a piece of land yet. Even if there was one piece for us, we would not know how to take care of it. We should put this into the true perspective of our lives today. We always liked to take pictures in a nice garden with blooming flowers. But, the garden belonged to other people. We did not grow one. When we cleared the forest to establish a new village, we did not plant new trees back in it. At first, we cut down big trees and soon we burned and cleared up weeds. As the years passed, dirt and dust were commonplace. For other people, when they cleared up the forest to build a new village, they planted their fruit trees in every empty space. In a few years the fruit trees such as mangoes, coconuts, pears, and lychees, just to name a few, would grow to take over the loss of forest they had cut down. For us, we liked to grow only short-term crops such as corn, rice, bananas, papayas, yams, and sugarcane. We considered the long life of fruit trees would take many years before they had fruit for harvesting. We even felt like the fruit trees would take a half century before they bore fruits. We could not wait until that day. We constantly moved before the trees bore fruit, whether there was a war interfering or not. Throughout our history, we did not build and preserve monuments. Instead, we destroyed them. We sometimes worshiped other people's Buddhas, but did not worship our own Buddhas. A Buddhas is a Buddha. Neither one can talk, nor can it move. The difference is that they painted theirs in gold, but we painted ours white or grey. We invented something today, but in the next few years we do not have it. For instance, the 1980s classic music and other things we produced now all gone. No one cared to collect them and store them in a good place. That's why the old political ideas were senseless to the younger ones. Therefore, when the older generation wanted to stay in the refugee camp and hold on to their fake titles, the younger generation wanted to go to other countries to get education.

In this crowded unpleasant place, I got nothing and did nothing due to my health conditions. One choice was to get out of there as soon as possible, but I was not sure where to go. The one thing I hoped for was to come to America. Going to a different third country was not a choice, but I hoped it was a survival situation for me. However, as a single person who was also underage at the time, my chances were very meager. I wished my brother who was in the camp would accompanied me to the US. But, he did not want to go to another country anymore. He actually had failed the interview process a couple years before I came. He was in the army before, but in the interview process they asked him some unrelated stupid questions which he had no clues about. After he failed the first time, the UN also called him back to interview for a second time. But, he was pissed and did not bother to show up for the second interview. Thus, he said he did not want to come to the US. Then I asked him to go with me to the UN office to separate myself from his family by making a new ID for me. The ID was called BV which stood for Ban Vinai. After I got my own BV, I tried the interview process through the UN two times without letting him know, but I failed.

Finally, in June 1984 the Minor Refugee Program accepted me to come to the United States with a simple interview process. In early July, I was set to go with a group of 12 other kids to Phanat Nikhom Camp in Chonburi (ชลบุรี), near Bangkok. There were one Vue, three Vangs, five Xiongs, one Lor, two Yangs, and I. I was the only Thoj. I consulted with my brother one more time if he decided to go to the interview process again to see if he could come to the US with me. He said he wanted to stay because my parents had just arrived in Chiang Kham Camp that month. He wanted to wait until my parents and brothers were ready to go, then he would be ready to go with them at the same time. This was my last intention of asking him to resettle in a third country. Once I got the answer from him not wanting to go, I thought it was time to look for my future, not his. While I was on my way to Phanat Nikhom or to the United States, if I became too sick and died, that would be my bad luck. On the other hand, I might get better after departing Ban Vinai Camp. I left the camp on the day that I was scheduled.

Life was even sadder as we were about to separate from one another. A couple days before my departure, my brother went to pick some corn in the field outside the camp, which we had planted in April. I told him to wait for another week when the corn would be completely ripe for picking. He said some of them should be ready to pick now. Since we went to plant them together, we should eat them together before I left. It struck my mind so deep upon hearing what he said because I was too young to think about the coming separation between us for a lifetime. Sometimes while in the camp, I was too sick, depressed, or very angry about everything. Thus, most often I did not pay as much attention to him as I should have.

Before my departure, some of my cousins told me the same corny story that had been told for many years that it was not such a good idea to go to another country because the Hmong former general was coming back to fight another war in Laos soon. They said it would not be too long before we all could go back to live in Laos peacefully. But, I thought I had suffered enough throughout my childhood before coming to this refugee camp. I did not want my body to get shot at by the enemies. It was senseless that people tried to create such a belief to influence me. Coming to America scared me to death, but I had no other choices. On the other hand, if I ever had a chance to go back to Laos, what would I do to earn a living? I would just go back to pound the dirt and repeat my parents' farming lifestyle again. But I also thought, what if the other side of the world was not like our own world. I saw a picture of my friend's brother who was living in California at the time. The picture was taken on the highway when he was returning from picking oranges. There was a basket of oranges next to him, along with his car. It depicted a background with only brown dried grass. It was a life without nature, I thought. It was very sad.

There were many problems brought up for the staff in the UN office to solve each day. Many families separated from each other in the camp. If the parents wanted to stay but the children wanted to go, they had to separate their family documents through the UN office.

Some newly married couples had to separate too, if the wife's family was ready to leave but the husband's family wanted to stay. The young couple had to divorce again to allow the wife to go with her family or vise versa. It caused the staff in the office to have a lot of headaches. When people did not want to go anywhere, then they reminisced what the foreteller said a few decades ago. This was what they remember the foreteller *Shao Joua Xue* said, "One day Hmong would gather in a place. Then the evil eagle *(Liab Nyug)* would howl from the trees to call Hmong people to go. Whoever slept face up and answered the call then they had to go. Whoever slept on their side would have to stay." Some interpreted it as when a person sleeps face up, that meant the person is dead. If you are dead, then you would go. The time had arrived. But it turned out that those who slept on their side were the ones who used drugs. They laid sideways when they smoked opium. They all failed the drug screening process. They did not have to go. Those who slept face up like what the foreteller said were the non-drug users. They passed the interview process and got to go. The evil eagle howling voice was the loudly speakers the UN installed on the high trees or the high posts throughout the camp. Whoever did not show up for the interview, their names were called very loud from the speakers. This story struck them big time. Therefore, they made every excuse to get away from the interview, so they did not have to go to a third country. That's why there were so many people who lingered too long in the refugee camp.

July 3, 1984, was the day I boarded the bus to Phanat Nikhom Camp. The heartbreaking moment had come when I was to leave my relatives behind in the crowded camp. I had only 300 baht, (about $14) in my pocket, which I had won in the Thai lottery, and relatives and one aunt gave me over 100 baht for my trip. My little suitcase was full of clothes which I completely packed the night before. By 7 o'clock the buses had already arrived on the hard dirt soccer field. The people who really wanted to stay in the camp did not care very much about me. They were not interested in pursuing a new life in a new country. They believed that coming to America was to bring one's body to feed the giant monster. Those who wanted to come, but did not have the chance, were desperate about my trip. They wished one day it would be their turn to pack and leave, just like I did. Most of my relatives, including my sister and brother-in-law, came to visit me early in the morning during breakfast time. They said it would be like I had disappeared forever after my departure. They were very sad to see their family members leaving for America and other countries every month.

By 9 o'clock it was goodbye time. I did not have anything left except to remember the place in my memory and keep the mental pictures for future souvenirs. I walked out of my uncle's house with tears on my face, carrying my suitcase, and gave my brother's three-year-old daughter a hug. It was very sad. It was the time to focus on my road ahead. It was the kind of emotion that happened to everyone who left the camp. My brother and some of the cousins walked with me for 10 minutes down to the dirt soccerfield where the six buses were lined up in a row to take us away. When we arrived, the early people had already boarded them. Alongside the buses, people old and young, tall and short, skinny and fat, reached up to shake hands with each other or pat one another on the heads to show their love for the last time. Friends and relatives cried to each other as the clock was ticking away. As I noticed, the ones who hurt the most, but were not able to express much of their feelings, were boyfriends and girlfriends. Some girls were leaving their boyfriends behind, or boyfriends leaving their girls. All they had was the hope that one day there would be a second chance for them to see each other again on this earth. While we were next to the bus before I was supposed to get on, one girl arrived on the scene behind her boyfriend who was leaving. She punched him very hard on the shoulder before she cried out and said why did he not tell her about his leaving. The man said his parents had not told him about their departure until the night before. So, he did not have a chance to tell her about it. What I heard the most was, "liar, liar...*ntsej muag dag*", in her cry through her palms covering her face. The young man slowly climbed on the bus with the words, "sorry, sorry and excuse me...*thov txim...thov txim*." She grabbed the strap of the bag hanging on his shoulder to pull him back, but he was at the door with crowds of people watching and getting in. So, she slowly let her hand loose to let him go. I thought it was good that I did not have a girl, so I did not have to deal with such emotions at this moment. Nothing tore my heart (liver) like those two people. There was a joke about this situation in the camp that the man told the woman it was time for him to go spend his American dollars. If he had some left over, he would send her some. This was the end for them. For some others, they might want to drink silver cleansing liquid acid *(haus tshuaj ntxuav nyiaj)* afterwards to end their lives.

Buses transporting refugees out of camp

My brother, along with my cousins and I, lined up next to the side of the bus for picture taking before I climbed in. In the meantime, the fourteen children in my group were on the bus already. One guy asked why I was so late. I did not say a word. Some people on the bus handed back candies and food to their relatives on the ground. It seemed this was a moment of heartache for everyone. All they did was to weep and wipe away their tears before the mountains, fields, and oceans separated them forever. Nevertheless, some of them might have become re-united somewhere by now in the United States, or someplace else. Others might still be separated, while some may no longer be alive these days.

After the pictures were taken, I climbed on the bus to look for an empty seat. It did not matter which seat I had to sit in as long as I was in the right bus. I pushed my suitcase under one of the empty seats and slid myself close to the window, so I could talk more to my siblings before the bus started to roll. From there I pushed up the glass window to extend my head outside to talk to them for a few more words. As they were watching, I told them to forget about me and go home because no matter what, I was leaving within an hour. It was time for us to say goodbye. Then they left the area.

At 11 o'clock the Thai bus drivers put on their seatbelts. The engines started to make louder noises. The people in the area cleared away by moving further to the side, making hand salute, watching the buses leaving this morning hot sun. Soon they were pulling out one by one off the dirt soccer field, two to three minutes apart, heading to the main road. Our bus was the third one to leave the field. When the buses were driving down the road with dusty orange clouds rising up, alongside the road from the soccer field to the edge of the camp, relatives were waiting to wave hands to their loved ones for the very last time while those passengers on the buses were throwing candies out of the window to their friends as goodbye gifts. The Hmong used to say that only mountains separated them, but no dirt separated them, which mean if they did not die, one day they would see each other again. *(Toj roob hauv pes quas xwb tsis yog av luaj quas ces yuav rov sib ntsib)*. The hot noon on the dirt soccer field was left behind. I thought there would be no more trips for me on that dusty road forever. The empty space of the burned buildings above the road was my last glimpse of Ban Vinai. The bumpy road, the dust, and cheer of the crowd on the sides of the street distracted us from paying attention to which direction the buses were going. In seconds everything disappeared behind us.

The trip took about a half day and a full night before we got to Phanat Nikhom Camp. About 5 o'clock in the afternoon, the buses stopped at a station to let us use the restrooms and stretch our bodies. In this location the temperature was cooling down as the night was coming. Even though I was far away from my family in the refugee camp, I was feeling fine. In Ban Vinai I was sick too often, but hoped I would be better in the new place. The stop was only 30 minutes before we were ordered to get on the buses again. We felt as though our heads were spinning, and we could not tell which direction we were going. What we saw was the orange sun still setting above the horizon. We knew that side of the earth was the west for sure. From the moment we were back on the bus, all I heard was the noise of the engine, and sometimes I felt the bumpy or smooth road.

Early the next morning when we arrived in Phanat Nikhom, the refugee processing camp in Chonburi, I was so tired. In my thoughts this place was either heaven or hell. If it was heaven, it meant that there would not be any police watching us again. If it was hell, it meant that we could be locked inside the fence with no way to get out. The buses stopped outside the fence to unload the people. The weather was clear and cool, but the sun had not risen yet. Some people, mostly children, were still sleeping. Once the buses completely stopped, the driver spoke in Thai language to us that it was time to get out. This was the place where we were to stay. Again, I hoped it was not a hell like Ban Vinai Camp where the police chased people around almost every day for no reason. At this time, we were supposed to grab our belongings from under the seats before leaving the bus. I extended my arm down there to search and pulled out my suitcase. I carried it off the bus. When I stepped out of the bus, I smelled some sort of bad odor. The orange sky in the east gave very clear light outside so we could see things better. Then I looked at my suitcase, it was stained with a lot of stool. Overnight, some children just pooped without sending anybody a message. When I extended my arm to search under the seat, the stool had touched my shirtsleeve already. Even though I smelled terrible with this unusual bad odor, I had to go to an office inside the fence to check in along with others. I smelled really bad. When I entered the room, the Thai personnel in the office did not want to get close to me at all. I told a young light skin Thai lady in Lao language, which she also understood, that I got some poop on my shirtsleeve and the suitcase, too. She spoke with an Esan accent. She went sort of, "What happened to you?" It seemed that she thought I was the one who had the accident. It was the kind of smell that made them process my paperwork faster, so I could get out sooner to wash off the bad smell.

Soon after we were done with checking in, they took us, the minors, to an empty building with tin roof and concrete floor. The place was dry and looked cleaner than where we had lived in Ban Vinai Camp. There were four buildings facing each other in this group. There was no hose for running water, but we were to fill water into two huge ceramic jars in the center for our use. After we dropped everything inside the building, two Lee brothers who had arrived two months earlier, came to visit us. They were our old classmates in KM52 village in Laos. Some of the youth who came with me were also my old classmates. The week before we left Ban Vinai, some of them wrote to the two Lee brothers that we were supposed to arrive on that day. So, they were expecting us. Since we did not have water for bathing yet, they took us to their building for baths. We smelled like pigs and chickens. The two Lee friends had a huge cement tub filled with water. The younger brother said that when they came there on the first day, they smelled the same. They were kind enough to let us use their water and said that we should wash ourselves good. We thanked them for their generosity. After the baths, the five of us had a meal of stir-fried vegetables with them in their room. After the lunch, we returned to our building to get our things organized. It was a relaxing and easy day for us.

Without much to do, on the third afternoon, we went to the field to play soccer in our tennis shoes. There were five of us in our group combined with some others to make up a total of 20 for two teams. It was super hot with the temperature close to 100 degrees. We thought we were tough and could sustain the hot weather. We chased the ball in the field with the hot sun on us for one hour until some of us dropped. Our bodies were sweating, our mouths were dried, and we were thirsty to death. Some had muscle cramps or pain in the groins. After we stopped, we came back home to our living quarters exhausted. The next morning some of us could not walk anymore. Our legs were sore, weak, and had become paralyzed. We walked like crippled people. For three days the five of us were not able to help others carry water from the tank to fill the jars. When the pain came, we realized that we had tortured ourselves in the stupid way.

In Phanat Nikhom Camp, it seemed there were very few Vietnamese. Most people were Cambodians who had been there for many years, waiting either to go to other countries or to be returned to their native land. The second largest group was the Hmong who waited for departure or for TB and drug treatment.

There was a Thai movie theater inside the camp with a 26-inch black and white television set. The entrance cost two baht per person per show. It was the only place that kept us from being bored. The flea market was still dominated by Thai people. Since the refugees did not receive as much food assistance as in Ban Vinai Camp, except rice, business went very well for the marketeers.

In our group there was a teenage girl who was supposed to help us do the chores in the traditional way, but she was sort of lazy, like a fox who hunts only when its stomach is very empty. She never helped us do anything. One of my friends called her, "THE MONK", meaning dutiless like the monks in the temple. Every mealtime one of my friend said, "Take the food to the monk." *Nqa zaub mov mus rau hauj sam.* It was good that we did not have to stay together for very long to cook for that lady.

While living here, we had many arguments because we did not coordinate things smoothly and did not listen well to one another. Everyone did not cooperate to do chores, so someone usually became very angry. Our team leader, Vue Vue, was younger than some of us, but he was stronger in almost everything. Some older people in the group did not respect his leadership. Whenever he told us to do something, people just did not move their butts. Some people slept until late morning as if they had their mamas to feed them when they got up. The team leader had to wake them up just as their parents had done when they were little. Instead of waking up before the sun, they let the sun wake them up. About this type of laziness, we said, "They let the sun burn their butts before they woke up." There were also three children younger than ten. We had to babysit them all the time. They needed supervision in doing everything, such as taking a bath, washing their clothes, and going anywhere. It was a tough situation. We learned from a group before us that they had even more problems than we did because they had a troublemaker leader, who misled the group. Our group leader tried to avoid troubles.

When many people were together, some people just did goofy things. One afternoon we went to take baths in the well with many other people. One of my friends tried to flirt with two girls who were from the far side of the camp. At some point one girl became angry. She was grown, but maybe she still had a child's mind and could not take jokes from guys. She ran to get my friend's clothes to drop them in the mud to appease her anger. She made the mistake of thinking the clothes she had in the mud were my friend's. After she dipped them into the mud, I told her they were mine. Then she was very embarrassed for making that mistake. Her face was red like a tomato. She almost cried. She gathered up everything and ran home without her friend. I was also very angry for not having clothes to wear. I really wanted to kick some butts, either my friend's or the girl's. I returned to the building with the wet underwear and boxer shorts on. The next day she came back to our place; she felt better. She said she was sorry. Another friend of mine asked how she could control her temper with her future husband if she behaved in such a way. She said, "I don't know, *kuv tsis paub.*"

The weather in Phanat Nikhom, Chonburi, was much cooler indeed. The breeze constantly brushed your face during the day, so you never felt sweat. During our stay here for two and half months, I never got sick with any symptoms. I was physically healthy and gained more strength. When it came to the beginning of September, the weather was even cooler at night. My only hope then was to wait to get on the plane to fly to America.

In the middle of September 1984, which was about six weeks later, our group leader left the camp for America. Our living situation was uncertain, but we did not bother to assign another person to lead our group. The week after our leader left, I was also transferred with the four younger orphan children, who we had to baby-sit, to the transit center on the other side of the road. During this time, I had to take full responsibility to watch over those little kids. The living conditions were very bad. In this place the toilets were even worse than those in the camp we had come from. There were two in a row with walls around them, but they were open holes in which you poop and pee straight down into the tank. We stayed there for a week, but I used the toilets only four or five times.

In this new place we did not receive any more food assistance because this was our waiting time for departure. We had very little money left to buy food. Each day I went to get free bean soup for us from a building next to the big market. I also went to the market to buy some meat they grilled on sticks for dinner because we were so hungry. Also, the four little ones did not have any money left. The UNHCR provided some little food to people who did not have money and had to stay there longer.

Our building did not have walls dividing the rooms. We stayed in one end and five Lao youths lived in the other end. There was one Lao youth from the next building, who came to beg me that he did not have any food to eat. He maybe was the same age as I was. If I was okay, then he would like to share food with us. I tried to be nice to him because we were from the same country. I told him that he may eat with us for a couple of meals, but not for too long. Once I allowed him to do so, he came to have meals with us every time. There was another Lao man with his family, who lived in another building next to ours, came to scold the Lao youth. The old man said the Lao youth should not just come to eat with us. He had to have his own responsibility for helping himself because food was expensive. The Lao youth told the old man he came there without anything. The old man scolded him for being lazy and not preparing for himself. Another reason was that the Lao youth should understand that we, the Hmong, were a minority group in Laos. The Lao people should not come to get help from us. Instead, they should be the ones to help us. By us sharing food with the Lao youth, the old man felt rather embarrassed that Lao people losing their identity and prestige. He said what the young man did was disgraceful to their people. Those Lao youths who stayed in the same building with us raised their eyebrows like they were nuts and whispered to each other. We did not hear exactly what they were talking about. But we assumed they were talking bad things about the Lao youth. After the old man scolded him, that evening he did not show up at our place for dinner anymore. It was a job well done by the old man.

Two days before our departure, Doug Hulcher, the man who coordinated the minor's program, came to see us with an interpreter. He brought a Down's syndrome boy with him. The boy was physically normal and healthy, except no speech. He used hands and body gestures to signal and perform works. Mr. Hulcher visited us a couple times in Ban Vinai before we left there. He also traveled back and forth to Ban Vinai Camp, Pak Chom, and Bangkok as well. After we talked for a while, the interpreter left. Mr. Hulcher took us to dinner in the market where the restaurant was in one end of the big market building. I could understand what he said, but was not able to respond to him. He bought each one of us a can of Pepsi, one sweet donut, and some grilled chicken sticks. While eating dinner, he asked me if I had any money left to buy a pair of jeans for the little girl. She had only skirts at the time. He said while on the plane the little girl needed to wear a pair of pants. Without saying very much of anything, I spent my 150 baht to buy the pair of jeans for the little girl after we finished the dinner. Then we came back to our place and he took off for some place else, along with the Down's syndrome boy.

11

DEPARTURE FROM ASIA

*"Dej hiav txwv quas ces yuav mus tas ib **sim** tsis muaj hnub rov los sib **fim**. Hmoob quaj thiab hais tseg tias mus ua neej nyob deb los thov cim ntsej cim **muag**, peb mam sib ntsib thaum peb rov mus muab tsho tsuj tsho **npuag**. Nov ces yog thaum tuag lawm xwb os lawv."*

On the 26th of September, our names were posted on the bulletin board to be leaving early on the morning of September 28. My reaction to it was a mixture of good and bad. The good part was that we did not have to live any longer in the dirty toilet place. The departure was what we had been waiting for a long time. The bad feeling was that the ocean might separate us, my family and me, forever, especially if my parents did not have the chance to follow me to America. The flight from Asia to America was like going through a dark tunnel. Some people still believed the earth was flat with a wall dividing Asia and America. The myth was that the airplane had to fly through a very dark hole in the horizon to pass to the other bright side in another world. When the plane left Asia, it was in bright daylight. It flew for an hour then the earth turned to be very dark. Then in another hour the earth became bright again. During the dark period the plane flies through the dark hole. When it turned bright again was when the plane was in the world on the American side. When people talked about this, it became a scary flight from Asia to America. What I heard people say so often was we would never be able to go back to Asia again. Once we were in America, to go back we had to go through the same interview process. Thus, when I left Ban Vinai Camp, my brother told me to write down the bus number, date, and month of departure for reference. He said without all this information, I would not be allowed to go back to Asia again. When I thought about all of this, it made me scared about my flight to America. Some people said it was too cold, but still the caterpillars were as big as newborn piglets. There was also a giant in town who liked to eat people. Some day we might be fed to the giant for food. It sounded scary. When I left Ban Vinai, I wrote down the departure date and bus number as: July 3, 1984, Bus # 10-0058, Nong Khai-40. On the side # 223-20 Oudon Thani Si Chiangmai. Leaving Ban Vinai at 12:10 PM. Departed from Transit in Phanat Nikhom at 10:50 PM on September 27, 1984.

On the afternoon of September 27, with a cooler temperature, we went to wait in the building for boarding the bus early the next morning to go to the airport in Bangkok. Upon arriving in the building, I met a lot of different people. They were Hmong, Mien, Lao, and Cambodians. I met two Xiong brothers who were coming to Minnesota. That night we stayed in the same building, but the next morning they boarded a different bus and also flew on a different plane to America. Later that year the younger brother and I were attending the same high school in Saint Paul. At 3 AM on the 28th, the bus pulled in to take us to the airport in Bangkok. The bus number in the front was 10-0119 Chonburi. On the side was #1633-2-1. Before boarding the bus, Mr. Hulcher came with a girl and the speechless boy who he had brought to see us two days earlier. The girl was fine. The boy knew only a few words of sign language and behaved very badly. He used to hit children in the past. Mr. Hulcher told him to stop being mean to other people;

then he seemed to be better for a moment. He wanted to be with Mr. Hulcher all the time because he did not trust anyone else. On the bus, he asked me to hand his little bag to him, but I did not understand what he was telling me. He was mad and bent his pointing finger at his chest to show me that I had a crooked heart, which meant I was a bad person. From that moment on, he hated me very much to the point he never wanted to look at or talk to me all the way from Bangkok to Seattle when he separated from us. I thought it was fine with me. Even if he did not want to talk to me, it would not make me shrink down two inches shorter anyway.

It was still very dark when we arrived in Bangkok at 4:10 AM and got on a Thai Airline plane to fly to Hong Kong. After we got on the plane, we had to wait for a while, and I did not look at my watch when it took off. When we arrived in Hong Kong without a breakfast on the plane, it was 8:55 AM. I did not remember very much of anything. One of the things I remembered was that Hong Kong Airport was very close to the ocean in a very low valley. After the plane landed, we were transferred to a China Airline plane. That plane took off at 9:05 AM and arrived in Tokyo, Japan, at 12:45 PM on my watch. I did not know why it took so long to get there or maybe it was in a different time zone. From Thailand to Hong Kong and from there to Tokyo, they did not serve us any food. The four little children, the Down's syndrome boy, the older girl, and Mr. Hulcher all were still with me in the same plane. When we got out of the plane in Tokyo, the weather was a little cooler than in Hong Kong. At the airport I saw Japanese people for the first time. It seemed they were very polite. Some of them had very light skin color, especially the females. In my thoughts, "Why are their skins so pretty?" We stayed there until 3 PM Pacific Time. Then we boarded the plane again to fly to America. When the plane took off, it was 4:35 PM. I thought that with all these times and bus numbers were recorded, I could go back to see my mother again in Asia. However, I might fail the interview because I forgot about the flight numbers. This was very sad, but funny, also.

I was sitting in a window seat and fell asleep soon after the plane took off from Japan. Even though when I woke up again many hours later, it was like only a couple of hours had passed. There was a tray of food sitting in front of me. Sitting next to me in the middle seat was a Caucasian, a middle age man. He looked at me but said nothing. Maybe I smelled bad because no bath for two days. My second thought was maybe the man might think what in the hell is this little Asian dude doing on this airplane, or something else. I watched him eat his food for a while, but did not feel like I wanted to eat mine. I turned around to see my fellow Hmong, who were sitting behind me, to see how they were doing. They were the four younger children, who were with me in the camp, the girl, and the Down's syndrome boy who was brought by Mr. Hulcher. The bigger boy of the four was suffering from motion sickness. The other three were fine. "They all were still alive", I thought. They had eaten some of their food already.

After turning around to watch them, I faced forward again to taste the food in the tray. I took a bite of the red apple, which I had never eaten in my life. It tasted so different. I put it back on the tray. I took a couple bites of the dinner roll, then dropped it on the tray. Then I opened the pack of butter and I had no idea what it was. It looked like a candy or a small ice cream pack quite similar to those in Laos and Thailand. I licked it. The taste was bland and even worse than the red apple. I put it down in the tray. I opened the little bowl covered with a clear plastic sheet. It was some small diced white chicken and rice with creamy stuff set on top. I used the plastic spoon to dig up a little bit and put it in my mouth. The cream was sort of bland, too. The meat was soft. The rice was rough. Since it was an emotionally stressed moment with unlikable foods, I left everything on the tray. That was my first meal on the plane from Asia to America; I will remember it for the longest time.

After tasting all the different foods, I stood up to give a signal to the Caucasian sitting next to me that I wanted to get out of there. He turned his knees and body toward the center of the plane and leaned back against the seat to give me a way to get out. I got out of my seat and walked to the back of the plane to use the restroom. Once I got there, one Caucasian just came out from the toilet and tried to shut the door again because he did not see me. When he saw me stand in front of him waiting to get in, he said a word, "Sorry" then left. I went inside to pee. After I was done using it, I pressed the latch to flush the toilet. The dish-like seal in the bottom slid open wider. Not much water came down. Rather it was more like air blew down the hole only. I thought maybe the water was gone. I came out of the restroom. There was another man waiting outside to get in. I said to the man, "The water is finish." He responded to me, "It's Ok." I got out. The man went in.

I walked back to my seat. The Down's syndrome boy still did not want to look at me. Back in my seat, I turned back to the girl sitting behind me to ask her where her parents were at the time. What she told me was, "All dead" without emotion. I though, "What kind of person is this." We talked for only a moment. I asked her who was in America where she would be living. She said her older sister was living in America. I asked her where her sister was. I meant in what state. She said, "Don't know. Just go until I see her." After this nonsense conversation, I turned back toward the front of the plane. I leaned back and tried to see if I could fall sleep again. At this time, it felt like the plane was motionless with the bright sunrays hitting on the portside of the plane. I knew we were going toward the sun, but still wondered why it rose so fast. Maybe it was like the story people told us in Asia that the plane flies through the dark hole to the other bright side. But that was only the old beliefs of the old people. The truth was the plane flew to where the sun rose, so they both must meet in a certain zone in the air. Then I also no longer thought about my family in Thailand because I believed they were in a good place already. The one thing I hoped was that if the plane did not crash anywhere on the way, I would soon meet my brother, cousins, and maybe also Marlin Heise, the Caucasian who came to see us twice in Ban Vinai Refugee Camp.

Above our heads in the center of the plane were some flashing small TV screens showing cartoon pictures. The cartoons appeared to be dancing and singing for a while and then disappeared again in a language I did not understand. I watched for a while since I had not watched TV shows many times in the past. It kept showing the same kind of cartoons over and over again. Then I leaned back in my seat and fell asleep.

When I woke up the second time, it was about late noon. I looked down on the earth. There was nothing other than the blue ocean. It seemed we had blue earth and blue sky rather than green earth and blue sky. Indeed, the flight had been a long day since we left Tokyo in the afternoon to arrive in Seattle at sundown on the next day, but it felt like we spent only a few hours on the plane.

Then we arrived in Seattle Airport where half of us would be separated from each other. Mr. Hulcher had to take the Down's syndrome boy to his sponsor's home. The older girl was going on her way, too. After we exited the plane, we had to pick up our belongings. It was difficult to follow directions while Mr. Hulcher was not with us anymore. At the gate I saw a skinny Asian man working there. He looked more like Vietnamese or Hmong, but not Chinese for sure. I did not bother to ask him to find out. The one thing I needed was to carry my suitcase and follow the group. For some reason after the Customs checking, I went one way and the rest went the other because there were too many people in the crowd. After a while, the children who came with me disappeared. I ran back and saw their backs; then I rushed to catch them. We walked for a while and ran down the escalators. Some of us could not control our balance and almost tipped over. Then we came to rest in the waiting area to catch our next flight. In Hong Kong and Tokyo, we saw a few Caucasians. In Seattle it was the opposite from Asia. Now we saw only a few Asians and mostly white people. In the crowd a man was holding a little girl's hand. She was about three or four years old. They were walking back and forth anxiously like they were expecting someone to arrive. Very soon a woman, maybe she was his wife, arrived carrying a little black bag hanging on her shoulder and pulling a bigger suitcase on the two-wheel traveling cart. She wore a white shirt with black skirt and black coat on top. Once she approached them, she ran and jumped on the man, assuming he was her husband, as the child was standing next to them. Both of her arms were over her husband's shoulders. She kissed him mouth to mouth. At that moment the four little children who came with me were shocked, with their eyes fixed on them for seeing that. It was the strangest thing we ever had seen. It was a culture shock to us!

Within 24 hours, we were in a new country, coping with a different climate, seeing a new culture, and finally, speaking a new language. After they were done with the kissing, she relaxed, held the little girl up high against her chest, and gave her some kisses on the cheeks. She held her tight while patting her back a few times. Then she let her down and the three left.

At this time, I had to accompany the four young children to the Minneapolis/Saint Paul Airport. Mr. Hulcher, the Down's syndrome boy, and the older girl left there before us without saying much. We waited until late afternoon to board the United Airlines flight. Once we were on the plane, there was a Caucasian sitting behind me. He was in about his mid-twenties and about six feet tall. Later when the plane was steady in the air, he left his seat to join me in the same row because the two seats next to me were empty as I sat in the window seat. He told me he was from Chicago, one of the popular US cities I heard about when I was in Asia. He seemed to be a very nice person with a lot to talk about while sitting next to me. He told me he was on a business trip. I did not ask him what kind of business he was working with because I did not know enough English to communicate with him. Even if he had tried to explain more the kind of business he was doing, I might not have had any clue anyway. It was like a human playing a flute to an animal's ears. I wished I spoke better English then. When I talked back to him in my broken English words, it seemed he understood me a little bit. Even though I was able to answer him a few words in a sentence, he kept talking to me all the way from Seattle to Minneapolis/Saint Paul Airport.

At dinnertime, the flight attendants did not serve food to us. When he got his tray in front of him, he asked me if I was hungry, but I shook my head and told him not really. He asked me to pull out my plane tickets for him to see them. I stood up to open the bin above, pulled out my tickets from my suitcase, and handed them to him. After he looked at them, he called the flight attendants to give us food because we had the tickets. I did not fully understand every single word he told the ladies. However, it seemed he told them that we were entitled to have dinner. Then one lady brought us the dinner trays. I thought to myself, "The Americans must have big hearts." When I got my tray in front of me, he then opened his food to eat and told me to eat mine. He did just as Asians do. When the person next to you does not have food to eat then you do not eat yours either. He was very generous. He should run for office to become a president because he had the good heart. As we were eating, instead of asking him how much our food might cost in the restaurant, I asked how much it would cost in the market. He told me the food might cost about $3 or a little more. I kept quiet while eating my food. Before finishing the dinner, I asked him something which I don't remember any more these days. He told me let's finish our food first. I was a little embarrassed that I might have talked too much.

After the food he forgot to answer my questions, but went on to many other things instead. He asked me about the weather in Asia and how we came to America. I answered him only half of the questions because some things I did not know the words. With talking to him on the plane for a few hours, it was a better flight than the flight from Asia to Seattle. It was not very long after dinner that we started to see some lights on earth. He told me we were close to Minneapolis/Saint Paul where the plane was supposed to land. After a while the loudspeaker announced something, but I did not understand a word. Maybe the four little children in front of me understood better than I did because they put their seatbelts on. He used hand signals to show me how to put my seatbelt back on because the plane was landing soon. In a few minutes, the descending motion of the plane made me feel that I would see my relatives for sure. Then I looked down on the earth again, it had even more lights shinning than the stars in the sky. He said it was nice talking to me. I thought, "It was nice talking to me?" I understood only half of the conversation and I did not even say, "Thank you." We leaned back, the plane touched down with a few bumps and the fast engine running sound. When we landed and came to a complete stop at the gate, he stood up, pulled his suitcase from the bin above, fixed his suit coat, and waited until the people behind us all left. He said goodbye to me before walking out to the door. We followed him to the gate. I saw him tell my relatives in the crowd when we were behind him. Maybe he knew exactly those people there were my relatives waiting for me. He walked past them and disappeared in the crowd of people ahead of us before I met my relatives at the waiting area. He disappeared forever without turning back once to see us. Then I approached my relatives. In the group were my brother, a few kind cousins, and Marlin Heise. Once I met them and took some pictures, I forgot to say goodbye to those four children who came along with me from Thailand. They separated from me at that moment without saying anything to me either. They were going to another place. I was not sure whether their relatives picked them up or they had to take another flight home. By turning to take a good look at my cousins, I was startled because some of them were healthy and chubby. They were completely different from when they left us in Laos. After the picture taking, we went downstairs to pick up my suitcase in the luggage claims area. Down there I looked around and did not see the nice Caucasian who flew with me from Seattle either. The four little children, whom I had been taking care of for the past two months, were gone, too. The old family was breaking apart, but I united with a new one. The nervousness of not being sure where to go was over because my relatives were there to pick me up.

As soon as we got my belongings, I walked with my brother and Marlin Heise to the parking ramp. Other cousins went into another car. The weather was a little cooler now. It seemed to be a happy moment for everyone. In the ramp the three of us got into my brother's manual drive Nissan Datsun, a two-door hatchback. He turned on the engine and pulled it back to the driveway to drive out of there. Inside the car

I was sitting quietly in the backseat listening to my brother and Marlin Heise talking on the way home. Once in a while on the road, Marlin Heise turned his head to check on me in the backseat to see if I was still awake. Obviously, I would not fall sleep soon either.

When we were about half way home, or I was not even sure how much longer we had to go, my brother made a turn to get off the road to stop at the front door of a big building. Marlin Heise took me inside with him while my brother was waiting in the car outside. Inside the building he asked someone to give him a little box, which I did not know what was in it, and he gave them some money. How much did it cost? He did not tell me, and I did not ask either. We returned to the car and my brother drove home. When we arrived at their home, we got out of the car. Marlin Heise grabbed my suitcase and carried it to the apartment. I walked with empty hands. I felt like the temperature was even cooler than when we were at the airport. We went inside the apartment and it looked good to me. I thought now it was the end of my hazardous journey as a refugee and it was the beginning of my new life in Minnesota. There were a lot more cousins waiting to see me inside like I was very special that evening. At that moment, without saying any word to any one yet, I already felt like I needed to use the bathroom first because of the long flight from Seattle to Saint Paul. I asked them for the bathroom and Marlin told me it was upstairs. I climbed up there for a while and returned to the living room again. They were having a loud conversation in the room. I did not talk to those cousins in the living room and they did not talk to me either. As I listened, many of them were talking about how difficult college life was. My thought was, "They go to college already?" I was half impressed and half shocked that they were in college already.

By then the dinner was ready on the kitchen table, which was prepared by my cousin's wife. They invited each other to enjoy the food, but I was too thirsty and asked for water. There were many pop cans on the coffee table in the living room. My brother told me they did not have water, but if I wanted to I could either drink a pop or the cold water from the sink. I told him I had too much soda on the plane already, so I would rather drink the water in the sink. He gave me a glass and I turned the cold water on to fill it half full. I drank it all. They invited me to join them with the dinner. I was not really hungry. Marlin Heise handed me the little box he bought on the way home. He said, "*Noj*" in Hmong language which meant, "Eat." I opened the box and took the whole thing out. I took a bite. It had bread with sesame seeds, beef, vegetables, tomatoes, creamy stuff, and many other things in it. It tasted sour, sweet, bland, smooth, and other flavors. I thought I would just chew and swallow everything down to see what happened thereafter. But, over the night my stomach was okay. It was my first acculturation in America, I guess. Later in the year I found out it was a Big Mac from the most popular American food chain of McDonald's. The place I landed in was 1584 Timberlake Road, Apt C, Saint Paul, Minnesota, where I spent my next two years like a poor orphan, sleeping in the dark, cold basement in the most civilized country in the world.

In reality, life in America was opposite from my imagination when I was in Thailand. The next morning when I woke up and looked down from the second-floor windows facing to the east, I saw nothing other than a whole bunch of cars in the parking lot. A few people were there and yelling at each other like they were ready to fight. I came downstairs and asked the cousin, who used to be a cow herder with me in 1975 in Pha Hoi, how many different kinds of people were living in the area. He said there were many different kinds and I would see them in the next few days.

Two more days in the apartment and September was gone. Then October arrived. In two weeks, the weather had changed rapidly to much colder than when I first got there. The leaves turned brown and fell down steadily as the wind blew. The gusting wind blew the leaves on the ground and piled them up in the corners and curb of streets, in the dents, and on the sides of buildings. There were no flowers blooming and no silver or gold decorated the side of the streets as I imagined before. Soon, one more month passed and then it was the beginning of November. Then trees became leafless for that year. The cold, white snowflakes started to fall from the sky like popcorn. Within hours it covered the ground or even stuck on the leafless tree branches. The window glass froze with a quarter inch thick of ice as the cold wind continued to blow. The ground was as bright as it could be when the sun rose up. When stepping outside with my Thailand thin pants, the cold windchill bit through my skin, making it feel like it was burning. Walking for five minutes against the cold wind to and from the bus stop each morning and afternoon, I had a lot of nose dripping. Some cousins told me taking a hot shower might help warm me up.

The first 5 months, from November 1984 to March 1985, were the longest time ever for me. The one thing I missed the most was the sunlight. I saw no caterpillars as big as piglets like the myths I heard in Thailand, but I was in a frozen ice place *(daus xib daus npu, ntuj tuag no teb tuag ntsim)*. By the time the weather was warm enough in April and I was able to sit outside in the backyard against the morning sun, I felt like I had gone to some place else for a year already. My tan skin turned lighter and it looked like I was pale. To see the flowers and green plants, my cousin had to take me to Como Zoo to see them in the greenhouse. I saw that it was the only place with flowers and green leaves in the winter. Everything I had thought of America had vanished in my first winter in Saint Paul.

In this new life I was very poor and sleeping with hunger. We did not have much to eat. Life was very depressing, but I did not want to tell anyone about my sadness. I thought maybe it was how refugees' life in America. I wished I could just fly home in Laos. However, my second thought was that I had escaped from the wars all those years to get to America, so I should endure the hunger, the emotional pain, and hope one day I might live in a better place. Even though I had nowhere to go, except confining myself to the basement month after month, some people still insulted me that putting myself in the dark would make me sick. Actually, I was sick every day from the cold weather. I thought when there was no father to guide, then I ended up in the wrong place.

Finally, one winter was gone and spring came to take its place. I did not learn very much in school either. What I realized was that my life was moving toward the challenging manhood stage that needed more decision making to survive in America.

BIOGRAPHY

Touayim was born in the 1960s, in war torn Laos. During his childhood, to escape fighting, he settled in many temporary places in the valleys and mountains. In the early 1980s, he abandoned his home and entered the neighboring country of Thailand as a refugee. He spent two years in the bad conditions Ban Vinai Refugee Camp. In 1984, he had the opportunity to come to Minnesota under the minor refugee program. In Saint Paul, he attended high school and graduated in 1988. He attended a year in community college, but it was difficult and unsuccessful. So, in the spring of 1989, he joined the United States Navy for three years. During his Navy days, he was deployed overseas twice. After being discharged, he returned to his home in Minnesota, and attended Winona State University for the next four years. In the spring of 1997, he walked with hundreds of graduates on stage to shake hands with the school president and received his diploma. He was the first child in his family to graduate from college.

BOOK SUMMARY

Near the Vietnam border, our village of Tham Thao was the entrance for the Pathet Lao and Viet Cong into Laos. From the middle of the 1950s to the middle of 1960s, my father was a delegate to the village council, serving our people divided by two major political influences, communism and capitalism. Life was always difficult, but Father and his colleagues had to face the distasteful political day to day activities as war penetrated our region. As the war boiled up with the interference from both, Pathet Lao and the Lao right wing, Father could not endure the disruption any longer. He then made the decision to abandon our century-old home and moved us to central Xieng Khouang from 1965 to 1969. Soon the war caught up with us with invading soldiers and bombing planes. In late 1969, we lost our second village, and had to move further west to Viang Chan province, where we had a peaceful life until 1975 when the Pathet Lao took over Laos. Right after the country fell, another war began. The people in our region rebelled and fought against the Pathet Lao government. During the next five years, we constantly moved to avoid the Pathet Lao rule. Between 1982 and 1984, our family escaped to Thailand as refugees. In September 1984, I was resettled for a new life in Saint Paul, Minnesota.

www.ingramcontent.com/pod-product-compliance
Lightning Source LLC
LaVergne TN
LVHW041743060526
838201LV00046B/897